APR 2 4 2013

DEC 3 1 2013

D1251816

# Maya Architecture

UNIVERSITY PRESS OF FLORIDA

Florida A&M University, Tallahassee

Florida Atlantic University, Boca Raton

Florida Gulf Coast University, Ft. Myers

Florida International University, Miami

Florida State University, Tallahassee

New College of Florida, Sarasota

University of Central Florida, Orlando

University of Florida, Gainesville

University of North Florida, Jacksonville

University of South Florida, Tampa

University of West Florida, Pensacola

# MAYA ARCHITECTURE

Kenneth Treister, FAIA

Foreword by George Stuart

# MAYA ARCHITECTURE

## Temples in the Sky

University Press of Florida

Gainesville · Tallahassee · Tampa · Boca Raton

Pensacola · Orlando · Miami · Jacksonville · Ft. Myers · Sarasota

To the memory of Alan Treister, beloved son, architect, and painter, whose world was his art.

Copyright 2013 by Kenneth Treister
Printed in China on acid-free paper

This book may be available in an electronic edition.

All rights reserved

18  17  16  15  14  13    6  5  4  3  2  1

A record of cataloging-in-publication data is available from
the Library of Congress.
ISBN 978-0-8130-4246-6

University Press of Florida
15 Northwest 15th Street
Gainesville, FL 32611-2079
http://www.upf.com

*Page i:* Copán, Honduras. Stela H with a resplendent scarlet macaw, the largest and most beautiful parrot in the world.

*Page ii:* Palenque, Chiapas. The seventh- and eighth-century palace displays a strong horizontality juxtaposed with and accented by a vertical element, the four-story observation tower. The wide sweep of its horizontal steps provides a solid, spreading base that leads to the main façades with rhythmical black openings of pillared galleries and tower.

*Page iii:* Copán, Honduras. Stela H (782 CE). A portrait of the richly adorned sovereign Waxaklajuun-Ub'aah-K'awiil emerging from the jaws of a jaguar in the role of the maize god as he danced at creation in the Maya Classic period's creation story. The intricacy and craftsmanship of the carved ornamentation at Copán are remarkable.

*Page iv:* Labná, Yucatán. The Puuc city covers a large area with a multistoried pyramid (El Mirador) with chambers and columned porticoes opening to terraces; a giant plaza; and the monumental arch with an adjoining inner compound. With only one large pyramid and temple, the ceremonial area was different from those of the Classic period, which featured multiple temple groups.

# Contents

*Bolonchen* (nine wells). Illustration by Frederick Catherwood.

# Foreword

Ken Treister's book—its title could not be clearer—is about one of the great architectural traditions of the human past. And as stated, it is also the accomplishment of one who is himself an architect. This combination greatly appealed to me, and I agreed at once to write this short foreword.

Early in my life, inspired by the stately homes and early public architecture of my hometown in South Carolina, I thought seriously about becoming an architect. That was before archaeology took over my life. But a strong interest in the history of building never really left me. I still recall vividly the day more than fifty years ago when I first encountered the wonders in stone created by the architects of the ancient Maya.

This happened in northwestern Yucatán state, Mexico, where I had been hired as an archaeological field assistant to Dr. E. Wyllys ("Bill") Andrews of Tulane University's Middle American Research Institute. My wife, son, and I had arrived in Yucatán, total strangers to that land and its languages. Soon after we were settled in Mérida, our new home, Bill drove me a dozen or so miles north of the city, to the archaeological zone of Dzibilchaltún.

Leaving the paved highway, we turned onto a dusty road that led through vast fields of henequen, or sisal, and several small settlements, then entered the ruins of the ancient city. We parked near a huge pile of rubble, one of many that rose above the arid thorn forest. Bill pointed to its summit, where many men were working, removing loose debris and building a system of scaffolding in front of what appeared to be a wall of carefully placed stones.

"They are uncovering a buried temple," Bill explained. "When we arrived here a few weeks ago, this was one of the largest of many mounds that define the archaeological zone. Making a closer inspection of it, Eugenio May, the leader of the workers, and I noticed a building corner sticking out of the rubble. It turned out to be part of a buried structure, probably intact."

The building that emerged from the great mound soon became known as the Temple of the Seven Dolls, so named for a cache of figurines discovered beneath its central chamber. The exposed temple and details of the stepped platform that supported it appear much as they did around 500 CE (except for the stucco that once adorned it) in two of Ken Treister's photographs in the final pages of his treatment of Maya architecture.

The superb images that fill the present work show examples of architecture and art over the entire Maya area and parts of Mesoamerica. In terms of time, they span

World's Fair
Columbian Ex-
position of 1893.
Photograph
courtesy of
George E. Stuart.

some three thousand years, from the Preclassic through the Postclassic periods and on into modern times, and include both Maya domestic styles and the richness of textile motifs. Treister's photography is complemented by appropriate images from past masters of Maya architectural recording and reconstruction, among them Frederick Catherwood (1799–1854) and Tatiana Proskouriakoff (1909–1985).

For me, one of the great values of this book lies in the author's knowledgeable treatment of construction methods and materials. Another is his discussion of the powerful influences on the architectural styles of the recent past and present, apparent in the works of Frank Lloyd Wright and other architects of our time, including the author himself.

As Treister points out, one of the most influential events in bridging the gap between past and present Maya architectural traditions was the great World's Fair Columbian Exposition of 1893 in Chicago. There on the Midway Plaisance, full-size replicas of portions of the imposing Maya structures of Uxmal and other ancient cities of Yucatán dazzled hundreds of thousands of visitors who had never seen such marvels.

Even unspectacular Dzibilchaltún once boasted such buildings, but none survived as intact as those at Uxmal and neighboring sites. Instead, they succumbed to time and the modern needs of road construction, surviving mostly as mere mounds of rubble with corners or facades of buildings exposed here and there. Reconstructing these buildings on paper with Bill Andrews's expert help taught me much about the genius of the anonymous Maya who designed them and oversaw their construction.

Since my memorable introduction to Yucatán and the world of the Maya, I have spent many years learning about the myriad forms and functions of the ancient buildings, settlements, and cities that dot the landscapes. I continue to do so, for such works are uniquely able to reveal much about the people who made and used them. Indeed, that is the grand lesson that Ken Treister provides for us in the work that follows.

*George E. Stuart*
*Former senior assistant editor for archaeology for*
*the National Geographic Society*

Copán, Honduras. Stela N, south face of
K'ahk' Yipyaj Chan K'awil (ruled 749–761 CE).
Copán was a major center of the Classic
Maya from 600 to 800 CE. With its success, its
forests were felled and its farmland covered
with construction until it finally succumbed
to the effects of its mushrooming population and the elite's pride in its architectural
and sculptural greatness.

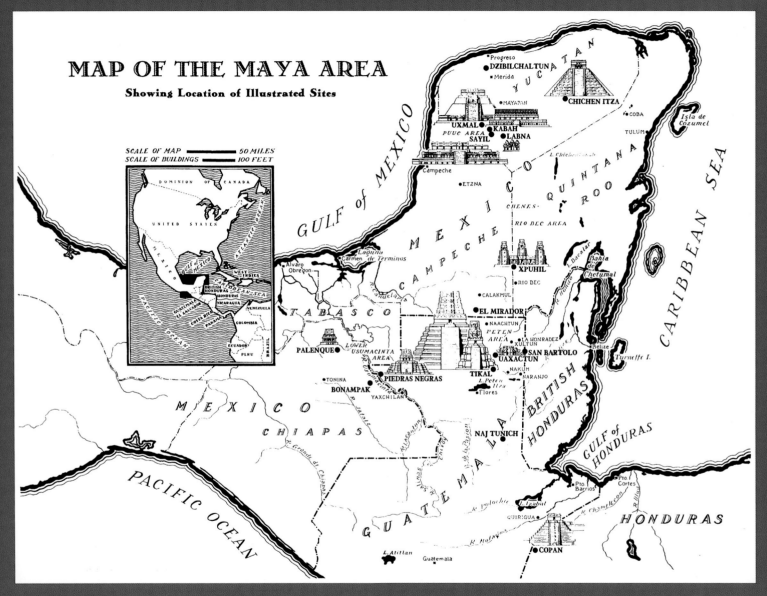

Map. From Tatiana Proskouriakoff, *An Album of Maya Architecture*.

# Introduction

## Through the Eyes of an Architect

*Ancient settlements resemble fossil shells. Both were purposely structured by organisms to support life, only to be stripped of vitality by time's retreating tides. Yet, preserved in these inert structures is an imprint of the different creative forces that cast both shells and sites into distinctive forms.*

Michael Edward Moseley and Carol J. Mackey, *Twenty-Four Architectural Plans of Chan Chan, Peru*

We all see the world through different lenses. Our interests, associations, profession, and education color our thoughts and understandings of the world. I am an architect and artist and observe the world in general and the Maya architecture in particular not as an archaeologist, historian, or anthropologist but as one who is keenly interested in the world of design.

A revolution has occurred in the study of the ancient Maya civilization in the last few decades. Although the Maya's books have largely been lost, the chronicles, mathematics, and astronomies still exist in hieroglyphic texts on stone, shell, and other media, in addition to architecture. We also have traces of their highly advanced civilization through their elite-commissioned architecture, rich with architectonic art.[1] Their elaborate buildings decorated with sculpture and hieroglyphics are often well preserved and reveal their cultural history, ideologies, and ontologies.[2] The decoding of the Maya hieroglyphics and the consequent broader understanding of their society have given a voice to the Maya who lived during their Golden Age. With these writings incorporated profusely on their architecture and sculpture, we can literally communicate with the elite rulers who commissioned these works. The ancient Maya can now talk to us as we visit their ruined cities, and scholars can interpret these words and relics that reveal so much of the Maya's social, religious, and cultural life.

As an example, since the archaeologist Alberto Ruz Lhuillier found the elaborate funerary crypt in the heart of Palenque's Temple of the Inscription, covering the tomb of a king, we can now deduce that many temples were funereal monuments dedicated to deceased rulers. This indicates that in addition to the power of the priestly class, there was great political authority in the hereditary rulers who perpetuated their remains within their architecture, as did the ancient Egyptian kings.[3]

But these details of the Maya's built environment now coming to light do little to help answer the basic question that this book ponders: How and why did this dynamic society, in a hostile environment and in a relatively short time, blossom and create such harmonious, architectural masterpieces? There have been thousands of civilizations during the world's long history, many with wealth and established in geologically friendly environments. Rarely, however, has one raised to the heights of architectural genius that the civilizations of Mesoamerica in general and of the Maya in particular did. Their astronomical and mysterious ascent and then collapse into relative obscurity is a phenomenon that baffles the mind.

Linda Schele and Peter Mathews, in their book *The Code of Kings*, tell us about the new Maya scholarship: "How different it is to walk through a ruined city when it has become a historical place—to 'read' a building and to know who looks out from a sculpted portrait. The ruins cease to be anonymous places admired only for their beauty and mystery."[4]

As an architectural designer, however, I want to know about this "beauty and mystery." I still have a thirst to learn how the Maya and their brothers in Mesoamerica, isolated as they were, and at one brief time in history, achieved the knowledge and, yes, the wisdom to create a magnificent design language that is both harmonious and wondrous—principles of design that others, including the contemporary architectural world, find so elusive and obscure.

Our visual and sensory environment affects our senses and feeling of comfort. Therefore, our goal should be achieving an aesthetic appreciation of the beautiful world of the Maya and trying to discover their rules of design for our individual well-being and that of our society.

Considering the historic breadth of architecture throughout the ages, the architecture of the Maya is unique in its beauty, totality, and harmony. The reality we find provides lessons in form, spatial relationships, balance, harmony, creativity, and unity. We can only imagine how glorious it was during its explosive life in the far reaches of Mesoamerica. Now we should try to understand and learn the lessons of the Maya artistic world, digesting its design principles, appreciating its forms.

Architecture consists of two elements, mass and space, and the interrelationship between the two. Mass by itself is falsely thought of as architecture, but if understood only that way it is merely an "object" floating in space or on the pages of a magazine. Architecture is the capturing of space, by both internal and external shapes. The awareness of these shapes and spaces and the involvement within them is the essence of true architecture. This is the lesson of the Maya. They created an architecture that defined space, enclosing the senses while involving their society and its whole being in them. These spaces are voids, or "empty" negative spaces, which anchored the surrounding mass. The structural volumes cancel the space, creating plazas and framing the precincts.[5] The current that flowed between the Maya's well-proportioned and handsome structures and their open plazas made up their universe. This symphony of volume and distance created a home for the Maya culture, religion, and art.

The expression of the spaces created by the Maya's built environment turns outward, unlike the Gothic structures, whose space turns inward. The architecture of the Maya is solid, solemn, set into wide esplanades to enhance its scale. The impression is always a backward or receding movement imposed by the projecting terraces and platforms, which allows the presence of the strong, stone monumental buildings to harmonize with the surrounding cityscape. The spaces of the city push against the buildings, and the generative syntax of this combination is surprisingly simple.[6]

The Maya architecture served as a background—a stage set with explicit iconography, framing private and communal rituals. Even when not in use, the architecture freezes in stone the aspects of ritual appropriate to that urban setting.

A hieroglyphic stairway set along a plaza without superstructure may be considered a building in the sense of enclosing space and giving a specific function to the area. These stairs may be incorporated into a larger assemblage, but their function is to accommodate numerous participants in a theatrical ritual. The architecture promotes specific memories and brings to all a mental slate with visual images and texts, perhaps a celebration of warfare or religious sacrifice.[7] The inclusion of these steps, as an architectural form with a specific function, is based on their important use for public seating during public events in Classic Maya centers. Some were amphitheaters with seating capacity estimated at as high as eight thousand. The steps and terraces at the Copán ball games are estimated to have seated three thousand spectators.[8]

This book combines a text that expresses the concepts of Maya architecture and cities, but those concepts cannot be understood without seeing them manifested in the reality of Maya architecture. The photographs that join the text, which I took over many years of travel throughout the land of the Maya, illustrate Maya architecture not as it was in its glorious past—painted brightly, adorned by sculpture and magical murals, animated by a colorful

people—but as it looks now. This offers only a teaser of what it was. The expression of harmony is only imagined, the gracefulness of its architectural composition of form and space only hinted at. Some of it is in ruin and some partially reconstructed, but none of it appears now as it once was. Lost is the interaction of the force of its masses and spaces that expressed the relationship between individuals and nature, individuals and their universe.[9]

The seemingly spontaneous generation, the blossoming, and ultimately the demise of Maya civilization, posed one of the great enigmas of the ancient world. Like the fossil shell found on a deserted beach, the architectural remnants of the Maya stand as some of the most salient—certainly the most visible—evidence of this once-living organism, and provide many of the most telling clues to its bygone existence.

Architecture is tightly interwoven into the larger fabric of man's civilized history, and much of our knowledge of ancient societies is gleaned from their architectural ruins. Ruins reflect more than a mere building process: they mirror the civilization's society, cosmology, and technology, its problems and solutions, its successes and failures. This hollow framework stands long after the culture dies, allowing us to see from the vantage of history a portrait of its grandeur and its despair.

In this book, I bring an architect's perspective to the physical remains of the Maya cities and, through observation and analysis, seek to elucidate the architectural aesthetic at work in this strange assembly of wonderful buildings.

Architecture not only reveals the physical blueprint of a society but expresses its spiritual and emotional "realities" as well. Maya architecture was the product of a creativity that flowed from a special and rare group of people in a way that has occurred only occasionally in the history of man. The Maya not only built their personal world, with all its functional requirements, but made it a total work of art as well.

In the history of world architecture, few civilizations have equaled the beauty and aesthetic harmony of the Maya and the pre-Columbian cities of Mesoamerica. I include all of Mesoamerica because the ruling elite and the societies in this vast area shared a common heritage and source of ideas. They had similar government structure and organization and were influenced through exchange and/or conquest by the events and traditions of each other. With similar cultures, they promoted cultural exchange, formed alliances, intermarried, and borrowed from each other. Because of this and the common abundance of easy-to-cut limestone, the Mesoamerican societies all created exquisite stone architecture and cities.

Over a period of nearly a thousand years, the Maya built dazzling cities more beautiful in their integration of art and architecture and better organized than any in the ancient world. In a dramatic burst of creativity, this Native American culture blossomed into a highly integrated civilization. Its achievements in creating monumental architecture, descriptive murals, sculpture, an accurate calendar based on an advanced astronomical system, epic literature, and an incredibly sophisticated hieroglyphic writing system stand out proudly among all the classic cultures of antiquity.

The grandeur of the Maya city fascinates all who gaze upon it. The totality of the Maya architectural statement has rarely been matched. The harmony, cohesiveness, and inspiring beauty of the architecture contrast sharply with the manifest chaos we frequently encounter in today's modern, frantic world.

The Golden Age of the Maya lasted not much more than eight centuries. Then, region by region, all such elaborate construction stopped, many cities were abandoned, the population scattered, and the accumulation of centuries of knowledge and creativity seem to have vanished—lost forever to the jungle. After its collapse, no new civilization rose to take its place. What could explain this sudden burst of creativity, organization, and greatness, never to occur again?

"Who were the people that built this city?" asked the nineteenth-century explorer John Lloyd Stephens, who, with the architect Frederick Catherwood, became one of the major early investigators of the Maya. Writing about the ruins of Copán in Honduras, Stephens queried:

> In the ruined cities of Egypt, even in the long-lost Petra, the stranger knows the story of the people whose vestiges are around. The place where we sat, was it a citadel from which an unknown people had sounded the trumpet of war? or a temple for the worship of the God of peace? . . . All was mystery, dark and impenetrable mystery, and every circumstance increased it . . . an immense forest shrouded the ruins, hiding them from sight, heightening the impression and moral effect and giving an intensity and almost wildness to the interest.[10]

The seemingly abrupt and still unexplained collapse left the Maya identity suspended in time and mystery. Dense jungle and volcanic residue have concealed for many years—and to a great degree still do—the secrets of this brilliant people. Their architectural ruins and scattered artifacts are all that remain of a once vibrant civilization.

The majesty of the Maya—like other great civilizations—expressed in large measure the integration of its arts and culture as a whole. Architecture and its allied arts were an integral part of daily living. Thus, the study of architectural precepts, clearly discernible in their ruins, can tell us not only about those who designed the buildings, but also, to some extent, about the cares, concerns, and thought processes of an entire civilization.

Maya art is not applied—objects floating in space—but is an integral part of the concepts and execution of the total culture, of the total architecture and city. It is an example of *Gesamtkunstwerk* (the nineteenth-century German concept of the totality of related art). Here the kings and lords, their architects and artists worked as one, creating a totality in the same way God creates a totality in the world of nature.

Monumental architectural art became an integral part of the Maya's architecture, from the Preclassic times. Buildings had sculpture imbedded into the surface fabric of their design. Giant monumental sculptures flanked the primary stairway of structures in addition to designs adorning piers, inset panels and cornices.

The Maya developed a hieroglyphic writing system with which they recorded, taught and perpetuated their language and culture. Unfortunately, many of their writings were systematically destroyed in the Spanish Conquest.

In 1566, the Franciscan Bishop Diego de Landa (1524–1579) wrote a detailed description of the Maya of Yucatán, this to help compensate for the loss of hundreds of their hieroglyphic books that he ordered burned as "tools of evil."

These people also used certain characters or letters, with which they wrote in their books about the antiquities and their sciences. . . . We found a great number of books in these letters, and since they contained nothing but superstitions and falsehoods of the devil we burned them all, which they took most grievously, and which gave them great pain.[11]

Although we now can decipher and read the Maya writings, we turn to the ancient stone structures themselves for a real understanding of this evanescent civilization. The Maya rank among the master builders of all time, and from their enduring edifices we can infer a great deal about the economic, political, and social foundations of their society.

Architecture is shaped by physical, psychological, and cultural forces: climate, topography, material, resources, and social organization all influence the physical surroundings we create. The anonymous Maya architects incorporated and manipulated available materials into original architectural forms, and they met all manner of topographical challenges to create their planned cities with order and beauty. What may have arisen spontaneously in the earliest periods ultimately became architecture designed by trained architects, whose formulae and precepts were codified and passed on from generation to generation.

We are able to trace the development of Maya building practices because of their unique system of historic preservation. The Maya seldom razed older buildings but built over them in successive layers, with the older buildings serving as the foundation for new construction. We can now peel back these layers and find a chronological history of architecture and culture.

Fortunately for us, the Maya were seemingly obsessed with building. Here our contemporary society can find a model for the planning and construction of a homogeneous environment that is at once humanistic and inspirational. From the Maya we can learn the proper use of natural materials; individual creation within a common order; the balance of form and function; and the integration of art, architecture, and society.

Even though there are many "styles" of Maya architecture depending on their time and place, the durable precepts of Maya architecture beautifully formed by the massing of stone structures gave us one of the highest levels of stone architecture in the ancient world. The Maya, with a unified code of design elements and a series of fundamental aesthetic conventions, gave us a simple code: the common use of stone to create a continuum between city and architecture; symmetrical buildings often asymmetrically placed on raised platforms; buildings complete unto themselves but interrelated with their neighbors both visually and physically; the capturing of negative spaces within their cities by the surrounding multifaceted structures; and the beautiful use of integral ornamentation.

Those who visit the Maya sites can appreciate their former splendor. The remnants of this proud and dynamic civilization impart to the jungle of Guatemala, Belize, Honduras, and Mexico, including the arid flatlands of the Yucatán Peninsula, a unique, transcendent beauty.

By observing these ancient cities, we may eventually unlock the secret of the Maya's collapse. The energy, enterprise, and pride that enabled this people to create such majesty may well have held the seeds of their destruction. In their buildings, we may find not only the mortar that held their civilization together but perhaps the causes of its ruin as well.

Viewing the sprawling city of Uxmal or the sweeping Great Plaza at Tikal, we sense the enormous pride of the people who conceived and built such places. Was their decline indeed foretold in their greatness, in their insatiable desire to build, in the egos of their kings and rulers? As our scholars discover, study, and read their ancient hieroglyphics, we learn what motivated the Maya to create these colossal stone cities and hopefully understand how they attained such a keen sense of design. The Maya spoke to us using their hieroglyphic inscriptions, which covered most of their architecture—their wall panels, columns, façades, stairways, stelae and altars placed in front of structures or courtyards—and constituted an integral component of their built environment.[12]

# 1

**Simple Principles of Maya Architecture**

Maya architecture is anonymous, about community and not the artist.

Maya architecture is about space—the captured space between.

Maya architecture is about mass and beautifully proportioned form.

Maya architecture is about harmony and stability.

Maya architecture exhibits continuity among a community of buildings.

Maya architecture exhibits continuity with past generations.

Maya architecture is organic: it grows from its own seeds.

Maya architecture is about a tradition of repetitious forms.

Maya architecture is about horizontality, a marriage with the earth.

Maya architecture is about verticality, pointing to the heavens.

Maya architecture is the integration of art and architecture.

Maya architecture is shadows and light, color and texture, murals and sculpture.

Maya architecture is about one material—stone.

Maya architecture is the total manifestation of exquisite design.

Maya architecture is a treasure—to study and understand.

Chichén Itzá, Yucatán. Pyramid of Kukulcán/Quetzalcóatl (El Castillo). What mysteries of human achievement still lie buried under the dense jungle? As their ruins are unveiled, it becomes evident that the Maya cities were not isolated fantasies of one celebrity architect or ruler but the evolving creation of a harmonic and beautiful environment. Illustration by Frederick Catherwood, 1844.

# 2

## Essence of Maya Architecture

### What Remains—What It Might Have Been—What It Must Have Been

*If the lintels had been of stone, the principal buildings of this desolate city would at this day be almost entire; or, if the edifices had been still occupied under a master's eye, a decaying beam would have been replaced, and the buildings saved from ruin. In the moment of greatness and power, the builders never contemplated that the time would come when their city would be a desolation.*

John Lloyd Stephens, *Incidents of Travel in Central America, Chiapas, and Yucatán*

As we encounter the remnants of the Maya world, our mind's eye permits us a glimpse of three discrete realities: that which remains in the present for us to see, study, and experience; that which our imagination tells us might have been; and that which we know must have been.

Standing amid the ruined Maya sites today, we gaze on great stone edifices competing with tangled roots under umbrellas of vast, overreaching trees. Cicadas and crickets sound a low, hypnotic rhythm to which exotic birds of the jungle add the melody. Macaws cry out in shrill judgment of our disturbance of this peaceful serenity. This consonance of man-made beauty, veiled by the encroaching jungle, is at once wondrous and unsettling for logic tells us that for millennia society has battled nature. It tells

us that once, for a short time, he mastered this tenacious enemy, but the jungle eventually emerged victorious and continues to trespass upon all he has created. What we observe, therefore, is the counterpoint of man's articulate and rational creation and that which was before, and may one day return after, man.

Confused by these competing beauties, our imagination cannot refrain from peopling these sites with the figures we find on painted on pottery, temple walls, and carved in stone. Romantically, we envision powerful godlike leaders, bedecked in huge feather headdresses, precious jewelry, and colorful ornament. We hear the chorus of talk and laughter of the throngs who gathered in the plazas for important religious and state occasions. It is easy to visualize magnificent processions and pageants enlivening these grand plazas and broad-stepped acropolises. Then, suddenly, all sound ceases and every eye turns upward to the top of the great pyramid, where the god-king stands silhouetted in the temple doorway—a demigod seen through a haze of incense and cloaked in bright cotton, gleaming with jewels and flowing feathers.

Even as we conjure up such images, our rational intellect reminds us of what also must have been. Reality must have superimposed conflict, jealousies, war, famine, and disease on this society as on every other. Here lived people who loved and warred, celebrated and starved, built and destroyed.

As we scrutinize Maya architectural design, we are led to both objective and subjective conclusions. Objective analysis demonstrates a people with a strong sense of aesthetic understanding, a code of fundamental design conventions, and the ability to master difficult design problems. Subjectively, we see evidence of a proud people with a strong and unique architectonic spirit. Characteristics common to Maya architecture portray a people possessed with an ardent communal purpose, a rational order. We see master organizers and urban planners.

Slaves can be forced to perform the mundane tasks of building, but a people in bondage could not have created the monumental complexity, the detailed ornament, the synthesis of design, the caring embellishment or the engineering and planning that we see in Maya ruins. This must have been a labor of pride—of community.

The architecture of the Maya demonstrates an appreciation and protection of their values, a love of knowledge, continuity and deep-rooted learning passed from one generation to another. The Maya built on their past both physically and spiritually. They valued the forms of their relations and incorporated them into their present. Subjective analysis tells us, therefore, that they must have cared deeply about perpetuating their ancestors' fundamental beliefs, traditions, and knowledge.

The Maya developed all the design and building skills required to express abstract principles in their architecture. In their building arts, they understood that a strong city form endowed their religion and society with symbolic strength. They also understood the importance of molding the building materials at hand, revealing to their sensitive minds all the materials' intrinsic strengths and qualities. They used stone well.

Maya architecture was a symbol of power. The ruler and his elite nobility obviously had to constantly reinforce their prominence within their own city-state as well as with their rival trading partners. What could be more demonstrative of their skill and power? The vast amount of technical knowledge and human resources needed to construct giant monumental architecture in itself demonstrates power. It was literally the power to move mountains—for the pyramids became the society's sacred mountains.

## Mirror of a Culture

The Maya's mastery of architecture was an integral aspect of their life. The spirit and even the reality of the Maya ruins have resisted erosion, and the continuous appeal of Maya architecture over generations is testament to its intrinsic value.

A people skilled in architecture, sculpture, and drawing . . . not derived from the Old World but originating and growing up here without models or masters, having a distinct, separate, independent existence; like the plants and fruits of the soil, indigenous.[1]

Architecture reflects the culture that creates it. It is the mirror image of all the complex elements, interacting forces, and material the society possesses. It not only houses its people but also graphically expresses the human condition. Architecture is shaped by its society, and society, in turn, molds its architecture. Neither works in a vacuum—both are symbiotic.

To understand the development of Maya architecture, it is also essential to consider each historical, geographical, and social condition.

## Commonality of Mesoamerica

Linguistic and architectural evidence indicates that the Maya existed as a distinct people approximately four thousand years ago. But there was human habitation in the Maya region for thousands of years before the appearance of a uniquely Maya culture.

The Maya region did not exist in isolation but was part of a larger area called Mesoamerica, a term coined by the anthropologist Paul Kirchhoff in 1943. This region comprises the civilized parts of pre-Conquest Mexico and Central America from the Caribbean to the Pacific, including Guatemala, Belize, western Honduras, and western El Salvador. Its pre-Columbian civilizations, in addition to the Maya, were the Aztec, Huastec, Mixtec, Olmec, Tarascan, Teotihuacan, Toltec, Totonac, and Zapotec. These different cultures shared certain distinct features, the most important of which was monumental stone architecture and cities, including stepped pyramids, ball courts, and stucco plazas, for which lime, mortar, and concrete were used in construction. In addition, they cultivated the ancient triad of maize, beans, and squash; had similar cosmologies, and a resulting solar calendar; practiced common religious practices, such as human sacrifice and self-mutilation; were adept at higher mathematics using numeration; used hieroglyphic writing systems; and established public markets with the cacao bean as currency. Within this complex cultural matrix, the Maya civilization thrived.

But alongside these common elements were vast diversities in language, social organization, government, city plans, building technology, architecture, and artistic style.

## Two Formidable Obstacles

The Maya and their sister civilizations, including the earlier Olmecs, of pre-Columbian Mesoamerica achieved a remarkable greatness facing two formidable obstacles. First, Mesoamerica was generally isolated and therefore its people were spontaneous in their creations. They were not a part of a gradual evolution of knowledge and skills. They did not have older and more mature ancient societies to lean on, to learn from, to inspire, to study. The Greeks learned from the then-ancient Egyptians and Persians: visiting their cities, their architecture, their libraries, their art, and their achievements. The civilizations of Mesoamerica did not have this luxury.

The second obstacle was that the Maya built their glorious cities in a geography that was often hostile to its development. Their homeland was a relatively small sliver of land in Central America washed by two opposing giant oceans and seas. It is a narrow strip, a wisp of land connecting the great landmasses of North and South America. It probably, in some distant evolutionary day, will vanish as it is further elongated and stretched like a rubber band. Even though Mesoamerica is blessed most of the time with glorious weather, a warm climate, a tropical sun, beautiful beaches, and a highland's bounty of cool eternal spring, they also are the victims of a devastating array of shattering natural disasters. They have catastrophic storms that attack from each side—typhoons from the west and hurricanes from the east. It is a land where the earth's crust is fragile and where volcanoes continually erupt and the land vibrates violently from earthquakes and tremors. It is a land of sudden violent tropical storms and cloudbursts that breed mudslides and destruction.

So when we think of their grandeur—conceived and built without older civilizations to build upon—in a land with rhythmical natural destruction, their achievements become even more amazing. This, then, provides a perplexing question—why and how? The answer may lie in a simply fact. Simply stated, it is a land of stone that is easy to find and easy to shape. The stone can be fashioned to build shelter: shelter that provides protection—for the storing and accumulating of literature for thoughtful progress and achievement.

## Maya and Egyptian Architecture

A similar phenomenon to the emergence of the Maya's stone architecture occurred on the other side of the world in the parched desert of North Africa. Here, nurtured by the rich Nile, the Egyptians also built a similar rare and beautiful civilization. The Egyptians, during their formative period, also had few historic references and precedents and lived in a relatively hostile environment. The one thing that both the pre-Columbian civilization and the Egyptians shared was an abundance of easy-to-work stone. Stone to build cities—cities protected from the elements; cities that sheltered schools that taught astronomers, architects, and administrators; cities that built societies that received the blessings of organized administration, inspiriting pageantry while exhibiting public beauty and illustrative art. The Maya and Egyptian silhouettes were similar as were their achievements.

These accomplishments, however, were not mirrored in the ancient nomadic cultivations that did not have stone with which to build. The nomadic Indian tribes of North America and the nomadic tribes of North Africa did not attain the achievements that the Maya and Egyptians did.

Early earthen construction of the Maya drew from Olmec antecedents on the Gulf coast and the Preclassic and Early Classic highlands of Guatamala and Honduras (at Copán).

## Origins of Maya Architecture

The Olmec culture located in the coastal plain of southern Veracruz and adjacent Tabasco, Mexico, was in many respects the cradle of the Mesoamerican cultures. The Olmec thrived from 1200 to 400 BCE and established patterns for all the other regional societies to follow. They carved gigantic basalt sculptures and were believed to have devised the Long Count calendar and the ability to write.[2] The Olmecs constructed cities on elevated areas in the swampy landscape. They built pyramids in the core of their towns and at sites like La Venta, placing parallel buildings at the base of their pyramids. They had ball courts and channeled water for water management.[3] All these achievements gave the Maya and other adjacent civilizations a beginning. An example of the first Maya civilization was found at San Bartolo, a small pre-Columbian

Uxmal, Yucatán. Palace of the Governor. The palace's central block and its wings are connected by lofty vaults. The giant triangular vault was originally open but later walled in and fronted with columns and lintels. Illustration by Frederick Catherwood, 1844.

Maya archaeological site located in the Department of Petén in northern Guatemala. San Bartolo's fame derives from its splendid Late Preclassic mural paintings still heavily influenced by Olmec tradition.

The great central Mexican city of Teotihuacan, located northeast of modern Mexico City and founded around the beginning of the Christian Era, was the dominant power of Mesoamerica until the seventh century CE. It was a metropolis with an estimated population of 250,000 by 550 CE. Its influence, along with that of other Mexican civilizations, such as Monte Alban, spread throughout the Maya region during the Early Classic period and was a great influence on the subsequent ascendancy of the Maya culture.

Within the Mesoamerican superculture, the Maya were a highly original and defined culture characterized by their own language and hieroglyphic writing system; construction based on the Maya vault; their own system of notating numbers; specific ceramics and sculptural designs; their own calendar, possibly derived from the aforementioned, earlier Olmec culture; towns that were well organized and landscaped; and a consistent body of architectural conventions.

Maya communities were linked together by trade, marriage, alliances, the need for diverse materials, and the simple exchange of ideas. This interaction throughout the Maya region contributed significantly to the development of a unified civilization and the blossoming of its unique architecture.

The Maya civilization ultimately extended over three distinct regions, covering 125,000 square miles of Central America and Mexico. The northernmost Maya habitation was in the arid flatlands of the Yucatán Peninsula of Mexico. Farther south, they populated the lush lowland Petén jungle of Guatemala and neighboring Belize. Below that, the Maya occupied the highland mountains of Guatemala, western El Salvador, and Honduras.

The Maya Miraflores culture of the southern highlands was centered at the regional capital of Kaminaljuyu. It was one of the greatest Maya cities located at, and now destroyed by, the urbanization of present-day Guatemala City. It flourished by trade in obsidian, salt, fish, shells, cacao, jaguar skins, feathers, and other commodities from the lowland jungles. This highland civilization collapsed about 400 CE when the Maya of this southern area may have become vassals of Teotihuacan. Representatives of this distant culture ruled the captive Maya people and built for themselves a miniature version of their Mexican capital. The colonizers were, in turn, molded by the strong Maya, and a hybrid culture resulted.

The Central Mexican culture, called Esperanza, eventually created at Kaminaljuyu an architecture that was not purely Maya. Their stepped platforms added a series of rectangular panels with insets placed horizontally over the traditionally sloped batter walls of the pyramidal base. The architects, who must have been from Teotihuacan, adapted to the lack of good building stone by using clay brick faced with red-painted stucco.

Each platform had a single, central stairway topped by a thatch-roofed or flat-beamed roof temple. Each successive platform housed a tomb. The amazing fact was that Teotihuacan was between 800 and 900 miles to the north, and yet their trade, colonizers, and architecture were transported with seeming ease over this vast distance.

By the sixth century CE, the Teotihuacan domination over all of Mesoamerica had diminished, and the Classic Maya civilization burst into bloom. However, the Teotihuacan rulers who came to Caracol, Tikal, and Copán started the royal dynasties that dominated much of the Classic period.

## Preclassic Period

Although the history of civilizations never falls into clearly defined periods, in order to understand civilizations better, historians arbitrarily divide their development into epochs. Maya history is traditionally divided into three major periods.

The Maya Preclassic period dates from as early as 2,000 BCE. Prominent Middle and Late Preclassic settlements were located in the southern Maya lowlands and the Guatemalan highlands. In 500 BCE, the Maya city of El Mirador was a massive metropolis with thousands of pyramids. It was the capital of several interconnected cities that may have supported up to 1 million people with a developed and complex society. The archaeologist Richard Hansen, who led the excavations at El Mirador, calls it "the cradle of Maya civilization." Its civic center is six square miles and has at its center one of the world's largest pyramids, La Danta.

This period reaching back from 150 CE to the first recorded settlements is characterized by the domestication of maize, beans, and other crops; the development of terraced farming; high-quality art; precise calendars; and the importation of exotic items from the Caribbean and Pacific coasts.

During this period, the Maya were one of several agricultural societies developing in Mesoamerica, all sharing similar religious beliefs. In the Maya region around the Mirador basin, according to Hansen: the Maya built monumental architecture; made the major transition from clans to complex societies with class hierarchies and unified ideologies; moved massive limestone blocks without metal tools or the wheel; collected rainwater in reservoirs; created historic stelae; constructed homes with posts, stone, and stucco; decorated their teeth with inlays; shaped their infants' foreheads; sustained their burgeoning populations; started the specialization of labor; and evolved a regime of religious and social control.[4]

## Classic Period

The central Petén was the site of the full flowering of the Early Classic Maya civilization. Here archaeologists have found stelae—freestanding carved stone monuments—and the Maya vault. All the elements of the Classic period were in place in the southern lowlands by 100 CE, though the period is generally thought to extend from 250 to 900 CE. Knowledge seemed to spread by acculturation among the Maya-speaking people, who shared a common cultural heritage.

The development of the Maya Classic period was roughly contemporary with the origins of the pre-Columbian civilizations of Central Mexico and Oaxaca. It has been characterized by vaulted stone architecture, monumental inscriptions, polychrome pottery, and the use of the Long Count calendar to date Maya monuments.

Over a period of close to eight centuries, the Classic Maya reached their intellectual and artistic heights. This flowering of their culture is characterized by the creation of many urban societies with refined sculpture, architecture, mural painting, hieroglyphic inscriptions, painted vases, clay statuettes, mathematics, and astronomy, which all flourished.

Maya civilization during this period was characterized by expanding populations, a thriving economy, and a dominant ruling elite. The sites containing the ruins we know today, plus many still hidden beneath the jungle canopy, appear to have been the capitals of autonomous city-states. The larger of these "supersites" exercised hegemony over the lesser ones. The Late Classic period witnessed increasing competition among these regions, probably the single and strongest force motivating their elite to build their elaborate and monumental building enterprises.

## Postclassic Period

The Postclassic period of Maya history spanned from 900 CE to the Spanish invasion in the sixteenth century. It defines one of the most interesting and mysterious epochs—the time of the Maya collapse. By the tenth century, most of the Classic Maya centers had been abandoned to the encroaching forest, the Maya people had dispersed, and the population had dwindled.

In the vacuum created by the collapse of this civilization, the Toltecs from the north brutally invaded the Yucatán Peninsula in 987 CE and established their new capital at the city of Chichén Itzá. (For further discussion of the collapse, see chapter 7.)

At Uxmal in the Yucatán Peninsula, the last building was finished in 900 CE. By that time, the great southern Maya cities of El Mirador, Tikal, and Uaxcatún had already been abandoned. Uxmal and other centers in the Puuc Hills were also abandoned under duress following the Toltec invasion and their rebuilding of Chichén Itzá, which, in turn, was abandoned two hundred years prior to the Spanish conquest. The confederation of cities, one under the banner of Chichén Itzá and the other under Mayapan, ruled the day. The Postclassic period did not find the Maya population gone, but rather on the decline over the next four hundred years. Some Yucatán and Puuc cities, however, survived until 1100 CE.

## Geography

Among the many riddles associated with this civilization is how the Maya rose to such heights in one of the most inhospitable areas of the world, and why, in the first place, they chose this region in which to live and build their great cities. The geography of the region ranges from almost impenetrable jungle and mountains in the south to the harsh, limestone shelf of the Yucatán Peninsula in the north.

Architecture in its simplest form is the answer to man's need for shelter. Few parts of the globe are as geographically diverse as Mesoamerica, which includes every ecological extreme from snow-swept waste of high volcanoes to parched desert and rain-drenched jungle. This mysterious landscape of arid limestone, rushing streams, placid lakes, and magic mountains provided a most unusual setting for this unique, creative play.

With the exception of northern Yucatán and the Guatemalan highlands, the Maya territory, lying south of the Tropic of Cancer, is characterized by a warm, humid climate. The steamy, tropical rain forests of the lowlands are host to mahogany, wild fig, and ceiba trees more than 100 feet tall, creating a great canopy over the forest floor. The Usumacinta River flows from the western edge to the heart of the Southern Lowlands region, known as the Petén, and along with other smaller rivers and waterways, provided important arteries of communication.

Northern Yucatán, on the other hand, consists of a dry, featureless, flat terrain covered by scrubby vegetation. The base rock is almost entirely porous limestone. The entire region lacks mineral resources and is exceptionally difficult to cultivate. "Yucatán is a land of less soil than any I know, being all live flat stones with very little earth, so that there are few places where one can dig down a fathom without meeting great banks of large rocks," wrote Bishop de Landa.[5]

## Spanish Conquest

The Spanish conquest of the northern Maya began in 1528, under Francisco de Montejo, but not until 1542 did the Spaniards successfully establish their capital in Merida in the Yucatán Peninsula. Unlike the Aztecs to the north, the Maya by this time had no centralized authority to be toppled. The last Maya center, located at Lake Petén-Itzá, did not fall to the Spanish until 1697. The Spanish were cruel conquerors, systematically depopulating the area by enslavement and forced migration. While the Maya civilization had already declined by the time the Spanish arrived, many elements of Maya culture and religion remained, only to be disseminated and destroyed by the Spanish.

The tumultuous east coast of the Yucatán Peninsula, part of the diverse geography of Mesoamerica, which includes almost every ecological extreme.

# 3

## Manifestations of Maya Architecture

### Sacred and Rational Architecture

Architecture to the Maya was sacred, a gift to the gods. It symbolized and embodied their ideology and transformed it into universal and permanent form. Their architecture rarely crystallized as one static vision but was constantly changing as the result of a dynamic kaleidoscope of people and place. The Maya built for their needs, but they also needed to build. When we behold the sheer volume of the Maya ruins and realize these represent only a small fraction of that still hidden by the jungle, it becomes clear that this vast consumption of energy and material far exceeded the needs of any civilization for shelter. The Maya ruins demonstrate a love, or even religious passion, for building. This drive to express their civilization ultimately became a competitive, consuming, and self-destructive obsession.

It is possible that the Maya cities were metaphors for a sacred landscape: the pyramids as mountains (the word for pyramid and mountain in the Classic hieroglyphic system was the same), the summit "temples" as caves, the open plazas as water bodies, and the stelae as trees.

Employing sound engineering and clear aesthetic principles, the Maya built a monumental architectonic civilization. With a limited vocabulary of architectural elements—stone, adobe, thatch, stucco, bas-relief, the arch and vault—they created their own expressive language of vision. Their rules of design were rigid, their plans—limited by their stone and concrete structural system—inflexible, but all the elements of this language were in perfect balance, creating a unified whole.

Their cities, sparkling jewels, set with precision in either the midst of tangled verdant jungles or a cleared area, were as beautiful as any in the history of man. Theirs was a rational architecture set apart from nature. It was an architecture sculpted out of the available indigenous materials by skilled craftsmen who seemed intuitively to understand the principles of good design. The Maya developed a palette of architectural elements, unified from the smallest detail to the largest monumental building. Recurring shapes, silhouettes, and patterns, used in a variety of original ways, provide continuity within diversity. The Maya created an environment that was nestled in untamed nature but at the same time defied it, expressing the supremacy of man. Much of their environment was created and designed, but unintentional landscape modification also occurred by the rule of pure chance or good fortune.

Their architecture was probably the product of a unified effort of a civic-minded community. The Maya probably did not understand the broader commitment they were making to the building of a multigenerational civilization. Their architecture was a result of rulers, a superior elite, talented architects, proud and cooperative masses, and an almost unexplained aesthetic sensitivity—all converging at one moment in time.

Their buildings and cities satisfied their need for importance. Within their powerful forms, there was an incredible multiplicity of design elements, but one can feel the ultimate charm of its totality without being aware of the complex design principles involved.

Within a hostile and diverse geography, the Maya created a rational and totally integrated equilibrium for living. Their architectural forms were rigid and geometrical, without the spontaneous naturalness found in many primitive cultures. The Italian hill towns, for example, appear to emerge organically out of the hills; the stone villages that hug the Greek islands express romantic ideas that blend land and water, copying natural shapes, forms, and colors. In these naturalistic societies, the line where man's work ends and nature begins is often blurred, but the demarcation line in the Maya-built environment is sharp.

Maya cities shout boldly, Our society creates this! This is ours—our forms, our cities, and our architecture! We are creative and brash enough to shape and mold our own language of vision.

The Maya designers, in deliberately establishing an architectonic statement, forcefully declared their mastery and supremacy over nature. Here was proof of man's superiority and unity with the gods and ancestors, testimony that man's intellect and his aesthetic sensibility could create original forms and spaces that did not copy natural forms found in the raw landscape.

Clearing miles of jungle, Maya builders constructed a multitiered stone landscape. On the top of level terraces, they built acropolises adorned with pyramids—many-faceted structures and temples. These "man-made hills" may have suggested nature's rough-hewn mountains, but with a sharp geometry, form, and symmetry rarely seen in nature.

The sum of Maya architecture attested to the fact that organized society could conquer and sculpt this natural environment. The Maya manipulated nature, cleared it, cut it, mined it, carved it, shaped it, hauled it, constructed it, and decorated it. Where nature is free-form, Maya architecture is linear; where nature is frequently small-scaled, Maya is always monumental; where nature has soft, curved edges, the Maya used hard, straight lines. Maya architecture became a counterpoint to nature, an articulate expression of a strong individuality and self-confidence.

## Coherent Architecture

Maya architecture is based on a rigid set of cultural, historic, and aesthetic conventions that endowed its form with an overall unity, even though it was designed and built throughout a vast region by different rulers over hundreds of years. The predominant architectural characteristics were its solid limestone masonry construction; the Maya vault and arch; the use of mortar, stucco, and concrete; integrating of older built forms; monumental size and scale; and structures animated with integrated architectonic art. Its primary design elements included a strong horizontality; specific functions for stairs; inherent plasticity; bright exterior façades facing large public plazas; and dark, narrow interior spaces. Its artistic embellishments employed an abundance of integrated ornamentation animated with art of strong color, deep bas-relief, sculpture, graffiti, and narrative murals. Their total built assemblages were symbolic, metaphoric, historic, ancestral, impressive, and a stage set for public ritual and performance.

Maya plastic arts were part of the city fabric and embraced elegant stone stelae, altars, carved bas-relief, roof combs, bright vibrant murals, painted stucco reliefs, and ceramic sculpture and pottery. At Palenque, the roof combs were four stories high and covered with carved-plaster embellishments and painted. In Classic times they were not perforated as they are today.[1]

The buildings were used for various functions and were generally referred to as the pyramids, temples, palaces, ball courts, steam rooms, observatories, markets, and ceremonial platforms. These buildings were combined with theatrical stairs, balustrades, false chambers, roof combs, hidden passageways, and tombs. They were linked together by connective features such as paths, roads, and defined, flowing public spaces.

The predominant shape among Maya buildings was the strong base made up of either batter or vertical walls or a series of stepped platforms. This form was probably derived in early formative days from the natural tendency of piled earth to form a sloped surface.

## Disciplined Architecture

The synthesis of the arts achieved by the Maya has rarely occurred historically in the myriad of world civilizations and then only in the most successful and sophisticated cultures. Maya archaeological ruins attest to the Mayas attaining a high level of innate design talent. They were highly organized and disciplined, possessing an abundance of pride. Theirs was a solid world of knowable proportions based on a continuum of fixed aesthetic canons, not a world in flux.

This was architecture of precise measurements and not one of chance or chaos. The uniformity, cohesiveness, and refinement of Maya architecture entailed formal schooling, planning, and a sound understanding of engineering principles. From their ruins and few surviving books, as well as from their murals and graffiti, we can see that as architectural draftsmen, the Maya excelled. By developing precise instruments of measurement, they produced construction techniques that involved exacting geometric forms, including the complicated requirements of modular prefabrication. They purposely built an environment that exalted balance, proportion, and symmetry.

Out of the wilderness, using only stone tools, the Maya chiseled massive cities and monuments without the elementary devices common to most early civilizations. They had no metal tools, wheeled vehicles, carts, or beasts of burden. There were no hoisting devices, cranes, winches, or other forms of tackle; they adapted using only the most rudimentary methods of transport, mostly their backs and shoulders. Their seemingly superhuman achievements were created by the sweat and muscle of humans and by the extraordinary organization of multitudes of people who had to be directed and disciplined by respected leaders in a precise and well-orchestrated manner.

Throughout their thousand-year Golden Age, generation after generation labored in the tropical heat of Mexico and Central America, felling trees, quarrying and hauling tons of stone great distances over difficult terrain, and then positioning and securing it. After this back-breaking effort, the edifices were then embellished with fine carvings and beautiful paintings.

It is doubtful that force or dictatorial power alone could motivate a civilization to build to such an extent. The monumentality and beauty of Maya construction required harnessing not only the muscle of multitudes but their communal dedication as well. The refinement of forms demonstrates a sensitivity, thoughtfulness, and devotion that cannot be commanded. Men captured in battle can be compelled to move and pile stone upon stone, but only pride and skill could produce the complex artistry represented in Maya architecture.

### Architecture and Allied Arts

The cooperative effort by the creative class—the architects, artisans, weavers, painters, sculptors, scribes, and masons—was the link connecting the vision of the elite to the reality the populace beheld. Building was directly connected with the ambitions of the ruling class, while religion undoubtedly provided a powerful motivation to the legions of the laboring class who toiled year after year to bring to fruition design conceived by their theocratic overlords. Building façades featured huge heads of gods for adoration and offerings. Later, in the Late Classic period, the decorations were placed on the upper façades of the pyramids in the construction of towering stone roof combs. The temples and their roof combs looked like gods enthroned on high.

Peasant laborers created the environment in which the nobility enacted their rites and ceremonies. These elite, in turn, guided every aspect of Maya life: keeping time, predicting future events, prescribing rituals and sacrifices, and promising prosperity and a happy after-life in return for work and obedience. The Classic Maya civilization appears to have been a product of the brilliance of a few superior and gifted leaders and the industry of tens of thousands whose work exhibits their pride and dedication to communal effort.

Maya architecture was more than a shell or exterior space. It was an organic unity of intrinsically harmonious elements—an all-inclusive environment. It was an expression of its own life. Its geometry was so clearly etched that it required no mental completion on the part of the viewer. It exuded a feeling of order in which its ornamentation breathed life into its soul. Its permanence and clarity of purpose rendered it an aesthetic experience that radiated the human condition, sheltered and secure.

The overall effect of Maya architecture on the viewer was pure pleasure, for it used the most unpretentious material—stone—luxuriously. It involved all the senses: sight was stimulated by the tonalities of its painterly walls of bright splashes of pure color; and sounds of everyday life echoed within the surrounding buildings of the public plazas, as did the music on festival days. The building shapes captured subtle nuances of the sun and bolstered the Maya fixation on time. The structures made everyone aware of the continuing process of life. The beautifully costumed Maya, with their resplendent dyed cotton and florescent feathers, added the human scale and dimension. Architecture and its spaces were a constant reassertion of the dynamic life of the society.

## Superimposition

Historic preservation, as practiced throughout the world today, means preserving an occasional historic building, often out of context with its new neighbors, or saving an entire district or neighborhood. The Maya, however, had a unique way of preserving their heritage. Their cities were continuously in a state of birth and rebirth. Their imposing palace complexes were always being added to, reshaped, and redesigned many times by the superimposition of new pyramids, temples, shrines, and palaces.

A lot of what we know about the Maya is reinforced by this one singular principle of Maya architecture—the practice of superimposition, or building a new and larger structure on top of an existing one. The Maya did not hesitate to build over a building when the structure no longer served its purpose or when it became politically expedient to build. Also, the Maya continuously remodeled or enlarged structures from their ancestral past, often with new functions and meanings.

The Maya centers grew continuously both upward and outward partly through this practice of superimposition. The construction was in multiple and distinct episodes with one structure often overlaying an earlier one and built with reused materials.[2] It was common for such construction to celebrate a royal birth, the ascendancy or death of a leader, a time cycle, or a new discovery. Superimposition provided continuity and a natural evolution of forms. Cities grew organically in a gradual, evolutionary process. In spite of individual differences in detail or subtle changes in function, the footprint of their ancestral architecture molded their future forms over centuries of building.

Although sometimes the space between the new, outer structure and the older inner, building was filled with rubble, in superimposition the earlier structure usually but not always influenced the shape and form of the new building. The new was invariably an expression of the past so that generation after generation of Maya builders perpetuated the traditions and principles given them by their ancestors. Each new structure was larger and grander than the one over which it was erected. A common "genetic" style was therefore created and lived.

Examples of architectural superimposition abound, the North Acropolis at Tikal being one of the clearest. Its maze of stone platforms, masks, and structures result from nineteen superimposed transformations. Another clear example is the Pyramid of the Magician at Uxmal, built over a period of three centuries and enclosing five superimposed pyramids.

By incorporating elements of earlier structures into new buildings, the Maya created a living, continuing form of urban renewal. The Maya approach to historic preservation was more fundamental than those in our contemporary society. Now historic preservation often means saving a single "historic" building, even though the neighborhood context may have radically changed.

A second and obviously better contemporary concept of historic conservation, used only occasionally, is the preservation of an entire neighborhood, where all the structures remain in the context of their original environment and scale. Two examples come to mind: the preservation

The original Group A-V at Uaxactún and the seven successive superimpositions that enlarged the complex are shown in this series of views. Examples of architectural superimposition abound, the North Acropolis at Tikal being one of the clearest. Its maze of stone platforms, masks, and structures results from nineteen superimposed transformations. Another clear example is the Pyramid of the Magician at Uxmal, built over three centuries and enclosing five superimposed pyramids. From Tatiana Proskouriakoff, *An Album of Maya Architecture*, composite from 111, 113, 115, 117, 119, 121, 123, 125.

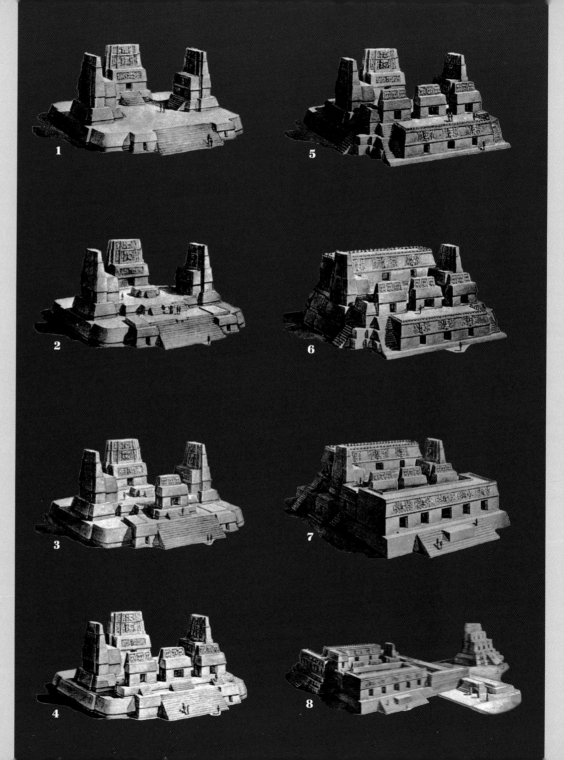

of the system of "green urban squares" in historic Savannah, Georgia, which provided a simple and human organization; and the South Beach Art Deco neighborhood of Miami Beach, Florida, where large areas of low-rise residential apartment houses preserve the scale of the architectural style.

However, the Maya had the best method of historic preservation. They kept the footprint, the genetic DNA, of their ancestors on which to create new forms and functions. The past, therefore, was not dead but living in the present. As the times and rulers changed and religious symbols were replaced, the Maya changed and enlarged their cities in a constant beehive of building activity. Their architecture, never abandoned, remained a living representation of their society at each moment in their history. This practice of superimposition has provided archaeologists with an invaluable resource. The erection of buildings on top of existing structures has often preserved the earlier structure in perfect condition, enabling archaeologists to study the development of successive Maya periods, styles, and techniques.

The Maya were obsessed with time. Their complex, interrelated calendars tracked both linear progression and repetitive cycles. The practice of superimposing buildings on earlier edifices may have reflected an important—even religious—process of spiritual renewal. For the Maya, along with other Mesoamerican cultures such as the Aztecs, the changing of the fifty-two-year cycle marked a time of regeneration, when buildings, works of art, and even domiciles were sometimes destroyed and rebuilt.

## Symbolic Architecture

During the Late Preclassic period, architecture began to serve a symbolic function in the Maya universe. It became a way in which the social and religious order communicated to the common people. The integration of Maya architecture into the overall cosmology of the civilization

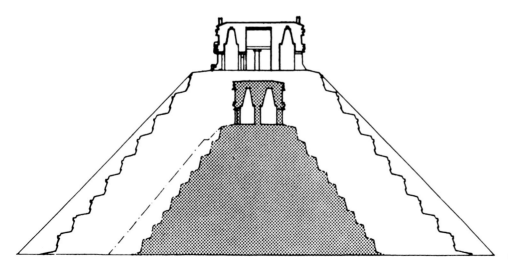

Section of the Pyramid of Kukulcán/Quetzalcóatl (El Castillo) at Chichén Itzá showing the two superimposed buildings: the first pyramid has been rediscovered beneath the masonry of the second. From Henri Stierlin, *Encyclopedia of World Architecture*, 438.

is nowhere as apparent as in the orientation of Maya buildings. The position of the sun, moon, and planets; the seasonal changes; and the solstices and the equinoxes determined the placement of Maya structures and their relationship to one another. Although the astronomical and cardinal orientation is not fully understood, many phenomena have been observed that relate to the positioning of Maya buildings and monuments.

One of the most spectacular examples of the manipulation of building orientation to create dramatic and symbolic effect is found at the Pyramid of Kukulcán/Quetzalcóatl (El Castillo) at Chichén Itzá. It was the creative product of a precisely planned and conceived work of architecture. Twice a year, a few days before and after the equinox, and a few hours before sunset, the sun enacts a visual drama written and orchestrated by the ancient Maya architects. The shadow of an undulating serpent is cast on the balustrade of the pyramid, ending in a giant sun-lit stone serpent's head. As the sun sets, the snake descends the steps of the pyramid in September and ascends in March. If this mystifies us, sophisticated and urbane as we are, imagine the mesmerizing effect that it must have had on the common Maya back then. I was fortunate to have made a documentary film on Maya architecture for the government of Yucatán state and observed this phenomenon.

The solar orientation of Maya buildings endowed them with the function of both clock and calendar, enabling the priests to use them as a magical and mystifying source for their prognostications. When predictable shadows appeared on the surface of the buildings, signaling the time to plant, harvest, or celebrate an annual festival, the brilliance of the prophetic priests was reinforced, suggesting deep knowledge and even supernatural powers.

Another of many examples of the symbolic orientation based on the sun is found at the ball court at Copán in Honduras. The court is positioned so that at the equinox, the center arches of the two opposing structures defining the space on either side are aligned perfectly with the rising and setting sun. At sunset, the sun completely lights the eastern façade without the thinnest shadow being cast by the north or south walls.

Additional archaeoastronomical phenomena have been discovered by the Guatemalan archaeologist Victor Segovia Pinto at the House of the Seven Dolls at Dzibilchaltún. At the time of the equinoxes, the placement of the windows on opposing walls is such that there is a precise alignment with respect to the sun. Also, the alignment and measurement of some of the edges of the various thick doorways were found to correlate with the phases of the moon. The projection of moonlight was obviously taken into account when the building was positioned and detailed.

The general orientation of buildings seems to have evolved during the Classic period from approximately fifteen degrees east of north in the Early Classic period to a true magnetic north by the end, suggesting the possible discovery of a magnetic device.

Within the city, the asymmetrical, and sometimes seemingly random, placement of buildings and complexes may be attributable to this need to orient structures according to astronomical phenomena.

Complementing the symbolic placement of Maya buildings, religious icons and historical imagery dominate the decorative elements of Maya architecture. Maya mythology and history were written explicitly on the buildings, teaching generations the cultural ideology through iconography and symbolic storytelling.

The city plans of Uxmal and Copán are particularly notable for the precision of their layout and for the fact that the baseline of the Pyramid of the Magician at Uxmal is parallel to the baseline at Copán. Standing on the pyramid at the vernal equinox, one can observe the sun setting along this line, while during the autumnal equinox, the sun rises on this same line.

# 4

# Building Materials

*Throughout, the laying and polishing of the stones are as perfect as under the rules of the best modern masonry.*

John Stephens on the stonework he found at Copán, *Incidents of Travel in Central America, Chiapas, and Yucatán*

The Maya buildings, both in the dry Yucatán Peninsula and the rain forests of Petén and Chiapas, are the most well preserved in Mesoamerica, a tribute to their ancient architects. Their ability to withstand time and invasion by the exuberant landscape results in large measure from the quality of building materials, particularly the excellent limestone that hardens after it is first quarried and carved, mortar, and concrete; the thickness of the walls, some exceeding three feet in thickness; and the strength of the Maya arch and vault.

It is quite obvious to an observer of the ruins that fine workmanship in the building process was a mark of character and pride within the Maya society. Poor quality in construction and an unattractive appearance would have been a travesty against the gods.

Unlike the megalithic construction of a simple stone pyramid, most Maya building did not rely on a singular mass. Rather, their sprawling cities were composed of millions of stones ambling along the face of their structures, delicately balanced and fashioned into wondrous, complex architectural forms and patterns. Considering the Maya's

limited resources and technology and their relative isolation, their architectonic achievement is truly amazing. Their inventive use of stone and concrete proclaimed an honesty of construction that was brought to life by the embellishment of integrated surface detailing.

## Lime and Concrete

The Petén and Usumacinta areas and the Yucatán Peninsula boast an almost inexhaustible supply of easily cut limestone that could be fashioned with fine flint and obsidian. The Maya of the lowlands discovered early that burning limestone created lime. Palenque limestone—at least that used in the finer carvings—is as dense as the famed lithographic stone of Europe; elsewhere the quality varies greatly.

Mesoamericans architecture, therefore, followed closely the discovery of this lime-burning process. This might have been the single-most important stroke of ingenuity that changed simple cultures into some of the world's greatest designers of the built environment.

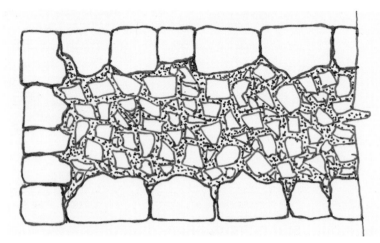

Section of a typical Maya wall with regularly hewn stone blocks surrounding a concrete core. Illustration by Kenneth Treister.

The technique of making and using plaster, mortar, and concrete from burned lime, then, played a decisive role in Mesoamerican building practices and influenced not only their structural forms but also the shape of their spaces and the character of their design. Initially, lime was used sparingly to provide an impermeable and smooth coating for plazas and a veneer for the wood lattice superstructures of the early perishable buildings. Its evolving use permitted massive rubble-concrete (not universally used) and masonry structures. Stucco was an excellent medium for unifying the diverse surfaces of stone and for stucco sculptural reliefs; it also was used as a base for painting and mural design.

The Maya structural, concrete walls were often formed by successive courses of dressed stone so that no additional forming was required and the wall was finished when the last concrete in the core set.

## Stone, Wood, and Brick

If one had to define Maya architecture, it would be as the capturing, on a monumental scale, of exterior spaces by a built environment, with stone and stucco being the common unifying elements. This is the essence of the Maya city—its shape, its texture, its permanence. Without everlasting stone, we would not be standing among the ruins, wondering and fantasizing. Stone was the measure of their art. It was a material quarried directly from the earth, shaped but unchanged. It was a material expressive of the Maya's desire to be part of the earth, rooted in their place. It was a simple building material that, when combined with lime, could be molded into any form, limited only by man's imagination, convention, and fashion.

Above all, stone gave the Maya continuity and a history. Their cities, and thus their society, were unified through the use of one material. If I had to choose between visual chaos with an occasional great building, or harmony, order, and unity without the occasional greatness, I would choose the latter. The Maya had both.

Earliest Maya structures combined beaten earth and wood, materials readily available in the rain forests of Central America, where gigantic trees often rose to heights of more than 100 feet. As building technology developed, limestone became the predominant building substance for monumental public buildings. In some areas, sandstone, rhyolite, and trachyte were also used, but always in a manner similar to that used with limestone. These relatively soft stones, which hardened when exposed to the weather, were quarried with tools made from flint and obsidian and transported on wooden rollers to the building sites.

Even after the advent of stone construction, the Maya continued to use wood and other perishable materials for private dwellings, for temples perched atop lofty pyramids, for lintels with ornamentation, as well as for scaffolding and supports required during the construction process. We can still find rare examples of skillfully carved wooden lintels in some of the most sophisticated stone buildings.

Where no stone was readily available, the imaginative and innovative Maya used kiln-fired brick as their basic building block. Comalcalco, in the north central Tabasco of Mexico, is the most important example. Interestingly, the brick slabs one finds there are often thinner than the layers of the joining mortar, which give it strength.

## Arches and Vaults

The highest structural achievement of the Maya in the building of their great civilization was the invention of concrete, which in turn gave birth to the so-called Maya arch and the subsequent vaults. This, like so much of Maya architecture, evolved from their basic residential hut. The Maya developed a concrete arch that could span short distances yet by repetitious positioning create vaults to create long rooms that were the basic rectangle of the hut. This was a revolutionary invention.

The Maya arch is not an arch in our traditional definition of a stone arch. A time-honored arch is a stone structure that is arranged in a radial pattern with thrusts that are counterbalanced so that the opposing walls end at the crown of their curve with a single keystone that ties the entire stone structure together. It is a system where all the masonry construction works together to span a space.

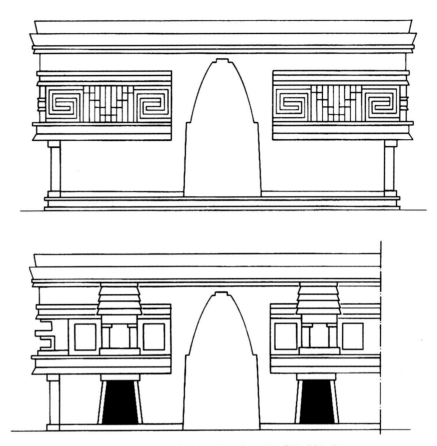

Arch at Labná, Yucatán. From Henri Stierlin, *Encyclopedia of World Architecture*, 431.

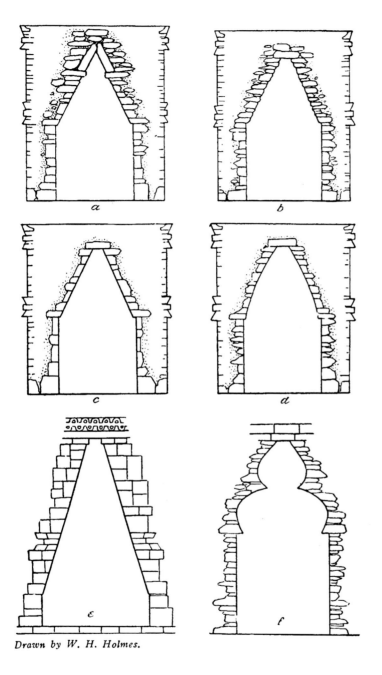

Drawn by W. H. Holmes.

The Maya arch is a concrete arch and not a "corbel arch," as has been mistakenly reported in numerous works on the Maya. The corbel arch, or false arch, is constructed with progressive cantilevering or corbelling of stone in horizontal rows from the two sides until they meet at their center apex, then fit with a keystone. This mischaracterization was made by authors observing only the exterior surface of the arches while not considering the interior structural strength of the lateral walls.

In early buildings in the Petén and Yucatán, the exterior-forming stones, used only to form the concrete, were corbelled in neat horizontal courses with each stone overhanging the one below, so that a quick observation led many to believe it was a "corbel arch." These arches, however, were actually held by the strength of the cement and rubble concrete and not by the dynamics of the corbelled stone itself.

The true Maya arch is therefore a concrete arch comprised of two adjoining concrete walls, each of which gets wider and wider or thickened as they get higher and approach each other until the space between is closed. These concrete walls enclosed the space and gave the Maya a structural system that was then repeated over and over, forming the modular basis of all their interior architecture.

Types of Maya vaults: (*a*) section of cuneiform arch with Acute apex, Chichén Itzá; (*b*) section of ordinary arch with flat capstone; (*c*) section of ordinary arch with dressed surfaces; (*d*) section of ordinary arch with dressed surfaces and curved soffit slopes; (*e*) portal arch with long slopes, showing masonry of exterior facing; (*f*) Section of trefoil, portal arch of Palenque. From George Oakley Totten, *Maya Architecture*, 31.

The stone facing of the rubble concrete walls that one sees is actually the concrete forms that were used to place the concrete. To build a wall, the Maya would start from the bottom by adding facing stones one above the other and then filling the subsequent void between the walls' two faces with rubble concrete. By using horizontal dressed stone as forms, the interior walls were finished when the concrete set, and no additional facing material was needed. Rubble was used in their concrete in place of the contemporary gravel, but the result was the same structural concrete.

The Maya arch and vault together was a singular, amazing engineering achievement that was strangely not followed by subsequent evolutionary changes of larger and more complex concrete structures. The Romans, who also invented concrete, developed the Roman vault that replaced the Egyptian and Greek post-and-lintel system, and then went on to create a plastic, free, concrete architecture of rounded forms using the arch, vault, and dome. The Maya stopped at the concrete arch and vault.

## Walls and Windows

As discussed above, the basic structural system in most, but not all, Maya architecture was the concrete wall consisting of a matrix of lime mortar embedding stone rubble. Some walls were composite, with their centers packed with pounded earth and rubble. The concrete walls not only formed the vertical structural surfaces of most buildings but also became the roof as they expanded toward the top to form the Maya arch. The concrete was surfaced with cut and dressed stone that was rectangular on its face and sometimes was tenoned into the concrete

wall in a triangular form. In early Maya structures, the facing stones occasionally contributed to the structural strength of the building, but by the Classic period, the stone facings served simply as a form to pour the concrete and as a veneer for the rubble concrete beneath it.

Although years of abandonment and natural decay have left only the uncovered stone that we see today, in earlier times the exposed surfaces of both the interior and exterior walls were covered with layers of smooth, glistening stucco, and often painted sculptures embellished the entry. Colorful cotton curtains closed off doorways.

Few Maya edifices had windows, as we know them. Archaeologists often characterized the tiny wall openings as "ventilation holes," but they are, in the strictest sense, windows. The Palace of Seven Windows at Tikal is an exception, containing a variety of windows of different shapes and sizes. At Palenque, we can find beautifully sculptured trilobite openings, and at Dzibilchaltún, the symmetrically placed windows form giant eyes in the anthropomorphic face created in the façade of the Temple of the Seven Dolls.

## Prefabrication

One of the fascinating aspects of Maya architecture is the technique of constructing ornamentation using the techniques of prefabrication—a concept commonly thought to have had its birth in the industrial age. Small ornamental stone elements were accurately carved in remote production areas and then assembled and placed into the façade as part of huge interlocking jigsaw puzzles. The resultant complex geometric patterns took on a vibrant life of their own when installed on the sunlit façades.

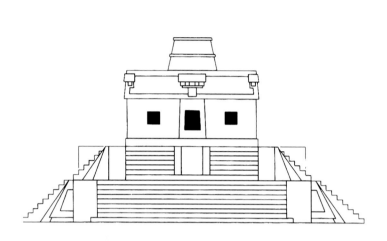

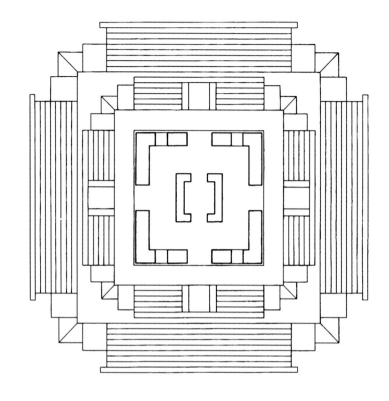

Dzibilchaltún, Temple 1. The only known example of the use of windows in Maya architecture. From Henri Stierlin, *Encyclopedia of World Architecture*, 427.

Such sophisticated mass production required a preconceived design, an organized and systematic method of manufacture, and an elaborately calculated system of spacing and mounting. The centralized organization that such a precise building technique required tells us a great deal about the highly structured Maya society.

One of the most beautiful examples of the mass production of stone components is found in the frieze of the Palace of the Governor at Uxmal. This interlocking geometrical pattern of lattice, frets, cubes, and zoomorphic figures is composed of more than twenty thousand mosaic blocks. These were not thin slabs of veneer but modular building components weighing 55–175 pounds each. There was little margin for error. Even slight inaccuracies repeated over the building's surface of 7,500 square feet would have had calamitous consequences.

The concept of modular mosaics inserted into the Maya's ornamentation also applied to their town-planning designs, where individual buildings or groups of buildings were inserted into a larger organized urban pattern.[1]

## Terraces and Foundations

One of the fundamental architectural forms developed by the Maya and the other pre-Columbian cultures were broad platforms used as substructures for their buildings. These artificial plateaus, often with battered faces, married the structure to the earth. These multitiered platforms created a gradual transition from the plaza to the building proper. The foundations and supporting platforms were made of beaten earth, rubble stone, or concrete, and if above ground, covered with a topping of cut stone and stucco.

The size and complexity of the stepped terraced substructures corresponded to the ruler's wealth or social status, or to the ritualistic function of a public building. Aesthetically, the use of diminishing stacked platforms graphically reinforced the horizontality of Maya architecture and the humanistic marriage of building and earth. This stacking of terraces forms the rudimentary design element, not only of the Maya pyramids but for all Maya

Kabáh. The largest and most beautiful of the Puuc Hill cities in Yucatán. The most decorated building, the Palace of the Masks, is raised on a series of stepped platforms. Its façade is covered with 250 rain-god masks, each made up of thirty units of mosaic stone, creating a texture that matches the structure's roof comb. From Tatiana Proskouriakoff, *An Album of Maya Architecture*, 67.

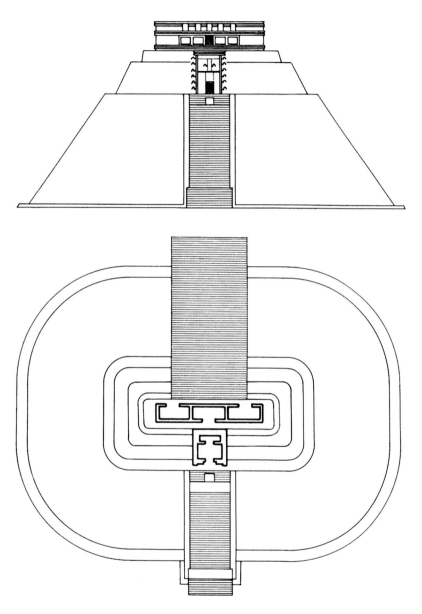

architecture. These terraces served as colossal pedestals with the important function of giving public structures *height, status, and visual significance.*

The spacious plazas where the Maya gathered for festivities and ceremonies were enclosed and defined by these surrounding stepped terraces. Broad monumental stairways graced their inclined surfaces, providing access to the top and reinforcing the strong horizontality of the architectural complex. The well-proportioned, elongated steps not only were strong elements of design but also served as reviewing stands for the repetitive cycles of ritual performances. From these stairs the populace could watch festivities and ceremonies held in the plaza or the ball court.

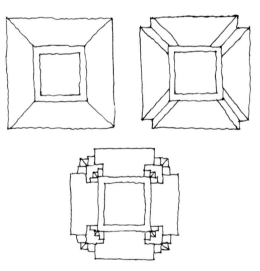

*Left:* Uxmal, Yucatán. Pyramid of the Magician. From Henri Stierlin, *Encyclopedia of World Architecture*, 434.

*Above:* The Maya were superb in architectural design. This diagram shows how a simple base can be changed into a noble work of art by the rhythmic articulation of the corners. The bottom sketch is of Temple 1, Dzibilchaltún. Illustration by Kenneth Treister.

Chichén Itzá, Yucatán. Temple of the Warriors, Column of the Plumed Serpent. Illustration by Kenneth Treister.

The manner in which a work of architecture rises out of the earth often helps determine its quality. The gradual, graceful marriage between architecture and the land was achieved by the Maya with a strong transition starting at the platform base and rising gradually on an inclined plane in a manner so measured that your eye travels skyward without discernable effort.

## Construction Costs

The archaeologist Richard Hansen estimated the labor cost for the construction of the Preclassic La Danta Pyramid at the Maya city of El Mirador: "We calculate that as many as 15 million man-days of labor were expended on La Danta. . . . It took 12 men to carry each block—each one weighs about a thousand pounds. . . . We've excavated nine quarries where the stones were cut, some 600 to 7000 meters away."[2]

## Integration of Art and Architecture

In our contemporary world, the fields of art and architecture are basically considered independent of each other and only distantly related. Both are taught and discussed as objects mystically floating in their own space. In the world of Maya creativity—art and architecture are one. The line where one begins and another ends is blurred; the two are inseparably fused. In the example shown, the column, one of two, at the entrance to the interior sanctuary of the Temple of the Warriors, at Chichén Itzá, is structurally important. It is also a magnificent sculpture of an open-jawed, plumed serpent, representing Kukulcán/Quetzalcóatl, with the rattler beautifully wrapping around the sculpture.

Chichén Itzá, Yucatán. Temple of the Warriors, portico column depicting the feathered serpent, Kukulcán/Quetzalcóatl, the cultural hero of Mexican theology. From George Oakley Totten, *Maya Architecture*, 132.

Copán, Honduras. An example of the integration of art and architecture is this painting, by George Oakley Totten, of a statue found almost complete on the Hieroglyph Stair, Copán. The colors are the painter's conjecture of probable colors. The green feathers represent the plumes of the quetzal bird. The stair was covered by hieroglyphs with intervals, like this, of seated human figures. From George Oakley Totten, *Maya Architecture*, 49.

# 5

## Building Types

### Houses

In ancient societies, form follows tradition as well as function. The distant forebears of the Maya were wandering hunters and gatherers who did not build permanent settlements. The domestication of maize marked the end of the Maya's nomadic existence and the beginning of an agricultural economy with fixed settlements. Ultimately the Maya would rise to take their place as one of the truly great civilizations of history.

The Maya domestic house dwelling, the building unit of early settlements, has been in existence for more than five thousand years, successfully withstanding hurricanes and all other natural phenomena. It was the progenitor of much subsequent Maya architecture during their Golden Age, showing the enduring attachment the Maya had for their original house form.

Their small dwellings, called *na*, were constructed of pole and thatch with walls of twigs covered with limestone plaster. These houses were generally rectangular with semi-circular ends, though other shapes were used. To the Maya, this oval shape represented the universe, and their houses were customarily oriented along an axis described by the rising and setting sun.

The houses were usually raised on low, rectangular mounds of earth and platforms faced with stone, protecting them from the summer floods and the dampness of the natural grade. Even today, one can identify these mounds around the periphery of the ruins of the Maya cities, frequently clustered along ridges where the soil was well drained. The homes of commoners were structures built of readily available local materials by skilled craftsmen following traditional conventions that rarely varied. Practical functional use was more important than any aesthetic or symbolic considerations. There were no fashions, just repetitive traditions.

In his *Yucatán Before and After the Conquest*, de Landa wrote:

In building their homes their method was to cover them with an excellent thatch they have in abundance, or with the leaves of a palm well adapted to that purpose, the roof being very steep to prevent its raining through. They then ran a wall the length of the whole house, leaving certain doorways into the half which they call the back of the house, where they have their beds. The other half they whiten with a very fine whitewash, and the chiefs also have beautiful frescoes there. . . . The roof drops very low in front as a protection against sun and rain; also, they say, the better to defend the interior from enemies in case of necessity.[1]

In dimension, the houses were higher than their length and width, and their internal space formed a great inverted "V" under the thatch roofs. This internal height, the orientation, the self-ventilating thatch, and the absence of openings that would have admitted the tropical sun kept the house relatively cool. Today the Maya do not cook inside their houses but in an adjoining lean-to. In the past, however, the center of the house always had a three-stone triangular hearth. This hearth was the center of family life symbolically and functionally, where the women prepared the food while the men were in the fields, called *kol*, raising maize, beans, squash, and chilies.[2]

The proportions, the shape of the interior spaces, the entryway, and the relative darkness of the house interiors are features that influenced later stone buildings. Even when the exteriors of Maya buildings are monumental and grand, their interior spaces reflect the simple pattern of their house.

The pole-and-thatch houses were often built in compounds, with several enclosed within a continuous stucco-covered stone wall. Such unified family groupings provided common protection and an enclosure for their livestock and domesticated animals, chiefly dogs and turkeys. The resulting hamlets were roughly 250 square yards. In the center, the farmers often created a small shrine or communal building. For every fifty to one hundred dwellings, a minor ceremonial center was built. This type of village growth occurred naturally over time and was the antithesis of the well-ordered Maya ceremonial city.

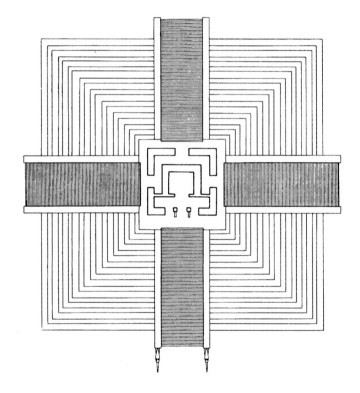

Chichén Itzá, Yucatán. Pyramid of Kukulcán/Quetzalcóatl (El Castillo). From Henri Stierlin, *Encyclopedia of World Architecture,* 438.

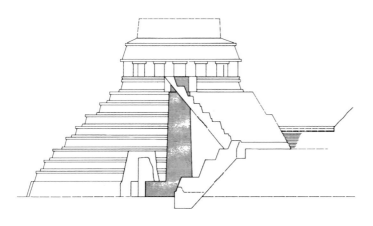

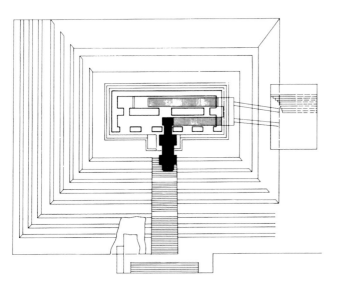

Palenque, Chiapas. Pyramid of Inscriptions. From Henri Stierlin, *Encyclopedia of World Architecture*, 429.

The houses, called *choazas* by the Spanish, were often depicted in ancient stone carvings and have remained virtually unchanged over the centuries. Since they are still used today by the Maya's descendants, they enable us to understand the connection between the earliest Maya buildings made of perishable materials and their successors in stone.

## Pyramids

The Maya pyramids were the most prominent image of the Maya built environment. Whether as the home of the gods or the honored dead, these structures formed the heart of the city, the link between the living and the divine. The pyramids, like those of ancient Egypt, probably evolved from the simple platform tomb. In Egypt, the *mastabas*—the single-story rectangular tombs with inclined walls—were stacked one upon the other in gradually diminishing sizes to form the original stepped pyramid. In Maya architecture, the platform served as a common building foundation, particularly among the Preclassic period Miraflores people, into a funeral platform where they entombed their rulers in a log-roofed chamber beneath the front staircase. The platforms were placed one on top of the other in successive burials, eventually forming the pyramidal shape.

The outer casting of the pyramid was faced with cut and dressed stone over an interior core of clay, earth, or rubble. The thick layer of stucco that covered the surface of the pyramid must have been dazzling in the clear tropic sun, particularly as most were painted dark red and were silhouetted against the dark-green mantle of the surrounding landscape.

Tikal, Guatemala. Temple 2. In 1941, a friend of the author, Edwin Shook of the Carnegie Institution of Washington, measured this pyramid, its platform, and the remaining portions of the roof comb. Note the beautiful articulation at the corners and the strong massing of this stepped pyramid. From Tatiana Proskouriakoff, *An Album of Maya Architecture*, 7.

The honored deceased was entombed in a seated position on a wooden bier, accompanied on his voyage to the other world by rich offerings, including eating utensils, shell trumpets, wood drums, pearls, rich textiles, jaguar paws, mirrors, utilitarian and art objects, and persons sacrificed for the occasion.

The pyramids eventually became man-made hills or symbolic mountains, establishing a vertical link between the Maya and their profusion of gods. The shape marries the underworld to the earth and the earth to the sky in a most gentle and gradual way.

This entire architectural system—the pyramid, grand stairway, and temple at the apex—provided a dramatic symbol within the Maya cityscape. Here the Maya priest literally ascended to meet the governing forces in the heavens above. The multitudes below must have found the silhouette of the pyramid, with its temple and towering roof comb, an awe-inspiring sight.

## Temples

Religion permeated every aspect of Maya life and embraced a pantheon of gods who helped the Maya understand their world and their place in its scheme. They had a god of rain, corn, light, sun, and childbirth, among many others. Theirs was a demanding religion that required fasting, abstinence, self-mutilation, and animal and human sacrifice.

The religion was administered by what we might call religious nobility, who counseled the chiefs in matters of science and ceremony. They wrote and read the books, conducted the temple services, taught science, kept the calendar, administered the religion, conducted festivals

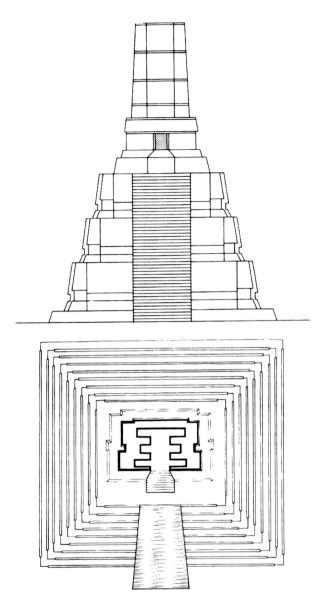

Tikal, Guatemala. Temple 2. Note the syncopated articulation of the pyramid's corners illustrating the greatness of Maya architecture. From Henri Stierlin, *Encyclopedia of World Architecture*, 427.

and ceremonies, practiced medicine, made prophecies, and recorded history.

Perched at the pinnacle of great pyramids, which themselves were often set on longer flat artificial terraces, gleaming in the sun, silhouetted against the sky, adorned by stone bas-relief, painted in brilliant colors, draped in bright cloth banners, and clouded in smoking incense, the temple was the spiritual focal point of the city. The pyramid represented the distant mountain, and the temple, the rock cave at its top where the gods emerged from their underworld to visit the earth and then proceeded to the sky above.

The temple evolved into a stone structure based on the simple residential form. All that remains of some of the early temples, made of perishable materials such as thatch and earth, are four post holes on the top of some of the pyramids. The temples were composed of one or more rooms with one, three, or five rectangular doorways facing the plaza below. Enclosed by the Maya vault, the tiny rooms held six or eight priests. Sometimes the rooms were grouped into two rows to expand the total interior space.

The temple's presence was often extended with the addition of a lofty crest of stone called a roof comb. This decoration richly embellished the building's silhouette and made it highly visible and more prominent while enhancing their symbolic relationship to the gods.

The manner in which a work of architecture meets the sky traditionally has been the element that helps establish a building's worth. The Greek temples fused their pedimental triangle with the clear Greek sky; the spires of the Gothic cathedrals pointed to heaven; the figures of the Baroque parapets danced, as if in court; the cupolas of the Victorian buildings characterized the spirit of their age;

and the Maya fine tracery of their temples' roof combs exhibited their masonry skills against the bright-blue sky of Mesoamerica.

## Palaces

The buildings that were called palaces or royal courts by the Spanish conquistadors are the most prevalent Maya building, but they were not palaces with spectacular reception halls in the European tradition. Rather, they contained many plastered and vaulted rooms that often opened to platforms, terraces, or interior courtyards. In addition to homes for the ruling elite and living quarters for the religious and secular leaders, their families and courtiers, these palaces were probably used as schools and administrative offices. Palaces were low structures compared to temples and had demonstrably residential functions.

Hernan Cortés, the Spanish conquistador who led the expedition that explored Mesoamerica and brought the

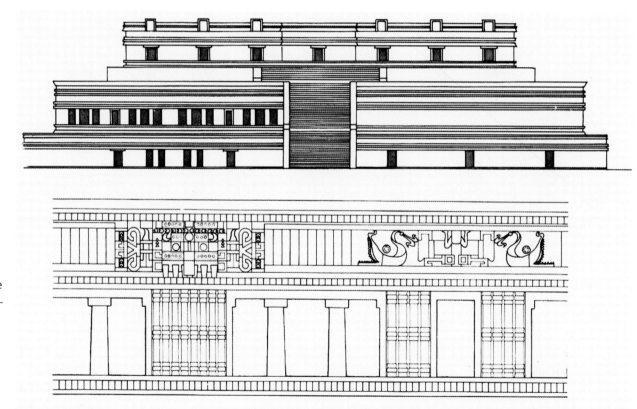

Sayil, Yucatán. The Palace. Elevation on top, detail below, showing the use of columns to open the spaces behind. On either side are engaged balusters representing in stone the original ties of historic wooden architecture. From Henri Stierlin, *Encyclopedia of World Architecture*, 435.

Sayil, Yucatán. The Palace. "In the region defined by this angle, named the Puuc from the Maya word for hills, was developed a style of architecture conspicuous for its careful workmanship in stone." From Tatiana Proskouriakoff, *An Album of Maya Architecture*, 55.

fall of the Aztec Empire—all in the name of the king of Castille—in the early sixteenth century, described the elite Maya house.

> There are houses belonging to certain men of rank which are very cool and have many rooms, for we have seen as many as five courtyards in a single house, and the rooms around them very well laid out, each man having a private room. Inside there are also wells and water tanks and rooms for slaves and servants of which they have many.[3]

Some of the interior spaces have windows, benches, and alcoves. Their forms are so general that their use may have changed during their evolutionary development. These long and monumental buildings were often set conspicuously on platform terraces, often as the dominant structure of a Maya city, indicating their significant role in daily life. Their room design, based on the restricted structural system, was not limited for a specific use as are the spaces in contemporary Western residences, such as living room, dining room, or bedroom. These functionally polyvalent and nonspecific rooms could be used interchangeably for many tasks—domestic, recreational, educational, or administrative.

Maya palaces are horizontal in design with lengths up to 300 feet. They were extended by the addition of supplemental vaulted chambers and not by enlarging the rooms themselves. Room size and floor plans were restricted by the structural limitations of the massive rubble concrete walls and the Maya vaults. Nevertheless, the interior plans of Maya palaces vary widely in number of rooms and corridors.

Some palaces were simple rectangular structures, while others, such as the Palace at Palenque, were intricate complexes with numerous wings opening to and enclosing a variety of courts. In some palaces, chambers communicate with one another, while in others each chamber is a separate room with access only from the exterior terrace. Some palaces were multistoried, the highest of which was the Palace of the Five Stories at Etzna. One variation of the palace, exemplified by the stepped palace at Sayil, is a multilevel form in which each successive story is recessed

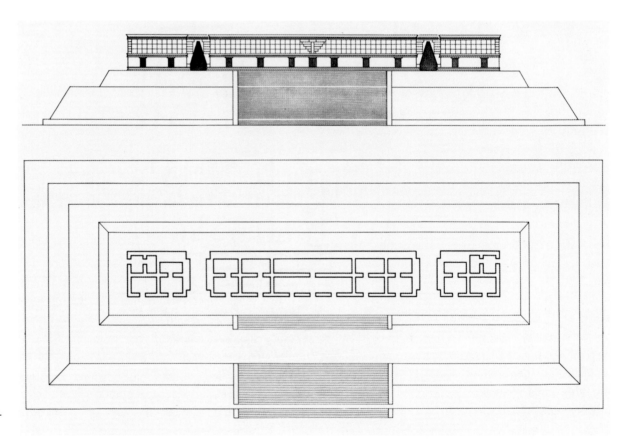

Uxmal, Yucatán. The Palace of the Governor is considered to be one of the finest residential palaces of the Maya. From Henri Stierlin, *Encyclopedia of World Architecture*, 432.

so that the roof of the story below serves as the entrance and terrace for the one above.

The activities of the hereditary religious and secular elite centered in the multifaceted palaces as the nucleus of administration and ritual. Here, new kings were installed, visiting heads of state received, wars declared, and captives displayed.

### Colonnades

The architects of the Classic period sought solutions to the problem of the small, dark rooms created by the limitations of the Maya vault. To this end, their architecture evolved to a system that used columns, either of monolithic stone or made up of several stone drums, to widen doorways that otherwise were restricted in size by their stone or wooden lintels. These columns, except in the Postclassic period, were not regarded as an adequate support for the vault and therefore did not successfully solve the problem of attaining larger room space within the building itself. However, it brought light into the otherwise dark room, making it more pleasant and useful.

The architects of the later Toltec/Maya period were the first to fully realize the advantages of the principle of post-and-lintel construction. In the *Mercado* (market) at Chichén Itzá, a new type of structure was created with the room's spaces no longer limited to the narrow width of the Maya vault. By using the column as a structural support, rooms could be spanned with several parallel vaults, permitting free circulation inside and increased light from the outside. The Mercado is a colonnade of alternating rectangular piers and round columns, with a gallery open to the court. These columns were painted in bands of contrasting polychrome color, as was the whole façade.

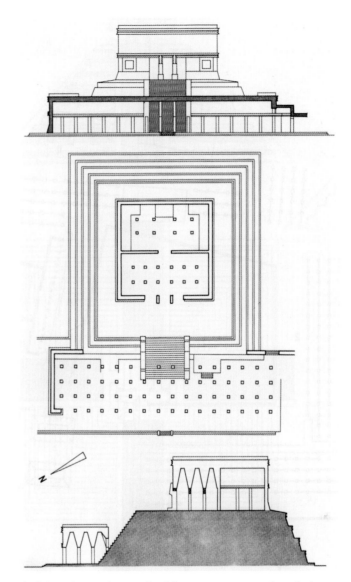

Chichén Itzá, Yucatán. Temple of the Warriors, Hypostyle Hall. The arrival of the Toltecs created new interiors using columns instead of vaults to support the roof. From Henri Stierlin, *Encyclopedia of World Architecture*, 440.

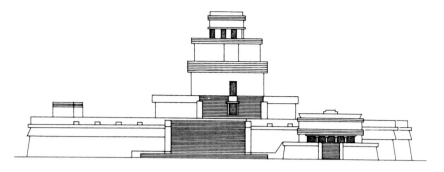

Chichén Itzá, Yucatán. Pyramid of Kukulcán/Quetzalcóatl (El Castillo). On the two yearly days of the equinox, September 22/23 and March 20/21, at sunset, the sun casts a zigzag shadow on the balustrade of the north steps, creating an image of a snake that ascends in March yet descends in September, culminating in the carved plumed serpent's head. Video frame from *The Mystery of the Maya*, produced by Raymond McPhee, Penelope McPhee, and Kenneth Treister.

The color scheme was apparently changed each time the building was repainted, and it is now difficult to correlate all the scattered bits of remaining color. If decoration was applied, it consisted of simple, low bas-relief carving on the surface of the columns or paintings in the horizontal zones.

## Observatories and Towers

The Maya's interest in celestial phenomena and the passage of time influenced the design and orientation of most of their buildings from the simplest house to the complex interrelationships of whole cities. The Pyramid of Kukulcán/Quetzalcóatl (El Castillo) at Chichén Itzá is an excellent example of the Maya fixation with astronomy and numerology. Added together, its 91 steps on four sides equal a total of 364. Coupled with the single large

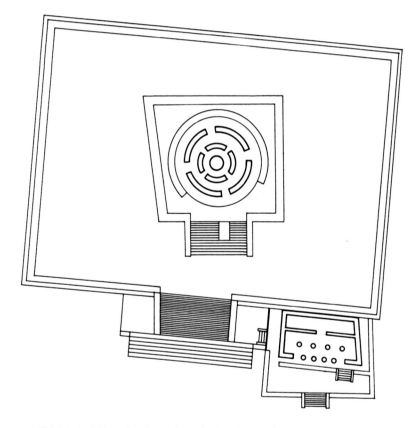

Chichén Itzá, Yucatán. Caracol, a cylindrical tower for astronomical observations. Built before the Toltec invasion, the structure has openings for celestial observations. From Henri Stierlin, *Encyclopedia of World Architecture*, 437.

step on the top, it totals the 365 days of one Maya solar calendar cycle.

One building form that possibly could have been an observatory appears to have been designed to facilitate heavenly observations, although it might have had other functions such as a watchtower. These square or round towers had observation rooms from which the Maya priest would chart the sight lines corresponding to the movement of the moon, sun, or the planets, particularly Venus.

By far the most interesting and architecturally sophisticated of these observatories is the cylindrical tower at Chichén Itzá. Built in the late ninth or early tenth century, it was one of the last buildings erected at the site and named *Caracol* (snail) by the Spanish for its internal spiral staircase.[4] Not well known is the limited-use form of circular structures like the Caracol in Mesoamerican architecture from the Middle Preclassic period through the Postclassic. They were built first by laying a circular plaster floor and then building successive timber superstructures. They probably all had a specific function—some as yet unknown—and were painted on their stucco surfaces.

## Water Management

Water—the lifeblood of any civilization—was particularly scarce in many regions of Maya habitation. Its collection, conservation, and control posed a demanding challenge to the Maya elite. The obvious solution was to situate their cities in areas where water was plentiful and accessible. The Maya often defied nature, however, expanding their civilization into regions where water was limited.

Just as the advent of house architecture coincided with the transformation into an agricultural society, other

This painting by Herbert M. Herget (1885–1950), with its white "virgin" (instead of the customary child) and its exaggerated pomp, is said to have launched a thousand careers in archaeology since its publication in the *National Geographic* in November 1936. Courtesy of George E. Stuart. Friar Diego de Landa, Bishop of Yucatán, wrote in 1566: "Into this well they were and still are accustomed to throw men alive as a sacrifice to the gods in times of drought; they held that they did not die, even though they were not seen again." From Gates, trans., *Yucatán Before and After the Conquest*, 90.

architectural forms developed as farming techniques advanced. The Maya extended their available land with a system of terraced fields that created level surfaces for cultivation. They built landfill projects that transformed swamps and lakes into fertile agricultural islands.

In order to control water, Maya engineers constructed huge stone cisterns and aqueducts such as the one found at Palenque. In Tikal, the plazas were sloped so as to collect and direct the rainwater to reservoirs. One of the largest cisterns, called *chultunes*, was situated under the Palace of the Governor at Uxmal and is a massive, 5-acre base esplanade. This and similar *chultunes* were lined with plaster so as to hold water. At most sites, particularly the large ones, all flat surfaces, such as building roofs, were made so that water could drain and be stored in artificial or natural reservoirs.

The Maya routed water from deep underground caverns. They developed hillside terracing for erosion control and silt entrapment. In the swamps, they artificially raised fields for cultivation, similar to the agricultural terraces built in Tenochtitlan on man-made islands in the lakes.

They drained marshy river basins and dug canals to take off surplus rainwater. These agricultural canals may have also been used for fish cultivation to provide much-needed protein. Many areas that today are covered with forests were actually savannah and grassland used for Maya cultivation more than three thousand years ago.

Due to the extreme rainy and dry seasons, the *cenote*, a deep natural water sinkhole in the natural limestone crust, was a vital source of drinking water for many Maya cities in Yucatán. Fortunately the porous limestone surface permits rain to collect in natural underground pockets that occasionally collapse, creating natural open wells.

*Cenotes* were considered the sacred home of deities. At the center of Chichén Itzá, offerings of value, as well as people for sacrifice, were thrown into the *cenotes*. Luckier mortals were allowed to swim back with messages from the oracles that mysteriously lived under the water.

## Ball Courts

Every Maya city had at least one ball court on which the ritual ball game *pok-ta-pok* was played. All of Mesoamerica was consumed with a passion for this game that was simultaneously a sport, a controlled form of intercity warfare, an occasion for high-stakes gambling, and a religious ceremony. The ball court represents one of the most interesting of the Maya building types since it established a cultural identity between the city and the sport. Standing in the Toltec ball court at Chichén Itzá, the largest and grandest in all of Mesoamerica, we are transported to another time when crowds filled the now empty plazas to cheer their favorite players and team to victory. Depictions of the game in Maya ceramic and mural art show an active game in the court, with spectators viewing from the periphery. Families, lovers with their arms around each other, nobility, and commoners are depicted enjoying an afternoon's recreation. As with modern football, soccer, or basketball, the sophistication and complexity of the ball games ranged from simple sandlot games to serious professional competitions.

Bordered by two parallel walls, the courts were narrow in the middle and open on the ends. The end zones were defined by walls set perpendicular, but not connected to, the lateral walls. We are not sure exactly how the game was played by the Maya, but scholars speculate that it was played with a solid rubber ball passed between teams

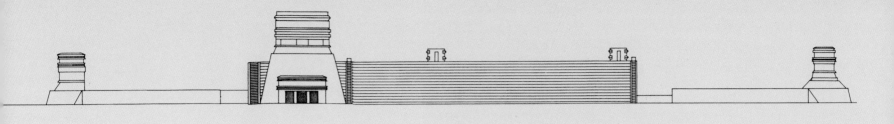

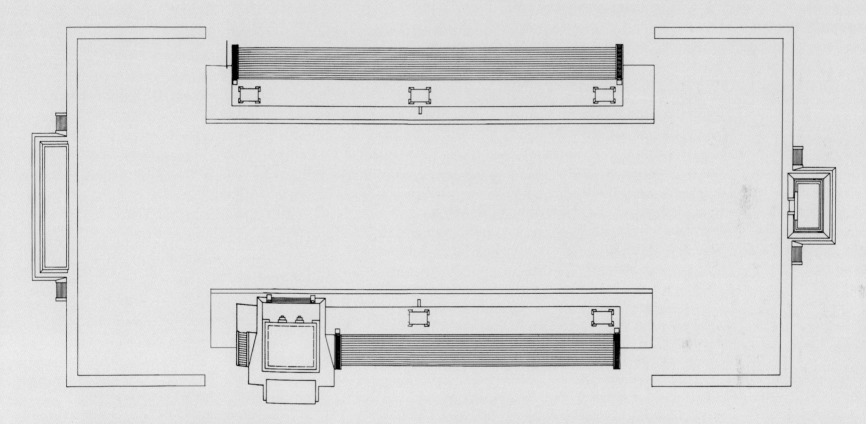

Chichén Itzá, Yucatán. The Great Ball Court, flanked by the three temples: the Temple of the Jaguar, the North Temple on the right, and the South Temple on the left. From Henri Stierlin, *Encyclopedia of World Architecture*, 441.

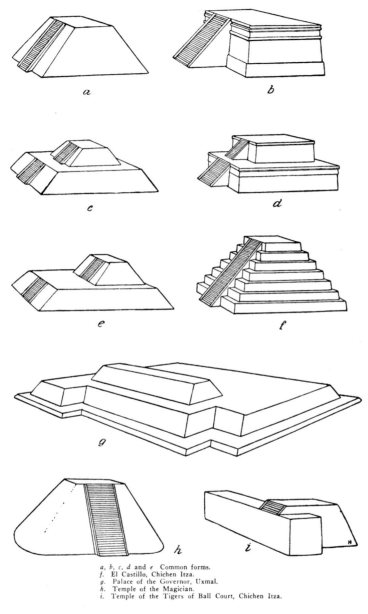

a, b, c, d and e  Common forms.
f.  El Castillo, Chichen Itza.
g.  Palace of the Governor, Uxmal.
h.  Temple of the Magician.
i.  Temple of the Tigers of Ball Court, Chichen Itza.

An illustration of the many types of Maya structures. From George Oakley Totten, *Maya Architecture*, 28.

defending opposite ends of the court. The players were required to keep the ball in the air, or bounce it against the two lateral side walls using only their knees, elbows, or hips. Use of the hands, feet, or arms was a foul. The players wore protective kneepads, helmets, a quilted arm guard, and a leather skirt or apron over the hips. The team scored by passing the ball into the opposing team's end zone. A point was lost by letting the ball hit the ground or by hitting it incorrectly.

In the Yucatán Peninsula, single rings of stone were set high on the sidewalls of the court. It must have been considered a particular triumph for a player to knock the ball through these rings. In what appears to have been a later Toltec addition to the game, the spectators sometimes forfeited the garments they wore to the lucky player.

The ball courts are stucco-faced masonry with a flat stone area between sloped side surfaces that kept the ball bouncing and in play. Sculptured stone markers probably used for scoring were commonly placed on each lateral wall. In some courts, three stone floor markers were set into the floor of the center court as well. The shape and size of the ball courts varied throughout Mesoamerica, suggesting that the game changed over the years and was played differently from region to region. In the Classic and Postclassic times, some courts introduced two rings, with one placed on either lateral wall, as part of the game.

Just as religion was integrated into so many areas of Maya life, so it was a fundamental aspect of the ball game. Important games were played as part of religious ceremonies and festivities. In extremely competitive games, such as intercity contests, the priests gave their blessing to the players, who may have been defending a city's honor or even independence. Skillful players were held in high

Chichén Itzá, Yucatán. Platform on the North Terrace. From Tatiana
Proskouriakoff, *An Album of Maya Architecture*, 95.

The joy of experiencing heat was an act of physical and spiritual purification.
From Tatiana Proskouriakoff, *An Album of Maya Architecture*, 27.

repute, and when the competition had religious or political importance, the losing players often paid with their lives.

## Ceremonial Platforms

Situated in many civic plazas of Maya cities were low, flat stone ceremonial platforms probably used for entertainment and other public uses. These platforms were usually about 20 feet square in plan, surrounded by four symmetrically placed stairways leading to the top. The shape of these platforms was similar to a cut-off pyramid with straight, vertical corners and stairs forming the batter sloped walls. The stairs, balustrades, and the platform's vertical walls were often embellished with stone bas-relief.

Bishop Diego de Landa described the platforms: "In front of the north stairway, at some distance, there were two small theatres of masonry, with four staircases, and paved on top with stones, on which they presented plays and comedies to divert the people."[5]

The stone carvings on the Platform of the Eagles at Chichén Itzá alternately depict eagles and jaguars, some holding what appears to be a human heart. These animals were symbols of Toltec military orders, suggesting that the performances staged on these platforms may have been connected with the art of war. On Platform 5C-53, at Tikal, the detailed ornamentation is similar to that found at Teotihuacan in Central Mexico, indicating the great influence in this entire area—either through political intervention by Teotihuacan emissaries, trade, or alliance—of this important Mexican empire.

*Tzompantli* is an Aztec word designating a wooden rack on which skulls of sacrificed prisoners were publicly displayed. The name was given to this Maya platform because its vertical walls depicted continuous rows of human skulls impaled on stakes. Skulls, while not a common motif, were sometimes found in Maya art, and human sacrifice also was shown. The depiction of skulls, in flat relief on the *tzompantlis* or in three-dimensional sculpture, as found in Copán, is a vigorous and sometimes grotesque statement of the interrelationship of sculpture and art to the religion and cultural customs.

In describing sacrifices, Bishop Diego de Landa wrote: "They made sacrifices of human beings as easily as they did of birds, and as often as their accursed priests . . . said it was necessary or as it was the whim or will of their chiefs."[6]

In contemporary architecture, buildings rarely express their function or the philosophical reason for their creation. Here, we find an example of the integration of architecture and social custom, where the purpose of the platform—human sacrifice—was displayed in graphic and simply understood sculptural relief.

The *tzompantli* at Chichén Itzá is located near the ball court, which dramatically underscores the potential seriousness of the ball game. The relief panels carved on the low vertical walls on either side of the ball court at Chichén Itzá depict the decapitation of a ball player.

## Sweathouses

Though we can only guess at the function of many structures found in the Maya architectural vocabulary, others explain their function clearly. One such form of structure is the sweathouse or steam room, called *temescal*. These vaulted structures, sometimes found near the ball courts, were similar in function to the Roman or Turkish baths. Sweathouses, such as those found at Tikal, are complete

with small sweat rooms; apparatus and special chambers for generating and condensing steam; a waterworks comprising reservoirs and stone-lined supply and drainage lines; and areas for the participants to cool off. At Piedras Negras in Guatemala, there is evidence of at least eight such baths that were probably used for hygiene, ritualistic purification, and the treatment of disease.

## Stelae

One of the most beautiful and important elements in the Maya's vast vocabulary of architectonic and sculptural forms was the stela. The stelae were usually vertical upright stone sculptures or wood slabs that often were beautifully carved and typically bearing a commemorative inscription and even a commemorative date. Many stelae, such as the magnificently carved ones at Copán, portrayed rulers and gave us archaeological evidence of the history and chronology of Maya civilization. By the end of the eighth century, the stela cult reached its heights with an abundance of monuments being built. By the ninth century, as the great ceremonial centers were abandoned, the stela cult fell into sudden decline. The building of stelae, it seemed, marked the high-water mark of the civilization, for even though the site remained populated, the construction of major new structures and stelae stopped.

Copán, Honduras. Stela N, as discovered in 1839 by John L. Stephens and illustrated by Frederick Catherwood, who made precise drawings, first with a camera lucida, and then with fine engravings on steel plates. The beauty of Copán's stelae is remarkable. From John Lloyd Stephens, *Incidents of Travel in Central America, Chiapas, and Yucatán*, 1:138a.

# 6

# The Maya City

*Clad in foliage and surmounted by ancient temples of limestone, grayish white against the sky, [the city] rose high above the surrounding treetops, like green volcanoes with summits wreathed in white cloud.*

J. Eric S. Thompson, *The Rise and Fall of Maya Civilization*

Copán, Honduras. The Acropolis. From Tatiana Proskouriakoff,
*An Album of Maya Architecture*, 31.

El Mirador, Guatemala. A painting of the Maya city El Mirador by T. W. Rutledge, from Ray T. Matheny, "An Early Maya Metropolis Uncovered: El Mirador," *National Geographic*, September 1987.

A wonderful painting by Chris Evans of Palenque, the great city in all its glory. This painting shows graphically the splendor and the majesty of the cities of the Maya. From David Stuart and George Stuart, *Palenque— Eternal City of the Maya*, 122–23.

Copán, Honduras. The ceremonial center is shown with thousands of spectators watching the ball game, which was more than a sport but a metaphor for contesting mythical concepts and beings. This painting by Chris Evans shows the ruler Yax Pac with his family watching from a temple terrace. From George E. Stuart, "City of Kings and Commoners, Copán," *National Geographic*, October 1989.

## Urbanism

The Early Classic period found the Maya civilization in full flower, with enormous urban centers stretching across the land. This period was driven by a fierce competitiveness among city-states, whereby they vied with one another in a continuous economic contest and over who could build the most beautiful and monumental architecture and sculpture.

This man-made landscape of stone was crowded with colorful temples, sprawling palaces, towering pyramids, and spacious stucco plazas. With an active imagination, one can strip away the centuries of overgrowth and visualize the city as it might have appeared more than a thousand years ago—busy, bustling, and prosperous.

The Maya moved about in a world of dramatic contrasts. Once a visitor entered the city from the raw nature of the countryside, he found himself enchanted by the splendor and dazzling architectonic art of the city. It was a stone landscape of never-ending stucco buildings punctuated by volcano-like pyramids silhouetted against the sky like the tops of towering trees. The remarkable disparity between nature's picture sequences and man's rational geometry made the experience of each all the more intense.

During this Golden Age, the population increased and the city centers expanded, becoming more complex. The architectural evidence of large urban populations in areas of limited resources attests to the Maya's sophisticated agricultural development, trade, and organization.

The Maya region was divided into city-states, each with its own ceremonial center and ruling elite. Nobles of the various city-states forged alliances, developed trade, and sent emissaries to other centers. Building competition among centers was keen, demonstrating competitive pride and power. The elite devoted itself to government, war, religion, and trade while their architects, high on the social ladder, drew plans for their expanding urban developments. The conventional assumption is that the Maya elite in the larger centers such as Tikal, Palenque, Quirigua, and Copán had a strong, centralized political organization. The architecture reflected a monolithic culture and society.

Maya society was highly stratified, with a hierarchy that placed the peasant farmer at the base and hereditary nobility at the top, similar to that of western Europe during the Middle Ages. Like the European aristocracy, Maya nobility filled the top positions in the priesthood and secular government, culminating in one supreme ruler. The lesser nobility comprised the upper class of warriors, scribes, bureaucrats, merchants, and architect-engineers. These specializations formed the basis of social groupings. Although there may have been some flexibility in the later years, class distinction and position were primarily hereditary.

The Maya created well-planned, integrated cities, complete with occasional triumphal entrance arches, large stucco plazas often dotted with freestanding sculptures, closely interwoven courts and quadrangles enclosed by buildings of simple, solid and graceful proportions. The plan of these quadrangles varied in shape, with some symmetrical and rectangular like the Nunnery Quadrangle at Uxmal. Others had irregular-shaped plans that created dynamic spaces that flowed and ricocheted off apposing walls. Some quadrangles resembled a coiled maze, a design pattern used by the Maya. One of the most beautiful quadrangles, in proportion, scale, and the intimacy of enclosure, is the Spectators' Gallery (762 CE) at Copán.

The quadrangle is recessed below the ground level and surrounded on four sides by continuous steps as its fundamental textual design element. Here, in addition to the well-articulated space, is a statue in high relief of the storm god holding a torch, beautifully sculptured as an integral part the stone stairs.

The Maya-built environment was a stage for "performance of human and divine dramas, centered on sacrifice, prestation, tribute giving, and ball playing."[1] The focus was on the participants rather than their setting. Buildings themselves were often dedicated to and decorated for a particular historic event, a ritual, or a person so that the building was personalized and literally became "alive."[2]

## Supercities

Let us examine some of the attributes of the Maya architecture and cities to see how they reinforced among the Maya a feeling of gratification, inspiration, achievement, and even superiority.

Cities, both large and small, functioned as the centers of trade, religion, and administration. As many as twenty supercities with large populations were sprawling centers of trade, well organized and planned. Dense residential settlements were clustered around the ceremonial core. In the ruins, we can recognize the elements of sound city planning with integration of architecture and urban design. The exact populations are difficult to determine since the family size and composition is unknown.

In what represented tremendous outbursts of civic pride, the architects, artisans, and laborers formed a team that created these magnificent cities all for the glory of their city-state. What resulted was an exceptional synthesis of the arts, where painting, sculpture, architecture, and city planning blended with the political, economic, and religious institutions to form a cohesive whole.

These were outdoor cities, where the arrangement of buildings, landscape, and roads was designed to glorify exterior spaces. Although there was regional variety in city plans and building styles, Maya cities shared a common architectural glossary that included acropolises, terraces, courtyards, quadrangles, esplanades, archways, and occasional causeways and planned landscapes. They shared a communal scale in which the most massive structures retained a sense of harmony with man. These features, combined with the use of the one material—stone—formed a common architecture that brought unity to the city.

The Maya cities were garden cities, a characteristic not easily realized when one visits their ruins today. These cities were pedestrian precincts for there were no wheeled vehicles and therefore roads, save for the *sacbeobs* (white roads named for their plastered surfaces) that served to connect cities and architectural groups. They were well landscaped with esplanades and deep hills, cultivated grounds with palm and shade trees; in some instances, reservoirs were planned as part of their urban diversity. The cities were bright with color; animated with sculpture; cool, clean, and openly spacious.[3]

The monumental scale of the Maya's built forms and the size of their great city centers symbolized the concentration of intense power in the ruling elite. The huge construction activity ordered and planned by the rulers and dedicated to their gods, ancestors, kings, and privileged persons were public in the sense that they were built by the masses of commoners tethered together with skilled architects, artisans, artists, and builders. Such powerful accomplishments must have inspired an overflowing sense of pride. So we have large architectonic mass and scale as an expression of the concentration of power in the ruling class directing the cognitive efforts of the entire populace.[4]

The Maya cities grew by accretion as temples, palaces, and entire complexes were built and rebuilt through the centuries. The cities were in a state of constant motion by virtue of their fluid public spaces exuding the impression of sanctity and power. The total visual reality imparted a feeling of a well-planned, organized urban center. Growth by superimposition and new construction put the cities in a continuous state of growth, yet at any one moment they had an inherent order, an architectural equilibrium.

The cities must have enjoyed long periods of peace, permitting the time needed to create, grow, and prosper. The major cities, such as El Mirador, Caracol, Calakmul, Uaxactún, Tikal, Palenque, Dzibilchaltún, and Uxmal, formed the nucleus of districts that, in turn, were subdivided into smaller, more rural zones. El Mirador, one of the largest and earliest Maya cities during the Preclassic and Classic periods, was a vast urban complex of 6 square miles supporting tens of thousands of people. Its towering pyramids (one was twelve stories high), temples, ball courts, palaces, and other public buildings were often oriented to the cosmos. Its broad causeways, over which many splendid processions must have passed, linked its vast plazas to the outlying neighborhoods, where thousands of its citizens resided, and on to outlying communities, from where tribute, food, and goods flowed into the city.

The reality of architecture is the contact between mass and space. If the interrelationship is fussy, then the form and quality of the architecture will be unclear. The cities of the Maya were external cities to be viewed and enjoyed from the outdoors in the bright tropical sunlight. They were a delicate balance between volume and voids, the voids being as important as the structures that enclosed them. The Maya architects, with limited structural systems, built mass with little concern of the enclosed interior spaces within each building. Their buildings' interiors were simple and based on the design of the one-room Maya house, which still survives in Central America today. This simple house plan was then reproduced in stone and multiplied many times. This house module was always long but never wide.

## Residential Neighborhoods

The long-standing debate over whether the great Maya ruins represented ceremonial centers visited by the populace only on festival or ceremonial days or were functioning urban cities has been decided in favor of the latter. These cities served both as the focus of population, commerce, and trade, and as ceremonial centers used for priestly ritual, pageantry, administrative and diplomatic affairs, trade, and markets.

As an example of the density of these cities, the total population of Tikal in Classic times was estimated to have been about 40,000–50,000, with a density of about 1,700 persons per square mile, while Copán's population was estimated to have been around 18,000.

The location of residential mounds indicates that population groupings fell generally into three categories: small clusters or hamlets of fewer than twenty houses; farming villages of fifty to one hundred dwellings; and satellite villages with more than one hundred houses and their own small ceremonial center. These clusters often stored water in reservoirs made by simply plastering over natural ravines.

Bishop Diego de Landa described the Maya cities as landscaped and orderly, following a comprehensive plan:

> Before the Spaniards subdued the country the Indians lived together in well ordered communities; they kept the ground in excellent condition, free from noxious vegetation and planted with fine trees. The habitation was as follows: in the center of the town were the temples, with beautiful plazas, and around the temples stood the houses of the chiefs and the priests, and next those of the leading men. Closest to these came the houses of those who were wealthiest and most esteemed, and at the borders of the town were the houses of the common people.[5]

Just as the advent of house architecture coincided with the transformation into an agricultural society, other architectural forms developed as farming techniques advanced. The Maya extended their available land with a system of terraced fields that created level surfaces for cultivation. They built landfill projects that transformed swamps and lakes into fertile agricultural islands.

Archaeological evidence supports de Landa's conclusion that social status determined one's proximity to the center. The peasants, living nearby their fields or *milpas* in the countryside, came to the ceremonial centers for religious observances or to trade on market days using beads, seashells, or cacao beans as currency. Gathered in the public plazas, they would be entertained by grotesquely masked men impersonating gods and by musicians with shell trumpets and rhythmic turtleback drums, dancing on the top of stone platforms.

## Plazas

Bishop Diego de Landa, in describing the plazas, wrote: "Around this structure there were, and still today are, many others, well built and large; all the ground about them was paved, traces being still visible, so strong was the cement of which they were made."[6]

The central areas of the Maya cities were most often placed on ridges, hilltops, or other lofty positions from which they were visible for miles. These summits were a combination of natural and cut stone, forming a juxtaposition of nature and the strong geometric forms of man. The basic ingredient of the built environment entails two elements, mass and space. In the Maya world, the essence of their architecture was the interrelationship between these two.

The core of the city was usually a great stucco-covered plaza surrounded and defined by horizontal bands of stepped platforms and the buildings that comprised their superstructures. One function of architecture is to create spaces to intensify the drama of living, and the Maya cities were all about drama. These spaces, enclosed by the sloped walls or stepped pyramids and bases, progressively opened up so that the negative shapes of the created space became an inverted hollow pyramid. Not only did this allow sunlight to illuminate the plaza, but it also expressed the sky as the dominant religious symbol of the city. No tall buildings plunged these cities into dark shade but only a gradual cascading of sunlight into stone. It was this negative space of the plaza as well as the towering pyramids that were the quintessential ingredients of the Maya city.

These well-organized public plazas were enlivened and decorated by multiple façades and friezes, by sculpture and color that embellished the surrounding buildings, creating a magnificent and awe-inspiring sight. Towering above these plazas, like giant punctuation marks, were the mighty temple-pyramids. These pyramids were difficult to climb, but their steep stairs not only gave vertical access to the upper platforms or temples but also helped articulate the upward movement of the entire complex where they were situated.

Standing in the midst of the now ruined and overgrown public plazas imparts a feeling both rational and emotional. The enclosing structures form a composition of strong shapes magically brought to life by the adroit handling of the tropical light as it filters through the surrounding forest.

### Acropolises and Esplanades

The Maya acropolis differs from the classic Greek acropolis, where the buildings were presented in stunning, isolated splendor. The Maya acropolis was a complex that emerged over time. It was a multitiered series of stepped plateaus rising gently from the plaza floor. These bases did not raise their buildings so as to cut them off from the cityscape but were more like springboards gradually transitioning them from the urban landscape upward into the superstructure of the built environment. On top of the acropolis, symmetrical building elements were placed in what seemed to be, but was not, a random order, creating an interrelated kaleidoscope of architectural forms. One common form was the triadic grouping arrangement where the top platform contained a central dominant structure flanked symmetrically by two, usually inward-facing, smaller structures. This triadic pattern of place-

ment, once established in the Middle Preclassic period, became popular for centuries.[7]

The cities and their acropolises expanded organically as small plaza groupings became multibuilding complexes, and complexes were superimposed over older complexes during centuries of building. The North Acropolis at Tikal provides a good example of the complexity of this urban metamorphosis. This 2.5-acre acropolis is 30 feet above the bedrock and 40 feet above the adjoining Great Plaza. Buildings were constructed one on top of another on this platform foundation over dozens of earlier versions. More than one hundred buildings lie under this mass of stone, attesting to the continuous organic maturation process that occurred.

The acropolis was seldom used in the lowlands of Yucatán. Here the Maya built huge, terraced esplanades, large open and level areas where people congregated. The amount of labor, all on the backs of man, required to create one of these vast esplanades, like the one supporting the Palace of the Governor at Uxmal, an area 600 by 500 feet, 40 feet high, was staggering. In mountainous areas like Copán, the Maya leveled hills for their esplanades before starting construction.[8]

### Courtyards and Quadrangles

The Maya city often contained enclosed courtyards or quadrangles, formed by balancing a series of horizontal buildings around a central plaza. One of the best-preserved examples is the Nunnery complex at Uxmal in the Yucatán Peninsula. Here, four long, low buildings completely enclose a large central courtyard, defining the enclosed negative space. The horizontal appearance

Piedras Negras, Guatemala. The Acropolis—"These walls and multiple doorways give the architecture a grace apparently never quite achieved by the
more conservative builders of Tikal and other cities of northeastern Petén."
From Tatiana Proskouriakoff, *An Album of Maya Architecture*, 15.

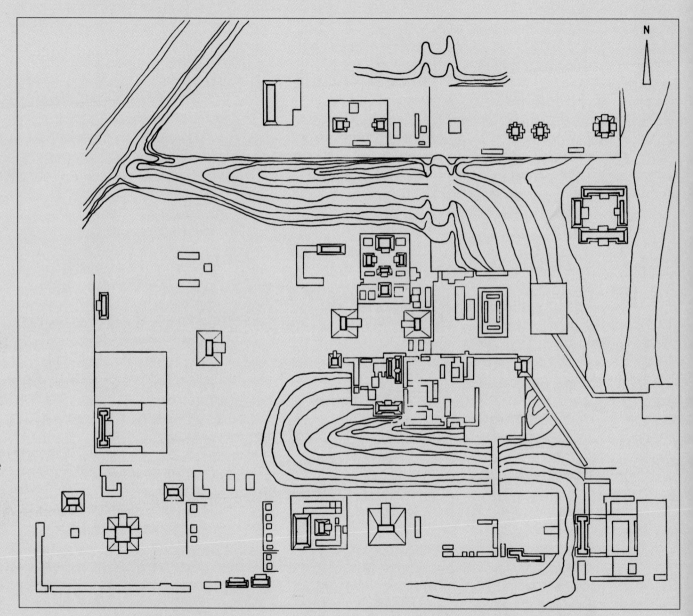

Tikal, Petén, Guatemala. The ceremonial center of this great city shows the rectangular layout of mass and space, creating esplanades and courtyards in a campus environment. From Henri Stierlin, *Encyclopedia of World Architecture*, 426.

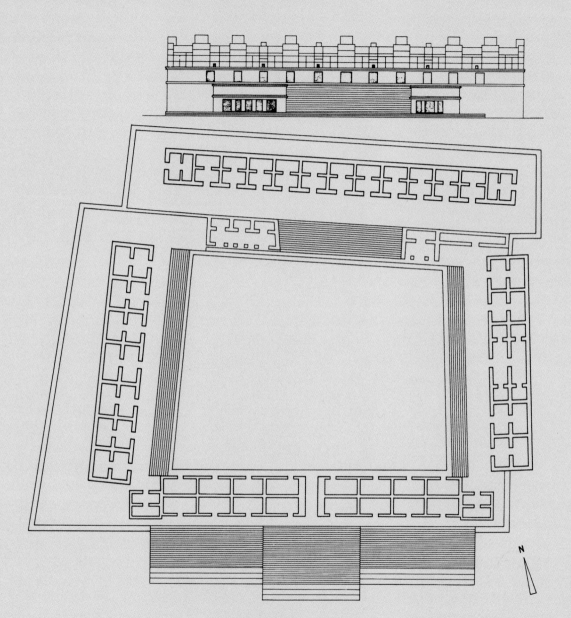

Uxmal, Yucatán. Quadrangle of the Nunnery. The enclosing of space in a quadrangle captures that space for human enjoyment and creates a place in human scale. From Henri Stierlin, *Encyclopedia of World Architecture*, 433.

N

Arch at Labná, Yucatán. The act of arrival delineated by architecture sets the
stage for the drama that follows. Illustration by Frederick Catherwood, 1844.

predominates, punctuated by the truncated Pyramid of the Magician that rises conspicuously behind the East Building.

The quadrangle is not a perfect square, and the buildings are set on different levels, all adding to the architectonic visual tension. This intricate quadrangle was probably the material reflection of a complex social governmental function that used this urban space.

## Causeways and Roads

The Maya cities were stone urban landscapes designed for pedestrians, perhaps landscaped with trees to welcome all with a clean, cool feeling of spaciousness. Esplanades and roads linked the building groups. Stone causeways called *sacbés* (white roads) ran for miles straight through the jungle, forming a network between some cities and often between neighborhoods within the city.

Citizens who lived outside the city center would have traveled along these roads on market or festival days to trade, to attend communal gatherings, or to visit neighboring villages. Often the point where the road entered the city was marked by a grand archway, such as the triumphal arch at Kabáh, which visually announced the traveler's arrival on the road from Uxmal.

These roads traversed swamps, hills, and jungle, and in a momentous feat of engineering, were almost always perfectly straight and perfectly level. In one case, its polished plaster top extended for 60 miles. There were some stretches, over low areas such as Cobán, where the road was more than 21 feet high, with one short length found to be 130 feet wide. The *sacbé* between Cobán and Yaxuma is the longest yet known at 62 miles.[9]

They were constructed of a rubble stone base supported on either side by mortared stone walls and covered with cut, smooth stone to which a hard surface of stucco was applied. They had a crown in the center for good drainage, and sometimes new layers were superimposed over existing roadways.

These long causeways often did not enter directly through the city but passed by their edges. Since they were built through thick jungle and often built after the cities existed, it is difficult to imagine how these roads were aligned to perfectly arrive at their destination. One possible suggestion, in addition to the continuous alignment of three stick markers, would be the use of smoke as a distant source of direction.

These causeways were marvels of engineering skill, especially when one considers their directional precision and that they were flat and elevated, often over undulating terrain. They required an amazing amount of labor and a tremendous quantity of construction materials, which had to be carried deep into the jungle, a seemingly insatiable task.

Intriguing questions abound. Why did they make these roads so wide since there were no carts or animals? Were the roads used only for walking or running? Why were the surface construction and foundations so sound when they had no heavy loads to carry? Was it solely to keep the masses busy building vast public projects?

We can only imagine the ornate processions of priests and noblemen parading along these high roads from one ceremonial city to another with hordes of spectators looking on.

Again in the Maya cities, the juxtaposition of both the horizontal and the vertical was clearly articulated in their built environment. The causeways, roads, paths, and open plazas created a horizontal dimension, while the steps and the terraces on the temples and pyramids provided the vertical path.

### Sequence of Spaces

As we observe their ruins, we see that the Maya cities were neither an isolated or spontaneous fantasy nor the single egotistical expression of one ruler or architect, but the creation, over centuries, of a quintessential harmonic special environment.

The Maya characteristically used contrast to emphasize dramatic differences in urban spaces. For example, the court is larger, more open, and brighter when approached through a narrow, dark entrance vault. The act of entering, be it into a plaza or a city, is reinforced by the use of an entrance arch that may have no other function than giving the participant the sensation of "having arrived." The planner Edmund Bacon states in his book *Design of Cities*:

> One of the prime purposes of architecture is to heighten the drama of living. Therefore, architecture must provide differentiated spaces for different activities, and it must articulate them in such a way that the emotional content of the particular act of living which takes place in them is reinforced.[10]

The unraveling of the multiple series of architectural spaces that flow together shows how well conceived and orchestrated was the Maya city's design. From a distance, the entire complex takes the form of a cohesive whole, but when one enters the sunlit brilliance of the first public plaza and the details of the city unfold, an explosion of space, mass, and detail is revealed that could not have been imagined before you stepped through the entrance threshold.

### Monumentality

The gigantic scale and monumentality of the great Maya cities was in itself a symbol of the power over time of the society and its ruling elite. The monumentality of the built environment was never hidden: it was visible to all at all times. The Maya cities created a continuous, always present, and profound impression among the populace of the raw hierarchy and social power of their society. The indigenous art, the painted buildings, the carved and inscribed murals, the carved lintels and plaques, all reinforced this constant form of propaganda that reinforced through pride and accomplishment the power of the ruling class. Where some interior spaces and palaces were available only for the elite, the large public spaces, courts, and the facades of the architecture and acropolises were part of the daily life of the common people and a constant reminder of this power.

### Contextualism

Contextualism in architecture refers to a building being in the context of its neighborhood. In archaeological terms, it often refers to the collection of collateral material to further the investigation of larger archaeological excavations. In this case, I am referring to the architectural definition.

Maya architecture is precisely designed, by its very nature, to be in the context of its neighbors and its neighborhood. Using similar forms, massing details of construction, conventions, and particularly common building materials, the Maya built entire environments as a coherent whole with a strong design thread, a unity of design. This is the opposite of contemporary architecture, a widespread practice of designing buildings as individual objects ("ego architecture"), as if floating in space and mind—the idolization of architecture without regard to its campus, context, or neighborhood.

One valuable urban design lesson we can learn from the Maya is the concept of campus unity. This is achieved by one of two methods: first, by the use of a common architectural style; or, second, by the use of a common building material. The Maya used both methods. As an example, we find in contemporary architecture the universal thread of a common style in the traditional Gothic college campuses, where one style sets the unity for the entire campus. In the case of a common building material, the city of Jerusalem is an example. Here the cladding of all buildings is regulated to be of "Jerusalem stone," so a wonderful unity prevails over the entire Holy City. When architecture exhibits this unity, or neighborhood contextualism, it creates a harmony of spirit, beauty, and peacefulness, where all structures in the related area whisper in unison, and none shouts for attention.

The architectural philosopher Leon Krier, in his book *Architecture: Choice or Fate,* comments on the architectural concept of contextualism: "It is impossible to conceive of isolated buildings cut off from the world. Whatever their size, buildings influence the world. They must be conceived as parts of a whole. Buildings are never neutral; they always have either a positive or negative influence. They are active."[11]

# 1

## The Maya Collapse

### End of a Civilization

The classic collapse of the Maya civilization lays the foundation for understanding Maya architecture, whose glory, perhaps, held the seeds of its ultimate demise. The mystery of why the Maya civilization, one of the most wondrous in the ancient history of man, collapsed over a relatively short time has perplexed archaeologists, Mayanists, and the general public since the remarkable ruined cities of the Maya were first uncovered.

The collapse of the Classical Maya civilization saw an age of turbulence when Maya farmers gave up their intensive farming; architectural monuments and grand ceremonial cities ceased to be constructed; and Maya kings gave up their crowns and crowd-pleasing pageantry. An estimated population of 3 million declined to under a half million in less than a century. Survivors moved into the crumbling architectural ruins or the jungle and the highland cities, now ruled by foreigners, were fortified.

The collapse of the Maya was marked by two events. First, the Maya stopped using the Long Count calendar, which dated Maya construction during its height. Second, the Maya stopped erecting stelae.

There are a myriad of scholarly books and papers offering theories as to why the Maya civilization collapsed, and I do not want to add one more to this bewildering list. My concept, or rather perception, concerning the degeneration of the society is a general one that has been discussed and touched on by many but never put at the head of the class. I must confess to a certain bias, for as an architect, I see events through the lens of my profession.

### Stresses

There are many and varied studies that expose the stresses that the Maya civilization endured, all of which probably played some part in its ultimate demise. The location and severity of each varied, but they all added to the heavy burden that the society had to sustain. Some of the stresses that scholars have identified can be simply summarized, not necessarily in order of importance, as follows:

1. Invasion of the Maya by strangers
2. Warfare among the Maya city-states
3. Overpopulation and eventual underpopulation

4. Degradation of agriculture due to thin soil layer and overfarming
5. Soil erosion, nutrient leaching, choking weeds, uncontrolled insects, and plant disease
6. Drought, irregular rain cycles, unavailability of water, agricultural failure due to climate change, and other ecological problems
7. Shortages of food and resulting malnutrition
8. Disease, including childhood illnesses, syphilis, yaws, and osteoporosis
9. A widening division between the elite and commoners
10. Trade and market failures
11. Political changes and competition
12. Natural disasters such as hurricanes, earthquakes, mudslides, and volcanoes
13. The decadence of society in its love for luxuries
14. The societal chain reaction involving many of these factors
15. The natural cyclical and evolutionary process that consumes all civilizations as a phenomenon of normal cycling

## Underlying Cause

Although the collapse of the Maya civilization was no doubt influenced and affected by all or most of the above list of potentially disabling processes involving natural, cultural, and historic phenomenon, we still should try to find the one underlying and fundamental cause—if one exists.

All societies are subject to stresses and pressures that can affect them individually at various times and in various ways. However, to have the diverse civilizations of Mesoamerica decline and die so drastically and completely points to one underlying reason that hung over them all—that started the dominos to fall.

Once a civilization becomes fragile due to a fundamental and continuous flaw in its basic structure, many fragmentary and secondary strains can contribute to its ultimate collapse. In the case of the Maya collapse, the secondary stresses were many and cumulative—attacks that toppled an already fragile society.

A most interesting fact is that after the classic collapse, there were seldom any recovery phenomena—no restructuring, no restoring, or regeneration. No subsequent civilizations or societies arose to grab the baton and inherit the vast accumulated knowledge and methods or records of achievement. There were no architects to learn from and carry on the Maya's great legacy of architectural wonder. The society just simply died and gradually disappeared under a verdant cloak of jungle.

## Common Thread

Let us find the common thread that binds the civilizations of Mesoamerica's geographic extent together, one that was present in all and that could have contributed to their shared success and, possibly, their ultimate demise. Mesoamerica, defined by customs and geography, covered a vast territory from north central Mexico to Costa Rica, comprising diverse cultures such as the Zapotec, Maya, Toltec, Mixtec, and Aztec. They shared similar calendars, hieroglyphics, religions, astronomy, cosmology, sculpture, agriculture, and, above all, stone architecture.

The concept that Jared Diamond, the author and evolutionary biologist, so elegantly postulates is that civilizations, to progress, must be able to produce an abundance of food so that some of the population can pursue endeavors outside of pure agriculture. With added time, they could raise the levels of the society's skills so that the civilization's wealth and potential richness could grow. The societies of Mesoamerica met that standard.

This theory, however, explains a civilization's growth and flowering but not necessarily its sudden collapse. So, to this important understanding of how a civilization sustains itself, I would add a specific, rational, elusive cause for the collapse of most Mesoamerican societies, particularly that of the Maya.

## Root Cause: Pride and Excess, Based on Excellence in Architecture

In this architect's view, the ultimate root cause of the Maya collapse was, simply stated, their brilliance in creating extraordinary architecture and cities.

The Maya reveled in the exciting act of triumphant building—the exuberance of pride, competitiveness, and overachieving that flows from that experience. This, I believe, was the underlying and fundamental cause of their ultimate collapse. Pride is a most potent force, for in addition to bestowing self-respect, dignity, self-esteem, and honor, it also often breeds arrogance, conceit, smugness, superiority, and self-aggrandizement. These, in turn, can lead to blindness on the part of the elite rulers and can bequeath hostility, antagonism, and aggression.

The Maya created illustrious monumental works of stone architecture and unequalled great cities to such a degree and with such a passion that their civilization, unable to sustain such glory, ultimately collapsed in the dust of its stone.

The premise that the Maya's excellence in architecture was the primary root cause of their demise can be better understood in the following sequence of cascading events.

1. At the top of a symbolic pyramid of causes and consequences is the Maya's brilliance in architecture and city building.
2. From that flowed a fierce pride and competitiveness among various city-states and their rulers. This blinding pride would only have merit and relevance if it were based on a real, almost unmatched achievement—wondrous architecture.
3. In turn this exuberant pride, justified and expansive, spurred the continuous development of ever-larger and more glorious cities.
4. The growth of cities then fostered an increase in population and density, intensifying the need for land, greater food production, and construction resources.
5. This resulted in large-scale deforestation: the clearing for building, the use of slash-and-burn agriculture, and the manufacture of lime for construction.
6. Finally, deforestation caused three problems, namely: (*a*) erosion; (*b*) a consequent loss of water-storage capacity as the swamps, rivers, rivulets, and reservoirs became filled with silt; and (*c*) diminished rainfall and consequential drought exacerbated by deforestation.
7. All of these amplified the society's continuous shortage of water, the staff of life. The Maya lived in lands with few lakes; in lands that had seasons of exceptionally low rainfall; and in areas where the earth's crust was thin and porous, sucking up rain when it did fall.

8. This cascading sequence of events weakened an increasingly fragile society that was susceptible to a multitude of ancillary stresses. Stresses that many societies encounter but, in the case of the Maya, were amplified by the dazzling heights that the Maya had attained—and then lost.

In the history of world civilizations, no other society created such wondrous architecture and cities. Cities of such extraordinary beauty and harmony raised passions so high that when it could not be sustained, the entire civilization quickly fell into an incredible abyss, a sudden precipitous fall into the dark, verdant jungle from whence it came.

# Oh, the Wonder of It All

The Maya in ancient days must have marveled at their spectacular cities hewn in stone, with their majestic sky-touching pyramids, capped by gleaming and brightly painted temples crowned by towering roof combs that literally entered the heavens.

As the Maya delighted in the beauty and grandeur of their cities, they eventually grew sightless to their opportunities for survival. Blinded by brilliant success and mind-numbing pride, the society expended a disproportionate amount of manpower, priceless and limited resources, and creative skill to the process of building.

We must consider the Maya elite and ruling class, who used their architecture to display their seemingly almost superhuman powers—their creativity and knowledge—while the commoners stood in awe and wonder. Could this brilliant and intelligent elite possibly have devised ways to avert the ultimate collapse? Perhaps, if they had reordered their society and their priorities when the first warning signs of collapse became evident, they could have taken corrective measures, made a midcourse correction, so to speak, that would have let them avoid or at least mitigate the projected doom. In this case, they could have stopped or slowed their intense, competitive construction activities. The fact that they did not take such remedial action has to be an essential part of the ultimate cause of collapse.

## Architecture of Mesoamerica

The lands of Mesoamerica produced one essential building material needed for the creation of great civilizations— stone. For it was limestone that enabled Mesoamericans to cut and fashion their monumental architecture and then to transform this limestone into lime that, in turn, was made into stucco, mortar, and concrete to bind the stone together. This was their common heritage, their common thread—the thread of stone.

The great civilizations of the ancient world shared a common characteristic. They all possessed an abundance of easily worked stone and produced permanent shelters that formed permanent cities.

The most obvious examples of great civilizations that created extraordinary stone architecture are the ancient civilizations of the Egyptians, the Persians, the Greeks, the Romans, and the Inca, to name a few. Even small civilizations, such as the one that flourished on Easter Island, had an abundance of stone to create substantial stone architecture and stone sculpture.

The reason is simple: stone architecture enables the civilization to create permanent and strong sociological and economic roots as opposed to the thin, surface roots that characterize the cultures of nomadic people. The stone societies that create permanent shelters have a place for intellectual pursuits to grow and flourish; for learning, schools, and libraries to store their collected knowledge; for shops to create tools that increase agricultural production; for workshops for skilled artisans; for governmental planning, organization, and the keeping of records; for the gathering and expanding of knowledge in mathematics, astronomy, and other studies; and, most of all, for designing their great architectural works.

Such pursuits, difficult without permanent shelter, all add to the cumulative wealth and growth of a civilization. The archaeologist Ray T. Matheny, when discussing El Mirador, states: "Ideas[,] . . . when exchanged and examined and reshaped, led to the flowering of Maya civilization."[1]

Stone architecture, therefore, encouraged learning, population growth, and agricultural productions by creating an environment where ideas could flourish and nourish the society under the protection of permanent stone shelters. With stone structures come stone cities, and with stone cities comes civilization.

## External Cities

The cities possessed plasticity, geometrically and rationally shaped and ordered, in contrast to the inhospitality of the surrounding jungle landscape. It was the same external architecture as that of the ancient Egyptians and Greeks. The Maya cities used a profusion of paths, steps, ornamentation, bas-relief, color, texture, and art coupled with a generous expanse of public, open space between their structures.

The Maya's external architecture was the opposite of Gothic architecture, which was primarily an internal architecture, to be witnessed and experienced from within; this included soaring spaces, defined arches, stained glass, exposed structural ribs, and, inside churches, the brilliant, dominant rose window. The Maya cities possessed a wonderful sense of human scale, even when viewed from the vast expanse of their public plazas. Their beautiful buildings enclosed and defined communal spaces—courtyards, squares, and quadrangles, all personalized spaces designed and proportioned for the individual. The citizens of each city must have felt that they were not merely observers but participants in a congregation that created the total drama of the city.

The cities were dignified and easy for all to understand, with patterned and repetitious forms and common materials—stone, plaster, bright color, sculptured reliefs, architectural hieroglyphics, and painted murals. The cities were a testimony to collective achievement and what can be accomplished when a people unite under enlightened leadership with a common purpose—and a liberal dose of pride.

## Vertical and Horizontal Cities

The great ceremonial centers of the Maya were cities that reached vertically to the gods while at the same time married all to the earth horizontally. The vast expanse of each city and the huts of the commoners stretched over the countryside in horizontal fashion, while the ceremonial heart of the cities possessed a religious verticality. The main functional buildings: the palaces, terraces, quadrangles, entrance gates, ball courts, observatories, and buildings for general use were horizontal in form and embellishment. Many were long and set on raised, elongated, horizontal terraces with horizontal steps. Their horizontal lines were pronounced with the addition of horizontal friezes, eyebrows, bands, bas-relief, and geometric decorations.

At the same time, the ceremonial centers were punctuated with pyramids that were basically vertical in form. One had to look up into the clouds to understand and feel the grandeur of the pyramids with their lofty temples perched on top that, in turn, were made even higher with roof combs added as a crowning glory. These vertical monuments could be seen from a great distance, piercing the jungle with their magnificence. Here civilization is seen as conquering nature, which again reinforces the society's communal feeling of pride, pride in their taming of nature, pride in their excellence in architecture.

This axiom of vertical and horizontal components within a design was also carried out in the surface decorations both in the large surface sculptures and in the smallest artistic details.

## Cities for Pageantry

The cities of the Maya were well-landscaped garden cities designed for the gods and pedestrians only. There were no wheeled vehicles and therefore no streets, alleys, or boulevards to crisscross and mar the beauty of their open plazas, courts, and public spaces. These ceremonial cities were perfect stages for wondrous days of pageantry and celebration. The setting was a palette of colors set against the bright whiteness of the thick, lime stucco carpet—the stone plazas. The towering, brightly painted buildings of red, festooned with their polychrome ornamentation, glistened when set against the bright blue of the tropical sky.

This was a magical setting for a day of pageantry. There was an excitement in the air. The elite, the architects, astronomers, scribes, and other scholars wore brilliant capes of many colors streaming down their sides, fashioned with the bright parrot feathers of the jungle. Visiting emissaries were crowded in the prime viewing stands along the steps of the pyramids. The scene was enlivened by the vividly colored banners and parasols that seemed to float in the air. The music of the orchestra was stirring—long wooden trumpets, conch shells with incised glyphs made of bright-red cinnabar, drums with drumsticks made from deer antlers, turtle-shell rattles, and pottery flutes created this music. The chanting added an intoxicating flavor to the mix. The king, carried in a beautiful carved sedan chair with a plumage top held by litter bearers, led the procession. He wore a magnificent cloak, jewelry, and a feathered headdress topped with towering, long and graceful quetzal feathers flying in the air. The procession—seen against the background of magnificent architecture and followed with an entourage of nobility with jaguar pelts and carvings of the gods, warriors, and dignitaries—created a feeling of wonderment and glory among the entire city. Impersonators of the gods lined the pyramid's steep stairs leading to the bright-red temple at its top where, among the gods, the king would stand. Chanting priests, rattles, smoking incense, the blare of the conch trumpets mixed with the drums created an overwhelming pageantry. Blinding pride was the blessing that day, but perhaps eventually it might be the curse.

Monumental stairs. Castillo at Tulum. Illustration by Frederick Catherwood, 1844.

Since in Maya tradition, one generation built on the works of another, there was a continuous pressure to build. A new ruler was obligated to the memory of his father, his grandfather, and his ancestors to continue the building process. This concept of a common lineage forced the powerful rulers to build with inspirited fervor and pride.

The cities were without a single, individual symbol. The city itself became the symbol. The city was the kingdom, part of a long ancestry and its roots. The rulers were not to be remembered by what they did, or even by what they said, but by what they built. This gave the society a mandate to preserve by building on the heritage of previous generations. The Maya were pressured to use their creative skills to strongly reinforce their sense of lineage, heritage, and, above all, pride—pride in their architectural abilities.

## Magnitude of Stone Cities

Nothing is gained without some cost and often unintended consequences. So let us now think about how this marvelous Maya architecture and their monumental cities could have put a significant and perhaps fatal strain on the civilizations of Mesoamerica.

The sheer magnitude of Maya construction was overwhelming. A vast amount of land, materials, and manpower was required to build these monumental works of architecture and cities. Diego de Landa advanced the reasons he saw for this massive building: the elite may have wanted to keep the commoners occupied; they often moved their communities; religious compulsion; a feeling of superiority compared to their descendants.[2] They destroyed, altered, remodeled, and abandoned existing structures only to build more. They built cities with temples, palaces, ball courts, observatories, markets, sweat baths, reservoirs, roads, and causeways. The main characteristic of the Maya-built environment is that it was huge, built with durable materials and on a large scale, all consuming a great deal of energy. The Maya elite deliberately undertook ambitious building programs. They integrated older built forms and their psychological associations into new structures.[3] The energy devoted to construction was often disproportionate to the other needs of the society. These were manpower, materials, and organizational and creative skills that could have been used for other, possibly more urgent, undertakings such as farming, irrigation, planning, and education when the society was in peril.

This apparent misdirection of energy is perceptible only in hindsight through the analysis of archaeological evidence. As Walter Witschey and Clifford Brown have shown through their growing digital atlas of Maya archaeological sites, such work has barely begun: of more than 6,000 sites catalogued so far, only a relative few have ever been subject to excavation, and in each of those only a small area has been analyzed. We do, however, know some of the more obvious causes of environmental failure.

The Maya deforested their land by three simultaneous processes: clearing vast land area for their ceremonial centers; slash-and-burn agriculture; and the manufacturing of lime. These three processes led to a continuous deforestation, the dire consequences of which were the erosion of the soil and the diminishing of rain, groundwater, and moisture in the air.

The eminent archaeologist George E. Stuart states, "Who cuts the trees as he pleases cuts short his own life."[5] This Maya adage, born of common sense and a close bond

This diagram shows the large amount of wood needed to create a relatively small amount of lime—and the Maya used lime in great abundance, denuding their forest and therefore causing erosion plus deforestation which itself reduced the amount of rain, so vital for survival. Illustration by Kenneth Treister.

with the land, is spoken in a language that uses the same word for both "blood" and "tree sap."

There is a significant relationship between deforestation and water supply and resources. When a large area of forest is removed, a companion degradation occurs in the environment and its biodiversity. When the forest is felled, the hydraulic cycle is broken, resulting in a significant reduction in the water content of the soil, the amount of both groundwater and underground water, and the moisture in the atmosphere. Although deforestation causes the greatest impact on water supply near the region where it occurs, its effects can be significant for great distances.

## Manufacturing of Lime

The construction of the Maya's magnificent cities required a great amount of calcified lime. From this lime, the Maya added water to make stucco; sand and water to make mortar; and sand, water, and aggregate or rubble to make concrete. These essential materials of stone construction that are still used in our time allowed the Maya to build amazing cities and structures that were large, well constructed, permanent, and homogeneous.

The creation of the vast amount of lime that was continuously required for the Maya's incalculable construction projects was an enormous undertaking. As an example, the lime stucco used to coat a single structure often consumed one thousand trees. The territories of Mesoamerica contained an abundance of limestone, the basic raw material for the creation of lime.

To manufacture lime where no kiln was used, the Maya would clear a large area of the jungle; collect a substantial quantity of fallen trees, often green trees to increase the heat generated by the fire; and create, with a considerable amount of labor and skill, a large cylindrical pile of logs about 6 feet tall and 15 feet in diameter. A center pole was placed in the pile; when removed, the resultant shaft acted as a flue. They then placed on top of the woodpile an approximately 2-foot layer of crusted limestone. The lime was first sprayed with water, and then the wood set on fire. Temperatures would reach 1,832° Fahrenheit to calcify the lime. The bonfire burned for a day. At the end, a white, powdery substance of lime was created and lay on the ground. The lime was exposed for some time before being ultimately mixed to make stucco, mortar, or concrete. This use of the rain forest to make lime made Maya architecture possible, but the resulting deforestation may also have been one of the contributing factors to the society's ultimate collapse. (See the discussion of lime and concrete in chapter 4.)

## Erosion

Simply stated, soil erosion is caused by deforestation. The roots of trees, which hold soil, are destroyed. When one tree is felled, there is simple erosion; when a forest is destroyed, the entire landscape and ecology changes. With erosion, the soil washes away with its rich topsoil and clay, diminishing nutrients in the soil that remains. The washed-away soil becomes silt that fills the natural water reservoirs: the lakes, canals, rivers, rivulets, catchments, seasonal swamps, and lowlands (*bajos*), robbing the society of much-needed storage areas for precious water.

## Force of Blinding Pride

We should think about what motivating force could have diverted the Maya's leadership class from the task of survival. The wise and educated elite—the kings, nobility, courtiers, elders, architects, engineers, astronomers, and mathematicians in so many diverse regions—all came under the influence of a strong magnetic force: *pride*, unlimited pride. Pride and its derivatives, competition and rivalry, are amazingly strong human instincts and powers that, in turn, breed an entire litany of aggressive behavior: antagonism, resentment, dislike, mistrust, struggle, bitterness, hatred, strife, anger, and war, ultimately causing great civilizations to crumble.

The eminent scholar Jared Diamond, when comparing the collapse of Easter Island and that of the Maya in his book *Collapse*, reinforces this theory by stating: "Maya Kings sought to outdo each other with more and more impressive temples, covered with thicker and thicker plaster—reminiscent in turn of the extravagant conspicuous consumption by modern American."[6] As a people, the Maya delighted in the beauty and grandeur of their cities, growing blind to opportunities for survival and expending a disproportionate amount of manpower and resources on the creative process of architecture and city building.

Perhaps at one point, equilibrium could have been maintained, a balance between their desires to design and create larger and more magnificent buildings coupled with the beautiful art within and their society's ability to survive. Yet once that point was passed, all was lost.

As reported by David Webster in his book *The Fall of the Ancient Maya*, David Stuart, the eminent Maya epigrapher, was quoted as saying that the late Classic period was the prologue to the ultimate Maya collapse.

> We see great Late Classic centers such as Tikal or Copán, with their huge buildings, grand palaces, and assertive art and inscriptions as the high tide of Maya civilization. Instead, [Stuart] suggests fatal weaknesses lurked behind this glittering façade. The causes of its failure were embodied in its apparent success.[7]

The archaeologist Richard Hansen reinforces this position on the Maya collapse when he explains the early collapse of the major Maya city of El Mirador between 100 and 299 CE. Hansen writes that the site was originally selected because of the high quality of the mineral-rich soil of its low, swampy areas. The Maya created high terraced agricultural fields and carried the mud up from the swampy marshes to grow maize, beans, squash, cacao, gourds, and other crops. Then, due to massive deforestation, there was soil erosion and the runoff of clay collected in these marshes, filling them. This deforestation was caused by felling trees used for firewood and for the manufacturing of plaster, which was needed for their massive architectural construction. The plaster covered everything, from major temples like La Danta and its acropolis, to the broad plazas, which, over time, got thicker and thicker. Hansen attributes this extravagance to simply "conspicuous consumption," which enveloped the Maya then, and later, during the Classic period, was the most significant factor in the Maya collapse.[8]

When we attribute the collapse to the excellence and efflorescence of the Maya's architectural creations, we must understand that this is just one contributing factor and not a specific cause of any particular collapse. Many factors combined directly or indirectly under the broad canopy of the overcommitment to create architecture and to build ceremonial centers at the expense of all else.

Many types of adversities can befall a fragile civilization. With a depleted forest, limited agriculture and intermittent natural calamities, the problems that the Maya faced must have grown. The tradition-bound leaders with their exuberant pride were probably unwilling to make adjustments to cope with these stresses. As the stresses multiplied, competition among the city-states became intense, and some began to impinge on the others' territories.

## Success Begets Excess—Excess Begets Collapse

The Maya were overwhelmed by their great success in architecture and their fierce passion to construct larger complexes of buildings. The Maya had grand architecture and monumental cities, and I believe that this phenomenal architectural success was the underlying cause of their collapse.

The building and rebuilding of their huge cities became an all-consuming passion, even obligation, of the elite, a source of pride and competitiveness that eventually undermined their strength, exposing them to a multitude of internal and natural stresses. The cycle of collapse had begun.

During the period from approximately 800 to 980 CE, the Maya civilization fell into a state of turbulence. The strangler roots of the banyan tree started to choke the magnificent stone architecture. Citizens took refuge in the crumbling relics that were once grand cities or retreated into the jungle, and the Classic Maya civilization came to an end.

The Maya passion for architecture ultimately ruined its wondrous prehistoric cultures. What survive are the magnificent fossil shells—the ruins of what were once vigorous and glorious ancient civilizations.

The Maya elite built and rebuilt their huge cities, an architectural fixation. In a similar fashion, also without the benefit of beast of burden, metal tools, or the wheel, the Easter Islanders devoted enormous manpower to quarrying, sculpting, and transporting their stone statues. The Easter Islanders, also with slash-and-burn agriculture, deforested their small island to procure wood for housing, transporting their images, and other communal activities, causing inevitable soil erosion.

As the creative projects grew larger and grander, more and more manpower was enlisted, all at the expense of agriculture and other necessities of survival. We know that at one point, most of the populations of both Easter

Island and the Maya were devoted to their creative activities.

Finally, the point of equilibrium was passed in both societies, imperiling their basic survival. The Easter Islanders toppled their beautiful stone sculptures, leaving them to someday be discovered by the curious, then retreated to their caves. The Maya retreated to the jungle, leaving their splendid cities abandoned and deserted. Is a lesson hidden among these ruins?

Palace of the Governor, the most important civic building at Uxmal, as conceived by Tatiana Proskouriakoff. From Tatiana Proskouriakoff, *An Album of Maya Architecture*, 75.

Uxmal, Yucatán. Palace of the Governor, an architectural gem built in the ninth and
tenth centuries, raised on an artificial substructure, and surrounded by an open plaza.
It has eleven exterior doorways and fourteen rooms. The lower walls are plain and the
frieze is a magnificent stone mosaic of Chac masks consisting of thatched huts, half-
columns, thrones, and feather headdress in the Puuc style.

# 9

# The Legacy

## Modernists and Maya Architecture

Contemporary architecture has generally ignored the Maya's legacy and does not use or even seem to understand elements or concepts available from the Maya's vast design and historic architectural vocabulary. In fact, modern architecture in many ways is the antithesis of the architectural heritage of the Maya.

Where the Maya relished integral ornamentation, the modernists have stripped their buildings clean; where the Maya were interested in human scale, the modernists often create monumental masses and spaces; where the Maya were interested in the movement of people between their buildings on plazas and courts, the modernists are concerned with the salutary, isolated building mass and its sculptural shape; where the Maya architects were anonymous, the modernists are egocentric; where the Maya used batter walls, multiple angles, and geometric forms, the modernists make a religion of the simple box; where the Maya used texture, sun, and shadow, the modernists use flat stucco or the hard surfaces of stainless steel, aluminum, or glass; where the Maya used color and painted murals to brighten their cityscape, the modernists use white and when tired of white, use more white; where the Maya built campuses with the structures interrelated and the spaces between the masses as important as the buildings themselves, the modernists build objects floating in space designed for the pages of the architectural magazines; where the Maya built and rebuilt based on their history, culture, and heritage, the modernists always start anew and shun architectural precedent.

## Frank Lloyd Wright and Maya Architecture

The relatively few exceptions to the abandonment of Maya architectural principles by world architecture were first seen with some fleeting references to them in contemporary Mexican monumental architecture, mainly in its mural-bedecked public buildings and its university campus planning with large, open public plazas.

Maya architecture also had a strong influence on the legendary work of Frank Lloyd Wright, possibly the premier architect of the late nineteenth and early twentieth centuries. Although Wright claimed that he only admired Maya architecture and denied copying any Maya architectural forms or details, this was probably due to his

Hollyhock House, by Frank Lloyd Wright, similar to the Nunnery at Uxmal.
From Anthony Alofsin, *Frank Lloyd Wright—The Lost Years, 1910–1922*, 236.

immense ego, pride of ownership, and the modern ideal that it violates some mythical moral code to copy or be influenced by anything of the past. Nevertheless, in his quest to develop a truly "American" architecture, Wright copied and was inspired greatly by the design concepts of the urban planning, construction techniques, and architectural designs of the Maya and other pre-Columbian civilizations of Mesoamerica, particularly during the first decades of the twentieth century.

Wright was a genius and, as such, not only mastered his own principles of design but easily absorbed and understood the concepts that he was exposed to and admired, namely: the work of architect Louis Sullivan, his teacher; the art of Japan; the Aesthetic movement; the Vienna Secession; and the architecture of Mesoamerica and the Maya.

It is unknown where Wright learned the concepts of Maya design, but it could have come first from the lavishly illustrated books by John Lloyd Stephens, *Incidents of Travel in Central America, Chiapas and Yucatan* and *Incidents of Travel in Yucatan*, both chronicling Maya architecture with beautiful illustrations by Frederick Catherwood, first published in 1841.

There were many opportunities for Wright to study Maya architecture. In the 1880s, Wright was in contact with Pierre Lorillard IV, a collector of pre-Columbian art who had financed one of Claude-Joseph Désiré Charnay's photographic expeditions to Mesoamerica. Along with notable scholars like Sylvanus Morley and Herbert Spinden, Charnay visited the Maya ruins and chronicled his visits. Charnay's book *Cités et ruines Américaines* (1862–67) covered pre-Columbian architecture and was an important early archaeological study with descriptions of numerous Mesoamerican sites. It is quite probable that this work circulated within Wright's social and intellectual circles. In addition, there were exhibitions of Teobert Maler's photographs of Guatemalan ruins at Chicago's Field Museum.

Wright would have had direct exposure to the pre-Columbian architecture exhibited in 1893 at the World's Columbian Exposition in Chicago, where he worked on the Transportation Building while in the office of the architects Adler and Sullivan. The exposition featured dramatic pre-Columbian, specifically Maya, displays at the Anthropology Building with Maya artifacts, reliefs, and large photographs. With this inspiration gleaned from Mesoamerican design, Wright, with his unusual ability to distill and understand basic principles of design, could translate and integrate them into his own personal vocabulary of design.

Wright used references to the Maya as his inspiration between 1909 and 1914 after he exhausted the Prairie style and became exposed to the pre-Columbian principles. He used architectural sculpture as part of integral ornamentation, using patterns recalling the mosaic of the Mixtec buildings at Mitla. The capitals of the slender columns of the "screen" in the hall of the Winslow house (1893–94) were based on the Maya frieze of the Nunnery at Uxmal.

Wright also used Maya elements, geometric patterns and scale in his detailing of the masonry panels for his Midway Gardens project in Chicago (1913, demolished in 1925).

In his book, *A Testament*, Wright wrote:

I remember as a boy, primitive American architecture—Toltec, Aztec, Mayan, Inca—stirred my wonder, excited my wishful admiration. I wished I might someday have money enough to go to Mexico, Guatemala and Peru to join in excavating those long slumbering remains of lost cultures; mighty primitive abstractions of man's nature—ancient arts of the Mayan, the Inca, the Toltec. Those great American abstractions were all earth-architectures: gigantic masses of masonry raised up on great stone-paved terrain, all planned as one mountain, one vast plateau lying there or made into the great mountain ranges themselves; those vast areas of paved earth walled in by stone construction. These were human creations, cosmic as the sun, moon, and stars![1]

The following are areas where it seems that Wright was strongly influenced by the wondrous architecture of Mesoamerica and the Maya.

Horizontality

The strong use of horizontality, marrying the building to the earth. Wright wrote his early principles at the turn of the twentieth century: "to associate the building as a whole with its site by extension and emphasis of the planes parallel to the ground. Extended level planes were found useful in this connection."[2]

### Exposed Stone

The abundant use of exposed stone, as exhibited in Wright's Imperial Hotel, where he balanced the patterned fabric of brick against lava (Oya stone) to create patterned and geometrically rich ornamentation.

### Courts

Wright used the quadrangle, interior courts, and defined plazas, often using long pergolas to enclose the courts and connect separate units of a building. Wright used this Maya quadrangle concept in his Midway Gardens, Chicago, Illinois, 1913; the Imperial Hotel, Tokyo, Japan, 1914; and in several large estates of his Prairie Home period. The close similarity of these two concepts is clearly apparent when one compares the Maya Nunnery at Uxmal, Yucatán, Mexico, and Wright's Hollyhock House. The historian Robert McCarter, in his book *Frank Lloyd Wright*, wrote:

> The beautiful ink-wash perspective drawing, apparently executed by Wright's son Lloyd in 1921, showing an aerial view of the Hollyhock House, is virtually an exact match with a view of the so-called Nunnery, a Maya structure at Uxmal. . . . [T]he walls are flat near the ground and slope back above, with a horizontal decorative frieze at their juncture; the proportions and dimensions of a thin long rectangular, flat-roofed massive volumes with roof terraces, set so that their ends do not align and their joints therefore remain open and of course the distinctive central courtyard. . . . [W]e are left to wonder if Wright provided this clue to confirm that, as has been suggested, he was at this time attempting to make a direct relation in his work towards the great monuments of the Maya in Yucatán—powerful examples of indigenous place-making.[3]

Concerning the Barnsdall House, McCarter wrote: "The drawing's massing details at the corners, and beveled upper proportions, closely parallels this view, and it is possible that the Wright drawing was begun by tracing over a photograph of the Nunnery."[4]

### Stelae

Wright's use of freestanding stone sculptures and pinnacles similar to the Maya freestanding altars, called stelae. Wright used freestanding sculptures, similar in size to the stelae, as beautiful punctuation points to animate his designs in such work as the Larkin Company Exhibition Pavilion, Jamestown, Virginia, 1907; Midway Gardens, Chicago, Illinois, 1913; the Imperial Hotel, Tokyo, Japan, 1914–22; and the Carnegie Library, Pembroke, Ontario, Canada, 1913. Wright also used exposed stone often in his residential designs to give warmth and texture to interior fireplace lintels and surrounds.

### Cornices

Wright used cornices, batter walls (a gradual backward slope in a wall), and ornamented bands of exposed stone, which were important features of Maya architecture. As an example, both Wright and the Maya used bands of mounding, commonly called the medial cornice, to separate the upper and lower zones of the façade. Horizontal bands were a common and important feature of most of Wright's works, executed in stone, plaster, and wood.

## Terraces

Setting the superstructure of a building on one or several strong horizontal and wide, usually sloped terrace, substructure or projecting bases. The 1924 Ennis House in California is an example.

## Batter Walls

The use of tall batter walls, often with no or few openings. The Ennis House and the Barnsdall House in California are examples. Wright used the batter wall as a horizontal banding, often decorative, above the flat lower wall, in a similar fashion to the Maya heavy mansard roofs, found at Palenque.

## Wall Construction

The construction method of building stone or brick-faced concrete walls. Wright copied the construction techniques of the Maya in the manner they built masonry walls to create arches or vaults, the essential elements of their architecture.

The Maya would place several courses of stone on either side of a space creating a cavity, with the outer face being finished stone. Then they would fill the space with rubble concrete. Walls were built on either side of an arch or vault in this manner, and the inner thickness of the walls would gradually grow until the opposing walls would meet at the apex of the arch or vault.

Frank Lloyd Wright used this same technique in building the exposed fieldstone tabby walls at his desert home, Taliesin West, in Arizona; in the brick walls of his Imperial Hotel in Tokyo; and later in the Textile Block Houses in California. Wright built the walls in ascending layers using the facing materials as his form, creating at one time a monolithic and perfectly veneered wall. This technique is described in the *Frank Lloyd Wright Quarterly* as follows:

> On a technical level, there are respondences between the construction of the Imperial Hotel and the textile block buildings that followed. . . . The structure was made from custom-manufactured brick laid up five courses at a time as both inner and outer walls, leaving an air space in between; at that point of construction, concrete was poured by hand into the cavity. As a result, the brick, in fact, acted as a formwork for the concrete structure that ultimately rose on the site.[5]

## Geometric Patterns

Both the pre-Columbian Middle American civilizations and Frank Lloyd Wright used repeated geometric, textured patterns as important architectural features in their designs. Good examples of Wright's work with continuous, repetitive bands of carved decoration are found throughout the work he designed in California in the 1920s, the so-called Textile Block Houses. The influence of the geometrical mosaic and fret motifs of the Mixtecs at Mitla (Oaxaca, Mexico) in their Palace of Columns—the grandest of their palaces—is particularly felt in Wright's work and iconography. Here the ornamentation is articulated in a strong contrasting play of varying rhythms: it is complex, but at the same time, when understood, simple. This geometry was obviously copied in Wright's archetypical, patterned details. These Mixtec zigzag designs were published in various contemporary journals that Wright most probably studied. Great architect that he was, Wright not only copied the design elements, details, and methods of the pre-Columbians but also captured the essence of their centuries-old architecture, an expression of design not acknowledged by contemporary modern architecture.

In addition to his California homes, the most obvious examples of Wright's Maya influence are found in his early Kehl Dance Academy, Madison, Wisconsin (1912), and the Albert Dell German Cold Storage Warehouse in Richland Center, Wisconsin, (1915). Here is Wright's manifestation of the pre-Columbian massing as a solid rectilinear structure with few openings, a monumentality perfect for a warehouse. The wide upper cornice articulation is typical Maya with its strong integral ornamentation. The contrast between this ornamental banding and the otherwise plain unembellished façade is a Maya principle embraced by other contemporary architects.

The architectural historian Vincent Scully Jr. notes the similarity in the use of multiple literal and visual references between the German Warehouse and the House of the Three Lintels at the Maya site of Chichén Itzá, Yucatán. He said that Wright's lattice, fret, and mask designs are similar to the fret elements and molding found in the roof combs and medial banding of the Maya of the Classic period.

Also, the entire concept of Wright's Imperial Hotel, in Tokyo, Japan (1911–22), is related to Maya architecture in its use of exposed Oya stone, its texture, details, and decoration. Their repetitive, patterned unit system gave the structures an order and organic rhythm. The most Maya-influenced design of Wright was the 1918 Yamamura Residence in Ashiya, Japan, with its stepped terraced platforms also using exposed Oya stone, the batter walls, and the ornamental bandings. The uppermost platform is crowned with a rectilinear enclosure similar to the temples placed at the top of the Maya pyramids.

It should be noted that Wright did not copy directly these details or designs but rather used them to learn the essence of pre-Columbian aesthetic design and then incorporated their principles in a fresh and innovative way to create his own genre of design. All architecture, like all knowledge, is based on an accumulation of past experiences and ideas.

Henry-Russell Hitchcock tells the story of the Maya influence on Wright in his book on the work of Frank Lloyd Wright, *In the Nature of Materials: The Buildings of Frank Lloyd Wright 1887–1941*:

> The other early block houses are not so interesting, although the Storer House should be mentioned for its grace, and the Ennis House for its majesty. Here—and this perhaps as much as the repeated units of formal pattern explains the suggestion of Maya influence— the great terrace on which the house stands is almost the most prominent feature.[6]

Anthony Alofsin, in his book *Frank Lloyd Wright—The Lost Years, 1910–1922: A Study of Influence*, writes:

> Wright's aesthetic experiments in ornament combined with an interest in ancient and non-Western cultures that extended throughout the decade of the 1910s and into the early 1920s to create the primitivist phase of his work. . . . Fundamental to these formal developments were Wright's associations of aesthetic, mystical, and social force with the geometric elements of his designs. . . . Wright's theory of architecture held that the social and artistic functions of design were inseparable. . . . These beliefs belonged to the tradition that

a Golden Age existed in which a culture's architecture expressed the true values of its people. . . . Instead of being simple influences, the forms associated with the pure origins of Mesoamerican architecture and sculpture became for Wright part of a universal language. This language existed throughout primitive and exotic cultures worldwide.[7]

The following several pages contain photographs of Wright's California Textile Block Houses, which were designed after Wright built the Midway Gardens and the Imperial Hotel. Prominent among these were the Hollyhock House (1917–20), a powerful statement using lightweight wood and thin stucco disguised as exposed poured concrete and concrete sculpture; the Alice Millard House, "La Miniatura," 1923; the John Storer House, 1923; and the Charles Ennis House, 1923. In these block houses, the geometric designs were fashioned in modular, concrete blocks that were exposed and stacked both horizontally and vertically, defining both the exterior and interiors spaces. The strong influence of Maya is immediately apparent in these examples.

Wright's block concept is ingenious for it is relatively inexpensive, flexible, and produces integral decoration. The method uses precast concrete coffered shells with reinforcing rods placed into the hollowed joints between blocks, then grouted. These concrete forms accept both tension and compression for walls or spanning members, plus create an insulated air space.

Hollyhock House, the residence Wright designed for Aline Barnsdall, was planned originally as a celebration of the arts, with several theaters, retail arcades, and apartments in addition to the private residence (which was built). The massing, batter walls and the "hollyhock"

bandings are similar to that of the Maya. This home particularly could have been influenced by the plaster model of Structure 33 at Yachilan displayed at the 1893 World Exhibition in Chicago.

Wright's Alice Millard House, "La Miniatura," in Pasadena, California (1923), was intended to house the archives of Mrs. George M. Millard's extensive collection of art and literature. The patterned integral woven decorations were evocative of Maya relief sculpture.

The last Wright-designed California home, the Charles Ennis Residence, is situated on a hill reminiscent of the Maya temples set on lofty pedestals and pyramids high in the sky. In this home, the hardware, ceramic tile, and ornamental ironwork have the tactile sense of transformed Maya geometry and hieroglyphics.

Wright wrote in his book *A Testament*:

The ancient American architectures of the Inca, the Maya and the Toltec are lying centuries deep buried in the earth where ages ago instead of the free soul of man, the cosmic-order of the sun, moon and stars inspired primitive man to level mountains and erect giant temples to his material power.[8]

## Maya Influence on the Author's Architecture

During my architectural career, I have studied and used many historic references in guiding my design decisions. I am not a believer in the doctrine that our modern times demand a completely new architecture, solely conceived for our time. Great civilizations are built on layers and layers of accumulated knowledge, a knowledge that is not always original or fresh but is still valid in its reality. This simple fact, often overlooked in our rush to "modernity," is what books, libraries, universities, and scholarly research are all about.

So I used the Maya as one of several wonderful historic sources on which to base my creative expression, and I did this without the camouflage of false pride. The clearest reference to the principles of Maya architecture was in my design for the shopping and entertainment complex Mayfair in the Grove, built in Coconut Grove, Florida (1979–85), now, unfortunately, mostly destroyed. In this work, I used poured, textured concrete in strong horizontal bands, and batter walls, rich in integral ornamentation. The details were first carved in the reverse in Styrofoam and then used as lining in the forms to permanently impress the integrated designs into the concrete.

## What We Can Learn

There were two powerful forces in Maya architecture that in ancient times had a sudden burst of glory—they were its stone architecture and sculpture illuminated in the blinding tropical light and accentuated by the deepest, black shadows; and then the scale of the Maya's vast cities, a perfect harmony of mass and space. Then suddenly it came to an end when the jungle conquered all. The occasional stone dot emerging from the green-carpeted landscape is all that is left. But the Maya legacy is with us today as its secrets are gradually uncovered by patient archaeology.

The Maya's dazzling and wonderful architecture can teach our generation important lessons—lessons of scale, beauty, form, space and the subtle harmony of a total, cohesive work of architectonic art that created garden cities in the midst of a most hostile, natural world. Can these lessons be learned as we continue to build our future, or are we only entertained by it all and destined to destroy the potential Garden of Eden that God has bestowed upon us?

\*   \*   \*

Following are nine photos of Wright's work showing Maya influence.

Midway Gardens, Chicago, Illinois, 1913.

Imperial Hotel, Tokyo,
Japan, 1914–22.

Hollyhock House, by Frank Lloyd Wright, for Aline Barnsdall, Olive Hill,
Los Angeles, California, 1917–21.

Hollyhock House, by Frank Lloyd Wright, for Aline Barnsdall, Olive Hill, Los Angeles, California, 1917–21. The pinnacles, which punctuate the skyline, are subtle references to the stelae of the Maya, which also punctuated the great plazas of the Maya cities. The continuous frieze of deep sculpture designs and the batter walls, where the walls have a gradual slope, are also an obvious part of the Maya design vocabulary.

Hollyhock House, by Frank Lloyd Wright, for Aline Barnsdall, Olive Hill,
Los Angeles, California, 1917–21.

Millard House (La Miniatura), by
Frank Lloyd Wright, Pasadena,
California, 1923.

Ennis House, by Frank Lloyd Wright, Los Angeles, California, 1923.

The Smiling Sprite, a Maya "stela" used by Frank Lloyd Wright in the Midway Gardens, 1914. Wright also placed "stela" statue variations on the projecting mezzanines at Midway. Wright also used the stela form named *Flower in the Crannied Wall* as a freestanding sculptural figure designed with the sculptor Richard W. Bock (1865–1948) in the entrance hall of the Susan Lawrence Dana House, Springfield, Illinois, 1902.

VIEW FROM SOUTHEAST
HOUSE FOR ZETA BETA TAU FRATERNITY
GAINESVILLE FLORIDA
FRANK LLOYD WRIGHT ARCHITECT

Frank Lloyd Wright's proposed Zeta Beta Tau Fraternity House, University of Florida, Gainesville, Florida, 1951. A strong horizontality of mass and the large circular terrace hug the hillside. The Maya used the horizontal terrace as a pedestal and an important architectural feature to tie their buildings to the earth. The author was the primary contact between Frank Lloyd Wright, the fraternity, and the university during the development phases of this design, which was never constructed. Rendering by Frank Lloyd Wright.

These five photographs of Mayfair in the Grove, Coconut Grove, Florida, 1989, by the author show the strong Maya influence on the author's architecture.

Kenneth Treister's architectural work with Maya influence (Mayfair in the Grove, Coconut Grove, Florida, 1989).

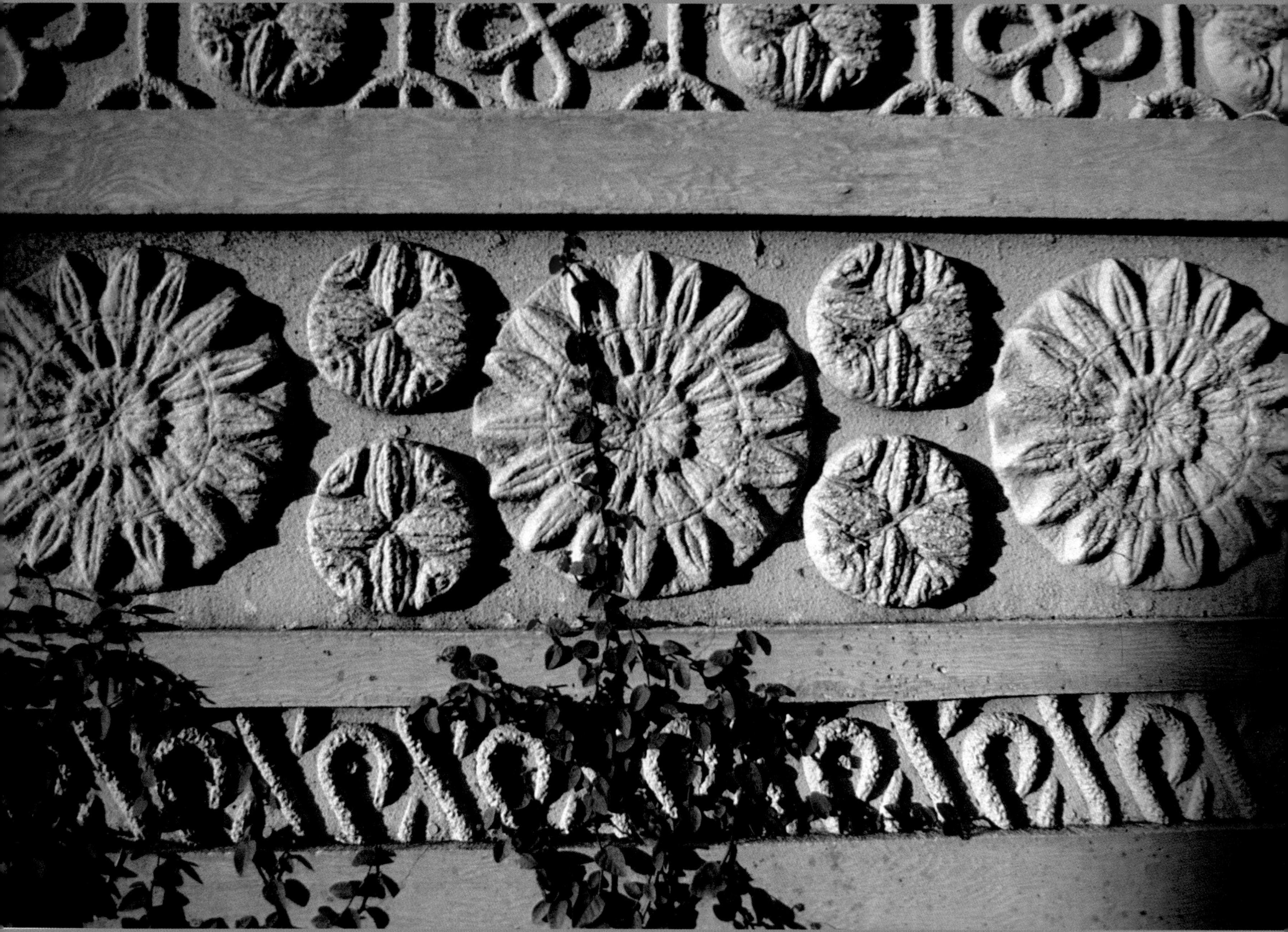

# 10

# The Cities

## Olmec

The Olmec Civilization, located in the coastal zone of Veracruz, Mexico, was the mother culture, beginning about three thousand years ago, from which the future complex cultures of Mesoamerica were born.

Olmec. La Venta, Tenochtitlan, Monument 1. One of four Olmec colossal head effigies at the park of the Museo de Antropología de Xalapa in Xalapa, Veracruz. The monolithic sculptured head wearing a helmet—a war helmet or one similar to those worn by the ball-game players—is a commanding portrait of an Olmec ruler, with facial features, hair texture, and cornrows.

Olmec. La Venta, Tomb A. This is a reconstruction of the tomb originally
built with giant basalt honed logs. It was literally an underground log cabin
containing the red pigmentation that once covered the bodies of two infants.
Also found in the tomb were rich offerings of jade and jewelry.

Olmec. La Venta, on the Gulf at Tabasco. Altar 5, a throne of an Olmec ruler, with the ruler sitting cross-legged with a crown in the image of a jaguar as the earth monster emerging from a mythical cave symbolizing the cave entrance to the supernatural underworld. The Olmec ancient ancestors came to the New World from northern Asia via the land bridge formed across the Bering Strait.

Olmec. Southern Veracruz and western Tabasco, Mexico. The Olmec are called the mother culture of Mesoamerica and flourished during the Formative period (1500–300 BCE). They created extraordinarily beautiful, brilliantly executed mural art, sculpture, jewelry, costumes, regalia, written codices, and architecture. Theirs was a complex, hierarchical society with a small elite governing specific political territories; they engaged in distant exotic trade.

# Palenque

Palenque, considered by many to be the most beautiful of the ancient Maya cities, lies at the northern edge of the Chiapas Highlands overlooking the vast coastal plain that stretches to the Gulf of Mexico, some seventy-five miles distant. The seat of a powerful court, Palenque reached its peak between approximately 600 and 750 CE. Much of the site still lies in the rainforest surrounding the beautiful temples.

Palenque, Chiapas. The Palace is a complex raised on a broad horizontal base composed of palaces, punctuated by the unique four-story observation tower. The palaces enclose and define cloister-like, human-scaled courts.

*Facing page:* Palenque, Chiapas. The Palace. The broad columns and rhythmical openings are capped by a horizontal, concrete mansard roof. This indicates Palenque's significant technological progress toward lighter construction. The heavy mass of rubble concrete of the older, typical Maya vaults was eliminated, and the roof became a relatively thin concrete slab. The internal ceilings remained hollowed out, while the load-bearing columns reduced the size of the supporting wall.

*Right:* Palenque, Chiapas. The Palace. This storied tower, unique in the Maya architectural vocabulary, served for astronomical observations or as a defensive watchtower. The square tower rests on four massive columns, one at each corner. These grow smaller at each level as the tower ascends. The top three façades have large central openings, while the tower is capped by a wide-brimmed mansard stone roof.

*Facing page:* Palenque, Chiapas. Temple of the Inscriptions. This 100-foot-high, eight-stepped pyramid, with a dominant temple, gets its name from the panels of glyphs found in the centered porticoed sanctuary. This pyramid was reconstructed three times. This represents the first phase with a narrow stairway. The roof originally had a roof comb. In 1952, a funerary crypt was discovered of K'inich Janaab' Pakal (ruled 615–683 CE). Originally the outer stepped cladding probably had a layer of polychromed stucco.

*Below:* Palenque, Chiapas. Like a giant pastoral, hilly park, the ruins of Palenque have their pyramidal substructures covered with green. Only the top temples (cella) are exposed. Shown here are the Temple of the Foliated Cross (672 CE), the Temple of the Cross (692 CE), and the Temple of the Sun (690 CE). The temples are crowned by mansard roofs with roof combs (*cresteria*). Site as photographed in 1985.

# Sayil

Sayil, a vast city of the Late Classic period in the Puuc Hills of Yucatán, is now overrun by jungle, but it displays one wondrous work of architectonic art—the restored three-story Palace, considered a masterpiece of Maya architecture.

*Facing page:* Palenque, Chiapas. Temple of the Foliated Cross (692 CE). Time has stripped away its front façade revealing a view of its vaulted concrete construction. The center vault is a typical Maya concrete vault with dressed stones used as its form. The weight of this massive rubble concrete is obvious to observe. On either side are vaults made in the shape of the graceful tilobe arch, a "key" form, found at various palaces at Palenque.

*Facing page:* Sayil, Yucatán. The Palace. View from the second-level terrace, which is the roof of the bottom level below, looking toward the colonnade façade. This section has six openings to the interior rooms: two are simple doorways, and four are porticoed openings, each with two beautifully shaped round columns, all holding the strong horizontal frieze of colonettes.

*Above:* Sayil, Yucatán. The Palace. Some of the freestanding columns of the mid-level porticoes are monolithic stone, while these shown are composite columns made of several circular pieces. Above all the columns are square stone capitals that distribute the loads more evenly from the roof and frieze to the columns. These thin columns, as opposed to the heavy, massively thick columns, open the rooms to the sunlight, creating lighter interior spaces.

Sayil, Yucatán. The Palace. View of the colonnade, looking out from the interior. By learning to use the post-and-lintel system of construction, the Maya liberated themselves from the long, narrow, and dark interiors spaces created by the concrete vaults. The columns are often bulbous at their centers like the classic Greek columns.

Sayil, Yucatán. The Palace. View from the interior of one of the second-story chambers with the vaulted-shape ceiling with horizontal rows of finished stone covering the concrete vault above. On the left is the open portico with a round column and capital holding the lintel above. The space is light and open in feeling.

Palenque, Chiapas. The Palace. This photograph of the interior of the vaulted, porticoed galleries with broad rectangular columns open to the great court shows the Maya vault construction method that was also used in Sayil. Rectangular openings on the left bring light to the secondary tier of interior chambers. This shows the technological achievements of creating lighter structures with the hollowing out of the interior space and reducing the materials used.

Uxmal, Yucatán. This section clearly shows the construction method of the Maya concrete arch and vault that was also used in Sayil. The exposed dressed facing stones that were decoratively finished and occasionally shaped as pointed triangles were the form work for the concrete rubble walls that are the real structural element of the Maya arch and vault. The two opposing concrete walls thicken as they ascend until they meet at the center.

135

# Labná

The city of Labná, in Yucatán's Puuc Hills, was one of the cities that experienced a revolutionary change in architectural design. The endless, flat terrain of Yucatán seemed to have inspired remarkable buildings noted for beautiful proportions and grace of ornamentation. Labná's great triumphal arch is a prime example as it welcomes visitors with a splendid architectonic experience.

Labná (fallen or ruined house), Yucatán. The arch, one of the most important structures in all Maya architecture. This richly decorated building is perfectly proportioned and balanced about the entrance arch. Its east façade is simple, while the west side is part of a group of buildings that form a defined and enclosed entrance court. As in all Maya groupings, the buildings, although different in detail and articulation, are wonderfully harmonious in architectural design.

137

Labná, Yucatán. This Puuc city, with an inner harmony that is characteristic of all Maya cities, has as its focal point and most spectacular work of architecture its monumental arch, located at the foot of the stepped pyramid Mirador. This arch is considered the finest portal arch of the Maya and served as a ceremonial passageway between courtyards.

Labná, Yucatán. Memorialized in stone, as decoration on the stone frieze on the arch to Labná, this rendition is of the typical pole-and-thatch house of the Maya. This common dwelling, used for thousands of years, has wattle-and-daub walls, a steeply thatched roof, and a single entrance. The interiors are shown in two photographs in the section on contemporary life of the Maya.

Labná, Yucatán. The Palace, Late Classic period. This is a large, three-storied building, built over several centuries. Its porticoed apartments overlook the main plaza, and their terraces are built over the roof of the level below and contain a built-in water cistern. The sculpture work is outstanding, with one of the largest rain-god masks ever sculpted and an open-mouthed serpent with a human head in its jaws on the corner of the cornice.

*Facing page:* Labná, Yucatán. El Mirador, a Puuc pyramid and temple, is the only temple within the ceremonial center. It faces south, away from the central plaza; however, the priests could still be on its high platform and look over the plaza to see processions arriving along the causeway (*sacbé*) through the arch.

*Right:* Labná, Yucatán. El Mirador. The surface of the upper temple, El Castillo, shows its exposed projecting tenoned, stone armature and its roof comb's open fretwork, both of which are all that is left of the once brilliant façade's high-relief stucco decorations.

Labná, Yucatán. Detail, entrance court group. This geometric pattern, created in carved mosaic stone and alive with sharp, layered shadow and bright sunlight, is a wondrous example of the design ability of the Maya architects.

Labná, Yucatán. The entrance court's inner compound wall behind the Great Gate. In the Puuc region, the name Labná means "the old houses." The trapezoidal door is aesthetically more pleasing and is structurally sounder. The slender, vertical stone columns, or bundle motifs, were simply a transposition of the logs or sticks used in the walls of the common Maya dwelling. The two intermediate, horizontal bands represent the ties and straw wadding that held them together. Their derivation is relatively unimportant; what is significant is the strong horizontal shadow of the thin frieze and repetitive shadows of the surface. The Maya were intuitively magnificent architects.

# Uxmal

The Late Classic city of Uxmal developed the style of the Puuc region to its greatest perfection. The city's main characteristic is its various quadrangles, each enclosing and defining an urban plaza. The flat Yucatán landscape is punctuated by the great Pyramid of the Magician, which is in juxtaposition to the long, low façades of the palaces, particularly the famous Quadrangle, the Nunnery, which it overlooks.

Uxmal, Yucatán. The sixth-century Pyramid of the Magician (Soothsayer or Dwarf), an impressive, unique, oval pyramid, located east of the courtyard. This pyramid was built in five successive periods over four hundred years. Its shape and mass are exquisite and sculpturally powerful.

Uxmal, Yucatán. Pyramid of the Magician. A detail of the corner of the central stairway showing anthropomorphic faces of Chac in a stepped, ascending line, a brilliant design concept to transition the steep stairs, "the ladder to the gods," to the pyramid's face.

Uxmal, Yucatán. A large public plaza is well defined by four surrounding horizontal and linear palaces. Here are the North and West Buildings showing the simple and beautiful massing juxtaposed with the intricate and delicate stone mosaic–textured frieze. The individually articulated façades of all four buildings complement each other and create one harmonious composition.

Uxmal, Yucatán. The west half of the North Building rests on the highest platform and has a broad, central grand stairway with two unsymmetrical, colonnaded structures flanking either side and opening directly onto the central plaza.

*Facing page:* Uxmal, Yucatán. The courtyard, the West Palace. This illustrates the design genius of the Maya, with the frieze considered the finest in all of ancient Mesoamerica. This façade is composed of a series of horizontal bands: first, the raised platform steps as the base; then a hard, thin, lower line of short columns with a projected shadow; then the plain, square-block main band with its negative door openings, each with a framed stepped frame; then the wide rococo frieze of intense decoration; and finally a thin projecting cornice—all working together in perfect harmony.

*Above:* Uxmal, Yucatán. The courtyard, Northern Palace, detail of one of three low towers of ascending anthropomorphic images of Chac. This quadrangle defined by four Puuc-style palaces is not a perfect square but has a trapezoidal ground plan that orthogonally is more interesting and inviting, like the later legendary Saint Mark's Square in Venice.

153

The omnipresence of the mask of Chac, the rain god, with its long, upturned nose, is a recurring anthropomorphic feature throughout Maya architecture and is particularly striking when placed at the building's corners and silhouetted against the bright-blue Yucatán sky.

Uxmal, Yucatán. The Palace of the Governor, standing proudly with a monumental central stairway and the rhythm of the openings capped by a wide horizontal frieze, creates a musical balance and humanistic beauty.

Uxmal, Yucatán. Palace of the Governor. This recessed entrance—one of two symmetrically placed that form an architectural punch—appears as an uplifting explanation point. Originally the entrance to the building's interior, it later was partially walled to form the back arrow.

Uxmal, Yucatán. Palace of the Governor. Over the central door, a beautiful stone mosaic sculpture of a ruler over his throne with a rich feathered headdress and framed by double-headed serpents.

# Copán

Copán, a city of astonishingly beautiful art located on the southeast Maya frontier, was distinguished for its innovations and skills in architecture and extraordinary sculpture, both in stone and stucco.

Copán, Honduras. Portrait of Waxaklajuun Ub'aah K'awiil ("18 Rabbit"), Stela H with scarlet macaws. One of the most ornate of Copán's stelae depicts the maize god with full regalia, plus symbols of sacrificial blood-letting. The stela is carved in a unique style with glyphs in a matte pattern, a symbol of royal power. It was part of the group of stelae in the northern part of the great plaza.

*Left:* Copán, Honduras. Portrait of Waxaklajuun Ub'aah K'awiil, Stela B (733 CE), a brilliant work of Maya sculpture. A realistic portrait of the Maya ruler named 18 Rabbit in his richly ceremonial costume. The eighth-century reign of this great lord witnessed the full splendor of the metropolis of Copán.

*Facing page:* Copán, Honduras. Altar G, dated 766 CE. A double-headed feathered snake wraps around the date, symbolizing the ruler's desire to connect with his dead ancestor. One of three G altars in a group on the plaza.

Copán, Honduras. Portrait of Waxaklajuun Ub'aah K'awiil, Stela C, in the great plaza facing the Cosmic Turtle altar with a rectangular altar behind. The turtle, carved with excellent realistic skill, is moving slowly, extremely slowly.

Copán, Honduras. This graceful Stela F, with Altar G2, on the east side of the Great Plaza, may be the most beautiful of all of Waxaklajuun Ub'aah K'awiil's freestanding sculptures, a masterpiece of gesture, fluid form, and sculpted detail. The rounded contours of the king's thighs and calves depict an athlete-warrior: hero of battle and the ball court.

*Facing page:* Copán, Honduras. Altar G (800 CE), is the largest of three similar altars located between Stelae F and H in Copán's Great Plaza, which was ruler Waxaklajuun Ub'aah K'awiil's showcase plaza and used for the commoners to enjoy public ceremonies. The altar depicts a double-headed serpent with its two opposing heads dramatically rearing up into the air.

*Right:* Copán, Honduras. Stela A, rear side with the hieroglyphic text. Such inscriptions are all over central Copán, and many texts also occur in the outlying valley associated with the larger buildings such as the Scribe's Palace. The texts are often short and simply relate to a specific ritual and the monument's dedication. The hieroglyphic stone carvings at Copán are magnificent examples of the fine and precise craftsmanship of the Maya sculptors.

165

*Left:* Copán, Honduras. Great Ball Court, Building 10. This beautifully executed masonry entrance misled generations of archaeologists into thinking the Maya used corbelled arches and vaults when they actually used structural concrete arches and vaults. The stone corbelling was merely the decorative finish and formwork used to hold the rubble concrete during construction.

*Facing page:* Copán, Honduras. Great Ball Court. Thousands of spectators packed into the ceremonial center near the Great Plaza to watch the spectacle of this national sport. The game was played for high stakes. It was an abstraction of a contest between mythical beings and concepts and had a relationship with the solstices and equinoxes that established the position of its structures.

*Facing page:* Copán, Honduras. West Court, the Spectators' Gallery. This three-dimensional sculpture, with a carved sculpture of the storm god holding a torch with the Ik sign (representing wind, sun, and life) is completely integrated into its architectural environment. It is the realistic focal point of this fundamentally calm and pastoral enclosed space. The hieroglyphic steps serve two additional functions: first, an aesthetic one, forming a continuous base of ascending parallel, shadowed lines; and second, as seats for the public during ceremonial events.

*Above:* Copán, Honduras. West Court, looking at Temple 11, with its strong rhythm of linear horizontality, and its Spectators' Gallery. Also facing this court is Temple 16 with Altar Q (not shown), a historically important sculpture that portrays the dynastic lineage of the rulers of Copán. The sixteen figures, all seated, are depicted in full body, four on each side of the monument, each ruler seated on the hieroglyph for his name.

Copán, Honduras. West Court. This is part of the Acropolis that included palaces, platforms, pyramids, spectators' galleries, the Great Plaza, and numerous public sculptures. Of all the enclosed public courts in the Maya realm—maybe even throughout the world—this simple, enclosed West Court (as it exists today) is one of the author's favorite exterior spaces.

# Chichén Itzá

Chichén Itzá is a combination of two civilizations blending
their creativity into one architectural reality. Originally
built in the Puuc style, it was rebuilt as the result of the
tenth-century migrations of warriors from the Toltec
capital of Tula into a magnificent new city, their capital.
Later migrations of the Itzá people added their name to
the former Toltec city of Chichén.

*Facing page:* Chichén Itzá, Yucatán. Pyramid of Kukulcán/Quetzalcóatl (El Castillo). This city was a merger of the Maya and the Toltecs of Tula cultures, ruled at its height by Lord Kukulcán, Quetzalcóatl (a snake), regarded as a god. It was the largest city of the Postclassic period. This magnificent symmetrical pyramid is flanked by four staircases bordered by a balustrade capped by a perfectly preserved upper temple. Each stair has 91 steps, creating 364; when one adds the extra step to the temple, the total is 365, the number of days in the year.

*Above:* Chichén Itzá, Yucatán. Pyramid of Kukulcán/Quetzalcóatl (El Castillo). One of the two sculpted heads of the plumed serpent, with open, menacing jaws at the foot of the north central stair of this Toltec-Maya pyramid.

173

Chichén Itzá, Yucatán. The stone ring of the Great Ball Court wall. This court was the largest known in the Mayan world. The hard rubber ball had to pass through this small stone ring mounted 20 feet high on the 27-foot wall. The ball could be struck only by the elbow, wrist, or hip, areas of the body covered with leather pads. A goal was rare.

Chichén Itzá, Yucatán. North Temple. Facing the Great Ball Court, this beautiful temple is elegant in its proportions, scale, simplicity, and grace. It shows the innate talent of the sensitive and inherently superb Maya architects. Compare this classical architecture with the instability of modern deconstructionist work.

Chichén Itzá, Yucatán. Upper Temple of the Jaguar in the Maya-Toltec style. This upper temple, with walls built on an incline, is built on a pyramid over the lower temple at the corner of the Great Ball Court. The portico is guarded by two huge plumes of feathers atop serpentine columns with raised rattle-snake heads that literally and beautifully embrace the structure by wrapping around it.

Chichén Itzá, Yucatán. Upper Temple of the Jaguar sitting high, balanced regally on top of the high east wall of the Great Ball Court. One of the most flawlessly proportioned Maya buildings, whose sculptural massing uses geometric forms to perfection.

*Facing page:* Chichén Itzá, Yucatán. Upper Temple of the Jaguar, east façade, with a jaguar forming an altar open to the large public plaza. The upper temple faces the interior of the Great Ball Court as a superior viewing box for the elite of the military-religious Toltec-Maya society. This is an example of the total integration of architectural forms and contextualism.

*Above:* Chichén Itzá, Yucatán. Platform of the Eagles. This square stage was created for the public display of the sacrifices performed by the Toltec-Maya priests; plays were performed here as well. The menacing plumed serpents guard the top of the stairs from the cornice molding. Its decoration shows eagles devouring hearts, warriors, serpents, and jaguars, as it was dedicated to the Toltec Order of the Eagles and Jaguars.

*Above:* Chichén Itzá, Yucatán. The Temple of the Warriors demonstrates the amalgamation of the Maya and Toltec cultures. The entrance to the interior space, created by the uses of load-bearing columns, was guarded by two sculpted serpent columns embracing the structure with open jaws at the bottom and rattlers above.

*Facing page:* Chichén Itzá, Yucatán. The Temple of the Warriors was a creation of the Toltec-Maya civilization when the Mexican city of Tula held a predominant influence on the Maya territory of the northern Yucatán during the eleventh and twelfth centuries. The Toltec used the fine craftsmanship of the Maya but added a new element—a structure that utilized the inside spaces created by large colonnades, whereas previously Maya buildings were outward looking.

Chichén Itzá, Yucatán. The Caracol (snail) is a unique building with a Maya base. The round tower has a beautiful overhanging apron-type cornice crowning the building, plus an interior spiral stair. It is an observatory with windows that locate the azimuths for the south, west, the equinoxes, and summer solstice.

Chichén Itzá, Yucatán.
The Church (Iglesia). This
highly decorated building
is named for its proximity
to the Nunnery. Its plain
lower section supports an
exuberance of embellish-
ments: a series of bandings;
a wide frieze with anthropomorphic masks in the
center and Maya masks
with a curved snout at each
corner; a unique negative-
batter wall; and above
all this, a roof comb built
of masks.

185

# Tikal

Tikal, in the heart of the Petén, was a giant Maya metropolis, the largest of the Classic Maya and one of the greatest in the New World. At its core was the Great Plaza flanked on the west and east by two towering temple-pyramids—two of six in the city—and on the north by a giant acropolis. The city was laced by broad causeways over which many resplendent processions must have passed.

Tikal, Guatemala. The Great Plaza. One of the most powerful kingdoms of the Classic period had an architecture that was also powerful. Their pyramids, of architectural immensity and amazing mass, were extremely steep and with towering roof combs that exuded authority. They were probably painted primarily in cream and red (the temples were also painted in red). The city dominated its neighbors politically, economically, and militarily. This plaza, dotted with stelae and altars, is enclosed by two great temple-pyramids and by the North and Central Acropolises.

Tikal, Guatemala. The North Acropolis, of staggering complexity—with more than a hundred buildings, dozens built over earlier ones—is 30 feet above bedrock and 40 feet above the Great Plaza. This acropolis is a multifaceted, giant sculpture of decorated temples beautifully modeled with polychrome stuccoed façades and huge masks bordering its stairways. It preserved the imprint of generations of creative architects.

Tikal, Guatemala. Temple I. Tikal, before being abandoned around the ninth century CE, had lasted for nearly two millennia. Temple I, along with Temple II and the vast Great Plaza, dominate this great Maya city. It has nine stepped layers that are united by a steep, central stairway in high relief, leading up its temple sanctuary; the temple is crowned by a magnificent lofty roof comb (*cresteria*). Access to the temple, the ladder between earth and heaven, was only for the elite members of the nobility and royal court in their opulent costumes.

# Kabáh

Kabáh is an important Maya city in the northern region with many scattered buildings still covered by jungle. The most extraordinary and well preserved is the Palace of Masks or Codz Poop, with a textured pattern of masks covering the entire façade.

Tikal, Guatemala. Temple I. This classical Maya masterpiece (700 CE), also known as the Temple of the Giant Jaguar, embodies many of the important Maya architectural characteristics: a terraced pyramid, with complicated changes of levels; strong rhythmical shadows; a strong, superimposed central stair; two pyramids seemingly joined by narrow indentations at its sides; and a high roof comb set to the rear of the temple 145 feet above the Great Plaza. In addition, it held a royal tomb with treasures of Maya jade, pearls, pottery, alabaster, and shells from the Pacific.

Kabáh, Yucatán. The Palace of the Masks is the second-largest Puuc Hills city of the Late Classic period. The Palace of the Masks, in the Chenes style, is also called "Codz Poop" (rolled mat), named for the imagined resemblance between a rolled mat and the limestone, stylized, mosaic masks of the large-nosed rain god, Chac, which entirely blanket the façade.

193

Kabáh, Yucatán. Palace of the Masks. This palace sits on a small platform on a high terrace opening to a court. The entire façade is richly textured, which is unusual in Puuc architecture, where usually only the upper frieze is highly decorated. In the interior, there are double rows of five rooms, one behind the other, each with a rain-god mask step between, similar to the rain-god steps at the entrances.

Kabáh, Yucatán. Palace of the Masks, detail. The Maya were mesmerized by the use of anthropomorphic faces, particularly of the rain god, Chac, with his long, coiled trunk. These sculptural constructions were manufactured in separate pieces, assembled and placed. The Chac masks at Kabáh are made up of thirty separate pieces, each prefabricated perfectly. The skill in mathematical planning was extraordinary for the number of masks, their size, the building's length, and the final aesthetic design that had to be preplanned with precision. The piercing eyes, the graceful nose, the sharp teeth, and the strong shadows create a menacing portrait with clear human emotion.

# Dzibilchaltún

The city of Dzibilchaltún, in the far northwest Puuc region of Yucatán—one of the centers that flourished despite the region's thin soil—was composed of elaborate and sophisticated architecture supported by a large population and well-organized urban society.

Dzibilchaltún, Yucatán. Temple 1, Temple of the Seven Dolls. This archaeological site located to the north of Merida is the stage of an archaeoastronomical event involving the alignment of the rising sun with the eastern gateway of the Temple of the Seven Dolls. When seen from the west side of the temple during this event, the solar disc is precisely framed by the gateway for a few minutes. This event was discovered in 1982 by the late archaeologist Victor Segovia Pinto.

# The Contemporary Maya World

*Facing page:* Lake Atitlán, Guatemala.

*Above:* The typical Maya house, which is primarily
the same after centuries of traditional use.

Typical Maya house interior,
where sleeping hammocks
have been used for centuries.

Eating is one of the many activities performed within the small,
multifunctional detached kitchen house.

Chichicastenango, Guatemala. Held on Thursdays and Sundays, Maya market days are full of colorful costumes and melancholic music. This market, more than eight hundred years old, is the largest market in Central America.

For more than four hundred years, the Santo Tomás Church
has been the focal point of Chichicastenango's market days.

The steps and interiors of Santo Tomás Church hold both Maya and Catholic rites with chanting, billowing incense, burning candles, and offerings of rose petals, pine needles, and harvested crops.

Colorful wooden masks and costumes enliven the historic dances preformed on Chichicastenango's market days.

*Above:* Chichicastenango's large open-air Maya market means trade and sustenance for residents of remote villages.

*Facing and following pages:* The beautiful, hand-woven *traje* of the Highland Maya are still proudly worn. They are unique for each village and language, representing the twenty-one different Maya ethnolinguistic groups.

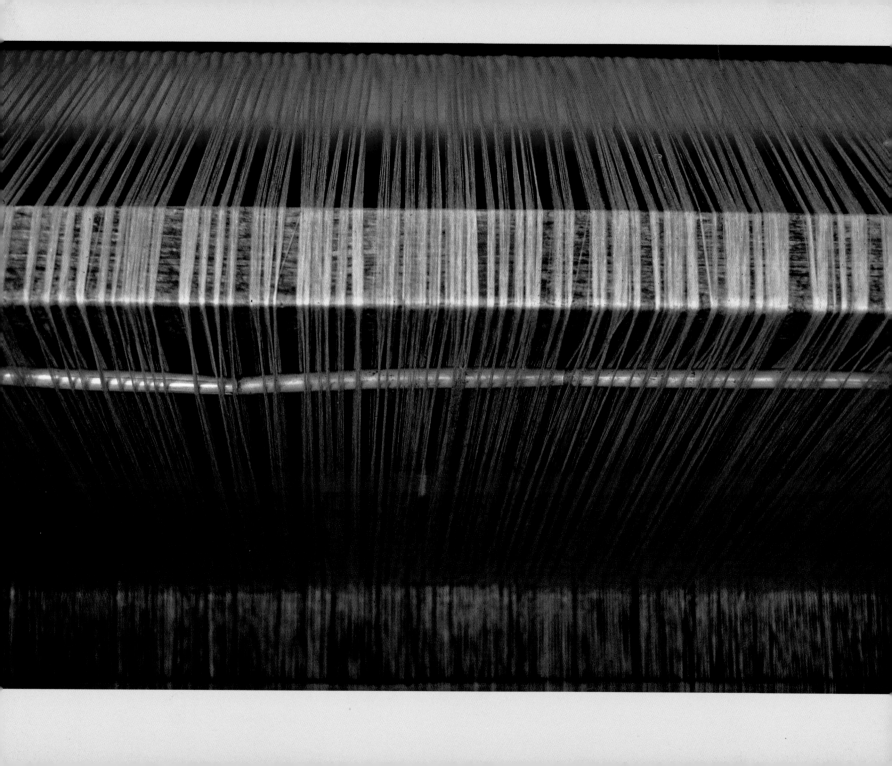

# Acknowledgments

For this book I am deeply indebted to Ves Spindler, a scholar and editor, who has helped me in every detail of the writing, editing, and composition of this book.

In my lifetime of architectural creations, I have strived for the noble cause of the integration of Art, Architecture, and Society. In my studies of architectural history, I found this dictum most prominent in the creations of traditional Japan and the Maya civilizations. I therefore visited and studied the great cities of the Maya and wanted to someday write about the architectural principles that they taught. That opportunity came when John Byram of the University Press of Florida encouraged me to write this book. The professionals at the press were of exceptional assistance: Meredith Morris-Babb, director, Larry Leshan, art director, Dennis Lloyd, Stephanie Williams, Michele Fiyak-Burkley, Amy Gorelick, Sonia Dickey, Kara Schwartz, and others.

In my studies of Maya architecture, my sole scholar was the world-famous and preeminent Maya archaeologist, George E. Stuart, who was the head archaeologist for the National Geographic Society in Washington, D.C. I worked with him for many years. George agreed to write the beautiful foreword for this book and then edited the final manuscript.

**Illustration Credits**

I want to thank the following for permission to publish their illustrations: the photo of the World's Fair Columbian Exhibition of 1893, courtesy of George E. Stuart; Henri Stierlin, for his precise drawings, (Photo Henri STIERLIN, Genève); Wendy Glassmire and the National Geographic Society for the three amazing paintings of the Maya Cities of El Mirador, Palenque and Copán; Joann Schwendemann and Dover Publications, Inc., for the map and perspective drawings of Tatiana Proskouriakoff; Indira Berndtson of the Frank Lloyd Wright Foundation for the historic photos and one rendering of the work of FLW (copyright The Frank Lloyd Wright Foundation, Taliesin West, Scottsdale, AZ); Jeffrey Herr, curator of the FLW's Hollyhock House, photos by the author (by permission of Hollyhock House, Department of Cultural Affairs, City of Los Angeles).

All photographs were taken by the author unless otherwise noted.

# Notes

## Introduction

1. Stierlin, *Living Architecture*, 7.
2. Johnston and Gonlin, "What Do Houses Mean?" 124.
3. Ibid., 35.
4. Schele and Mathews, *The Code of Kings*, 13.
5. Miller, "A Design for Meaning in Maya Architecture," 187.
6. Stierlin, *Mayan Architecture*, 177.
7. Miller, "A Design for Meaning in Maya Architecture," 192, 194.
8. Fash, "Intention and Design in Classic Maya Buildings at Copan and Other Sites," 124.
9. Bacon, *Design of Cities*, 15–16.
10. Stephens, *Incidents of Travel in Central America, Chiapas, and Yucatán*, 1:104.
11. Gates, trans., *Yucatán Before and After the Conquest*, 82.
12. D. Stuart, "The Fire Enters His House," 373.

## Chapter 2. Essence of Maya Architecture

1. Stephens, *Incidents of Travel in Central America, Chiapas, and Yucatán*, 2:442.
2. Stuart and Stuart, *Lost Kingdoms of the Maya*, 24–25.
3. Schele and Mathews, *The Code of Kings*, 39.
4. Hansen, "Continuity and Disjunction," 36–49.
5. Gates, trans., *Yucatán Before and After the Conquest*, by Bishop Diego de Landa, 95.

## Chapter 3. Manifestations of Maya Architecture

1. Hunter, *A Guide to Ancient Maya Ruins*, 143–44.
2. Abrams, "Structures as Sites," 124.

## Chapter 4. Building Materials

1. Stierlin, *Mayan Architecture*, 175.
2. Brown, "El Mirador," 46.

## Chapter 5. Building Types

1. Gates, trans., *Yucatán Before and After the Conquest*, by Bishop Diego de Landa, 32.
2. Schele and Mathews, *The Code of Kings*, 17.
3. Pagden, *Hernan Cortés*, 30–31.
4. Stierlin, *Mayan Architecture*, 106.
5. Gates, trans., *Yucatán Before and After the Conquest*, by Bishop Diego de Landa, 90.
6. Ibid., 91.

## Chapter 6. The Maya City

1. Webster, "Classic Maya Architecture," 26.
2. Ibid., 29.
3. Stierlin, *Mayan Architecture*, 180.
4. Webster, "Classic Maya Architecture," 34.
5. Gates, trans., *Yucatán Before and After the Conquest*, by Bishop Diego de Landa, 26.
6. Ibid., 90.
7. Hansen, "Continuity and Disjunction," 77.
8. Stierlin, *Mayan Architecture*, 132.
9. Stierlin, *Encyclopedia of World Architecture*, 426.
10. Bacon, *Design of Cities*, 19.
11. Krier, *Architecture: Choice or Fate*, 31.

## Chapter 8. Oh, the Wonder of It All

1. Matheny, "El Mirador," 336.
2. Webster, "Classic Maya Architecture," 10.
3. Ibid., 18–19.
4. D. Stuart, *The Fall of the Ancient Maya*, 148.
5. G. Stuart, "Maya Heartland under Siege," 95.
6. Diamond, *Collapse*, 177.
7. Webster, *The Fall of the Ancient Maya*, 348.
8. Brown, "El Mirador," 46.

## Chapter 9. The Legacy

1. Wright, *A Testament*, 111.
2. Kaufman and Raeburn, "Prairie Architecture 1893–1910," in *Frank Lloyd Wright: Writings and Buildings*, ed. Kaufman and Raeburn, 45.
3. McCarter, *Frank Lloyd Wright*, 128–29.
4. Ibid., 129.
5. Smith, "The L.A. Textile Block Houses," 9–10.
6. Hitchcock, *In the Nature of Materials*, 77.
7. Alofsin, *Frank Lloyd Wright—The Lost Years, 1910–1922*, 221.
8. Wright, *A Testament*, 62.

# Selected Bibliography

Abrams, Elliot M. "Structures as Sites: The Construction Process and Maya Architecture." In *Function and Meaning in Classic Maya Architecture*, edited by Stephen D. Houston. Washington, D.C.: Dumbarton Oaks Research Library and Collection, 1998.

Acosta, Jorge R. *Teotihuacan Official Guide*. Córdoba: Instituto Nacional de Antropología e Historia, 1978.

Aguiar, Walter R. *Maya Land in Color*. New York: Hastings House, 1978.

Agurcia, Ricardo F., William L. Fash Jr., Thomas Loomis, and Vito Vliz. *Copan, Yesterday and Today (A Brief Guide)*. Tegucigalpa, D.C., Honduras: Instituto Hondureño de Antropología e Historia, 1986.

Alofsin, Anthony. *Frank Lloyd Wright—The Lost Years, 1910–1922: A Study of Influence*. Chicago: University of Chicago Press, 1993.

Alonzo, Gualberto Zapata. *An Overview of the Mayan World, with Synthesis of the Olmec, Totonac, Zapotec, Mixtec, Teotihuacan, Toltec and Aztec Civilizations*. Merida, Yucatan, Mexico: M. Esquiliano, 1983.

Andia, Justo Paucar. *Machu Picchu*. Cusco, Peru: Andina, 1980.

Bacon, Edmund N. *Design of Cities*. New York: Viking, 1967.

Baines, John, and Jaromir Malék. 1980. *Atlas of Ancient Egypt*. Oxford: Phaidon, 1967.

Blanton, Richard E., Stephen A. Kowalewski, Gary Feinman, and Jill Appel. *Ancient Mesoamerica: A Comparison of Change in Three Regions*. Cambridge: Cambridge University Press, 1986.

Bloomgarden, Richard. *The Easy Guide to Chichén Itzá, Balankanchen and Izamal*. Mexico City: Litográfica Turmex, 1974.

———. *The Easy Guide to Cuernavaca and Surrounding Highlights*. Mexico City: Litográfica Turmex, 1984.

———. *The Easy Guide to Palenque*. Mexico City: Editur, 1982.

———. *The Easy Guide to San Miguel de Allende and Guanajuato, "The Cradle of Independence."* Mexico City: Editur, 1983.

———. *The Easy Guide to Taxco and Environs*. Mexico City: Editur, 1984.

———. *The Easy Guide to Uxmal*. Mexico City: Derechos, 1981.

Braun, Barbara. *Pre-Columbian Art and the Post-Columbian World*. New York: Abrams, 1993.

Brown, Chip. "El Mirador: The Lost City of the Maya." *Smithsonian*, May 2011.

Calvanio, Vittoria. *The Maya*. Geneva: Minerva, 1976.

Culbert, T. Patrick, ed. *The Classic Maya Collapse*. Albuquerque: University of New Mexico Press, 1973.

Diamond, Jared. *Collapse*. New York: Penguin, 2005.

Fash, William L. "Intention and Design in Classic Maya Buildings at Copan and Other Sites." In *Function and Meaning in Classic Maya Architecture*, edited by Stephen D. Houston. Washington, D.C.: Dumbarton Oaks Research Library and Collection, 1998.

Ferguson, William M., and John Q. Royce. *Maya Ruins in Central America in Color: Tikal, Copán, and Quiriguá*. Albuquerque: University of New Mexico Press, 1984.

———. *Maya Ruins in Mexico in Color: Palenque, Uxmal, Kabah, Sayil, Xlapak, Labná, Chichén Itzá, Cobá, Tulum*. Norman: University of Oklahoma Press, 1977.

Garrett, Wilbur E., ed. "La Ruta Maya." *National Geographic*, October 1989.

Gates, William, trans. 1937. *Yucatán Before and After the Conquest*, by Bishop Diego de Landa. Publication no. 20. Baltimore: Maya Society, 1937.

Gendrop, Paul. *A Guide to Architecture in Ancient Mexico*. Mexico City: Minutiae Mexicana, 1987.

Hammond, Norman. *Ancient Maya Civilization*. New Brunswick, N.J.: Rutgers University Press, 1990.

Hansen, Richard. "Continuity and Disjunction: The Pre-Classic Antecedents of Classic Maya Architecture." In *Function and Meaning in Classic Maya Architecture*, edited by Stephen D. Houston. Washington, D.C.: Dumbarton Oaks Research Library and Collection, 1998.

Hitchcock, Henry-Russell. *In the Nature of Materials: The Buildings of Frank Lloyd Wright 1887–1941*. New York: Da Capo, 1973.

Holmes, William Henry. *Archaeological Studies among the Ancient Cities of Mexico*. Chicago: Field Columbian Museum, 1895.

Houston, Stephen D. Introduction to *Function and Meaning in Classic Maya Architecture*. Washington, D.C.: Dumbarton Oaks Research Library and Collection, 1994.

Hunter, C. Bruce. *A Guide to Ancient Maya Ruins*. Norman: University of Oklahoma Press, 1994.

Johnston, Kevin J., and Nancy Gonlin. "What Do Houses Mean? Approaches to the Analysis of Classic Maya Commoner Residences." In *Function and Meaning in Classic Maya Architecture*, edited by Stephen D. Houston. Washington, D.C.: Dumbarton Oaks Research Library and Collection, 1998.

Kaufman, Edgar, and Ben Raeburn, eds. *Frank Lloyd Wright: Writings and Buildings*. New York: Meridian, 1960.

Kelly, Joyce. *The Complete Visitor's Guide to Mesoamerican Ruins*. Norman: University of Oklahoma Press, 1933.

Kerr, Justin, and M. White. *The Olmec World: Ritual and Rulership*. Princeton: Art Museum, Princeton University, 1995.

Krier, Leon. *Architecture: Choice or Fate*. Windsor, U.K.: Andreas Papadakis, 1998.

Krober, A. L., and T. T. Waterman. *Source Book in Anthropology*. Berkeley: University of California Press, 1920.

Lhuillier, Alberto Ruz. *Uxmal: Official Guide*. Mexico City: Instituto Nacional de Antropología e Historia, 1973.

Martin, Simon, and Nikolai Grube. *Chronicle of the Maya Kings and Queens*. New York: Thames and Hudson, 2008.

Matheny, Ray T. "El Mirador: An Early Maya Metropolis Uncovered." *National Geographic*, September 1987.

McCarter, Robert. *Frank Lloyd Wright*. London: Phaidon, 1997.

Miller, Mary Ellen. *The Art of Mesoamerica from Olmec to Aztec*. New York: Thames and Hudson, 1986.

———. "A Design for Meaning in Maya Architecture." In *Function and Meaning in Classic Maya Architecture*, edited by Stephen D. Houston. Washington, D.C.: Dumbarton Oaks Research Library and Collection, 1998.

Morales, Demetrio Sodi. *The Maya World*. Mexico City: Minutiae Mexicana, 1987.

Moseley, Michael Edward, and Carol J. Mackey. *Twenty-Four Architectural Plans of Chan Chan, Peru: Structure and Form at the Capital of Chimor*. Cambridge, Mass.: Peabody Museum Press, 1974.

Pagden, Anthony, ed. *Hernan Cortés, Letters from Mexico*. New Haven: Yale University Press, 1986.

Proskouriakoff, Tatiana. *An Album of Maya Architecture*. Norman: University of Oklahoma Press, 1963.

Rubio, Alfredo Barrera. *Official Guide—Uxmal*. Mexico City: Gráficas Monte Albán, 1985.

Sabloff, Jeremy A. *The Cities of Ancient Mexico: Reconstructing a Lost World*. New York: Thames and Hudson, 1989.

Scheffler, Lilian. *The Mayas—History, Art and Culture*. Mexico City: Panorama Editorial, 1987.

———. *Uxmal, Kabáh, Sayil, Labná*. Mexico City: Labná Editora de Periódicos, 1988.

Schele, Linda, and Peter Mathews. *The Code of Kings: The Language of Seven Sacred Maya Temples and Tombs*. New York: Simon and Schuster, 1988.

Scully, Vincent, Jr. *Frank Lloyd Wright*. New York: George Braziller, 1960.

Smith, Kathryn. "The L.A. Textile Block Houses." *Frank Lloyd Wright Quarterly* 16, no. 3 (Summer 2005).

Sten, María. *Codices of Mexico and Their Extraordinary History*. Mexico City: Panorama Editorial, 1983.

Stephens, John Lloyd. *Incidents of Travel in Central America, Chiapas, and Yucatán*. Vols. 1 & 2. New York: Dover, 1969.

Stierlin, Henri. *Encyclopedia of World Architecture*. Cologne, Germany: Tashen, 1994.

———. *Living Architecture: Ancient Mexican*. London: Macdonald, 1968.

———. *Mayan Architecture*. London: Oldbourne, 1964.

Stuart, David. *The Fall of the Ancient Maya*. London: Thames and Hudson, 2002.

———. "The Fire Enters His House: Architecture and Ritual in Classic Maya Texts." In *Function and Meaning in Classic Maya Architecture*, edited by Stephen D. Houston. Washington, D.C.: Dumbarton Oaks Research Library and Collection, 1998.

Stuart, David, and George Stuart. *Palenque: Eternal City of the Maya*. London: Thames and Hudson, 2008.

Stuart, George E. "City of Kings and Commoners, Copán." *National Geographic*, October 1989.

———. 1992. "Maya Heartland under Siege." *National Geographic*, November 1992.

Stuart, George E., and Gene S. Stuart. *Lost Kingdoms of the Maya*. Washington, D.C.: National Geographic Society, 1993.

———. *The Mysterious Maya*. Washington, D.C.: National Geographic Society, 1977.

Taube, Karl. "The Jade Hearth: Centrality, Rulership, and the Classic Maya Temple." In *Function and Meaning in Classic Maya Architecture*, edited by Stephen D. Houston. Washington, D.C.: Dumbarton Oaks Research Library and Collection, 1998.

Thompson, J. Eric S. *The Rise and Fall of Maya Civilization*. Norman: University of Oklahoma Press, 1954.

Totten, George Oakley. *Maya Architecture*. Washington, D.C.: Maya Press, 1926.

Webster, David. "Classic Maya Architecture: Implications and Comparisons." In *Function and Meaning in Classic Maya Architecture*, edited by Stephen D. Houston. Washington, D.C.: Dumbarton Oaks Research Library and Collection, 1994.

———. *The Fall of the Ancient Maya: Solving the Mystery of the Maya Collapse*. London: Thames and Hudson, 2002.

Willey, Gordon Randolph. *Essays in Maya Archaeology*. Albuquerque: University of New Mexico Press, 1971.

Willey, Gordon Randolph, and Dimitri B. Shimkin. 1971. "The Collapse of Classic Maya Civilization in the Southern Lowlands: a Symposium Summary Statement." *Southwestern Journal of Anthropology* 27, no. 1 (Spring 1971): 1–12

Wright, Frank Lloyd. *A Testament*. New York: Bramhall House, 1957.

# Index

KENNETH TREISTER is a Fellow of the American Institute of Architects and is an internationally known architect, painter, sculptor, photographer, and author. He has published five books, including *Havana Forever: A Pictorial and Cultural History of an Unforgettable City*, and four documentaries on architecture, urban culture, and photography, as well as in over fifty journals throughout the world. He sculpted the Holocaust Memorial, Miami Beach, Florida, and has exhibited in leading museums including the Sirball Museum, Bass Museum, Lowe Museum, Harn Museum, and the United States Holocaust Memorial Museum. He was an adjunct professor of architecture at the University of Miami and the University of Florida. He is a member of Reial Acadèmia Catalana de Belles Arts de Sant Jordi, Barcelona, Spain, and has lectured at universities in the United States, Chile, China, Israel, Indonesia, India, Malaysia, and Bali. Mr. Treister received the Silver Medal and the Lifetime Achievement Award from the American Institute of Architects, Miami.

The University Press of Florida is the scholarly publishing agency for the State University System of Florida, comprising Florida A&M University, Florida Atlantic University, Florida Gulf Coast University, Florida International University, Florida State University, New College of Florida, University of Central Florida, University of Florida, University of North Florida, University of South Florida, and University of West Florida.

# Texas Caves

Number Thirty-one:
The Louise Lindsey Merrick Natural
Environment Series

# Texas Caves

## Blair Pittman

Foreword by Francis Edward Abernethy

Texas A&M University Press
College Station

GRANDVIEW PUBLIC LIBRARY
GRANDVIEW, TX

Copyright © 1999 by Blair Pittman
All rights reserved
First edition

Photography by Blair Pittman unless otherwise credited

The paper used in this book
meets the minimum requirements
of the American National Standard for Permanence
of Paper for Printed Library Materials, z39.48-1984.
Binding materials have been chosen for durability.
(∞)

Library of Congress Cataloging-in-Publication Data

Pittman, Blair, 1937–
       Texas caves / Blair Pittman ; foreword by Francis Edward
    Abernethy.
            p.   cm. — (The Louise Lindsey Merrick natural envi-
    ronment series ; no.  31)
       Includes bibliographical references and index.
       ISBN  0-89096-849-7
       1. Caves—Texas.   I. Title.   II. Series.
    GB605.T5P57   1999
    551.44'7'09764—dc21                              98-27196
                                                          CIP

Dedicated
to those
who will protect
our Texas caves

# Contents

# Illustrations

# Foreword

Texas travelers long have admired the landscapes of Big Bend and the Big Thicket. They've seen the Rio Grande Valley and the Panhandle, the Hill Country and the Piney Woods, and just about everything in between. But few are the folks who have gone below the state's surface and viewed those wonders below ground that equal the beauties above. Blair Pittman's *Texas Caves* is an introduction to this seldom-seen world beneath the surface of Texas. This state is rich with caves, and it welcomes those who wish to explore another dimension of Texas' natural history.

The great seas that stood over Texas millions of years ago rained down the makings of thick layers of limestone. The land rose and the seas fell; millions of years of rainfall leached out hollows, deep pits, and underground stream beds and left acres of aquifers far below the surface where the dinosaurs once roamed. Ice Age animals followed, and some wandered or fell into these caves and left their bones, as did the Indians and the Spanish and the later westerners who chanced by.

All the while, during the times of the dinosaurs, then the mastodons, and later the buffalo, these deeply hidden inner worlds were building a silent beauty. Water solutions trickled through their ceilings and created delicate starbursts of crystals, butterflies, soda straws, huge columns, and flowstones as white as the cave was black.

Texas has over three thousand known caves and sinkholes, most of them in the Edwards Plateau area of central Texas. Some of the grand-est and most dramatic of the Texas caves for many years have been equipped with lights and graded with trails that allow ordinary folks to explore their interiors. Longhorn Cavern, a state park near Burnet created in the 1930s, has a trail that is wheelchair accessible. Cascade Caverns and Cave Without a Name, both near Boerne, and Wonder Cave of San Marcos have had cave tours for many decades. Natural Bridge Caverns at New Braunfels and Inner Space Caverns at Georgetown are recently developed caves of the 1960s, as are the Caverns of Sonora—consid-ered, for the splendors of its cave formations, to be the best tour cave in Texas.

The traveler who wishes to deepen his knowl-edge of the geography and geology of Texas has ample opportunity to explore less developed caves. One can schedule guided flashlight tours of Kickapoo Cavern near Brackettville, and an elementary course in caving is available in the half-wild crawl caves at Colorado Bend State Natural Area, near Lampasas.

Those hikers who plumb the depths of the show caves must not forget that these, too, were wild caves—with no lights, guides, piped-in music, or paths to follow—when cave explorers first started roping off into the darkness below. The Texas caves bred an enthusiastic population of explorers around mid-twentieth century. Some went caving for the sheer adventure of it; some went as geologists and biologists—scien-tists looking for new ways to look at life. All went, like Columbus, looking for a new world.

The most serious cavers are the members of the Texas Speleological Association. Its members methodically have discovered, explored, and mapped hundreds of Texas caves. They have made detailed studies of cave origins and of the physical and chemical attributes of the caves.

I was a semiserious caver for twenty years, starting from the late 1950s, the time that Blair Pittman calls the Golden Age of caving, when our paths first crossed in the caving world. During those years, the most exciting times in my life were planning a caving trip, getting all the gear together, and flying down the road in an old red Jeep to caves unknown. And the most interesting people in my life were cavers.

I cringe when I think back on some of my early caving days. I had a wife and five (*five!*) kids. Living on a beginning teacher's salary, we were crammed into a two-bedroom white frame house, and I would take off for a week or ten-day caving trip as if it were the most natural thing in the world for a husband and father to do. Even now I remember that it took considerable serious loin girding before I worked up the nerve to tell my wife that I was heading out to West Texas or Mexico to go swinging off into caves. Considering the circumstances, she handled it well, even when her first inkling of an upcoming trip came when she found a pile of ropes and climbing gear stashed at the back of the garage. Really, she handled it better then than she does now, when she can work herself into a rage thinking what I put her through.

We assembled a crew at Austin once and met at this cavers' den that was a two-story house in a decent enough neighborhood. I wish I had photographed the front room of that house. I wish I could have photographed the *smell* of the front room of that house. Ropes piled and hung on the wall, seat slings and Jumars strewn and draped, tents and cots, water cans and camping gear, hard hats and muddy boots and mildewed clothes—these filled the front room and spilled over into the next. They had everything in that room *except* a cave—which they didn't really need, because the whole house smelled like a cave that recently had been visited by a host of diarrheic bats. This was the den of dedicated cavers.

Why—in the name of all that is sky-blue and grass-green—*do* all these cavers go into caves, when the world has a wealth of beauty and adventure in the sunshiny outdoors? This is a question frequently asked by mothers, wives, and friends, particularly those who were raised on Vernon Dalhart's rendering of "The Death of Floyd Collins," whose "body now lies sleeping in a lonely sandstone cave." I'm convinced it's genetic. Cavers crawl into the Earth's bowels because they were born with the curiosity of a 'coon, eternally poking and prying and exploring from the cradle to the grave. One television program attributed this exploratory inclination to a "novelty-seeking gene" that causes certain folks to search continually for the outer edge of every experience. Add adolescent conditioning by *Boys' Life, Field and Stream,* and *National Geographic,* along with Frank Buck, Richard Haliburton, and Jack London, and you have people who will go into a cave—or a jungle or a mountain, the Moon or Mars—in a New York minute.

More personally, I would not have gotten any cavier than Carlsbad Caverns had it not been for Robert Mitchell, a biospeleologist and natural history photographer now living in Bandera. Mitch has been my main educator for over half of my life, and he took me into my first wild cave. When I met Mitch, he was considered a qualified big-time caver because he had been in the Devil's Sinkhole. I was impressed.

Mitch and I were teaching at Lamar Tech in the late fifties, and he took a field class of us into Station C Cave near Vanderpool one springtime midnight. He tossed in a one-inch rope and saw to it that we all made it to the cave floor, thirty feet below. This was elemental caving. It was a great little cave, with lots of beautiful formations, a copperhead, spiders and crickets, and a few bats. When leaving time came, only three of us were able to overhand the rope to the ledge above. Thereafter we hauled folks out, which eventually got easier, as we had more above than below. That was *not* a professional caving expedition.

For our next cave—Mexico's Sótano de Huítzmolotitla, whose entrance is 364 feet straight down—we borrowed a cumbersome cast-iron hand winch and bought four hundred feet of quarter-inch cable that could have cranked in a Mack truck. The first person in began a spinning scream on the way down, so we had to retrieve him, go into town, and purchase enough quarter-inch rope for a stabilizing line. That expedition was more engineering than it was caving, but we did make it to the bottom and back.

Soon thereafter we fell in with the Austin caving pros and learned that caving was like mountain climbing, only backward, and that cavers could use this keen mountain-climbing gear—with hard hats! We could rappel down a rope with friction bars and then climb out with Jumar Ascenders. We graduated into the next class of cavers.

Twenty-odd years later, I climbed out of a hundred-foot pit cave behind a young woman with souped-up Jumars, the latest in climbing gear. She scrambled up that line like a spider checking out a fly. I pumped and pulled and hung and finally made it, but I achieved a world of wisdom the hard way. I have not climbed a rope out of a cave since then—and won't now, even if the opportunity is offered.

A cave, especially a pit cave, can be intimidating on one's first encounter, but entering a cave arouses excitement and curiosity thricefold more compelling than any accompanying fear. To wonder what lies below and ahead—what depths, what formations of life and limestone—is enough to start one on the way. Going into a cave is like going up a river; you've got to go around one more bend for the great discovery of the throne room, or of long, rolling walls of flowstone, or of millennia-old stalactites reaching down to the stalagmites reaching up and the helictites reaching across.

Sometimes the search is simpler. Instead of one more bend in the cave passage, the attraction is one more look under one more rock or in one more pool or crevice. The very next pool of cave water may contain blind fish or a cave salamander. Lift one more rock, perhaps, and you may find one of the rare and delicate creatures of this underworld—a spider, earwig, or silverfish; a cricket, millipede, or centipede—all white and blind and moving carefully to conserve what little energy its finite food supply affords. Dusty Rhodes lifted one more rock and found a half-inch cave scorpion now named *Typhlochactas rhodesi.*

Or one may find that others have been here before.

I belly-buttoned across a narrow ledge into a short passage that ended in a cul-de-sac with a three-foot-wide basin of drip water. As I leaned against the cave wall, resting before my return, I saw an inch-square piece of green rock at the edge of the basin. When I leaned over the pond to pick it up, I saw another piece of equal size nearby. The two pieces were alike and were handmade, and as I studied them I looked up and saw a third green stone of the same shape. Much more carefully now, I lifted the third piece from the pool floor. The three parts came together as a bored jade pendant with the face and headdress of an Indian man. My mind spun out into space, trying to bring back that ancient speck of time when some person, sitting where I sat, broke a jade pendant in three pieces and tossed them into this silent pool.

Once we squeezed through the tightest of cracks, skidded down a mudslide, and ended in a long, vaulted hall that was filled with the finest of ancient pots, from pitchers the size of one's fist to waist-high ollas. And there was not a footprint in sight.

And sometimes the goal is an affirmation of life.

We got to Bracken Bat Cave about mid-afternoon on a hot and dry Texas summer day. We climbed down the slope to the cave entrance and walked back into the darkness under a quivering ceiling of Mexican freetail bats stretching out as far as one could see. The guano floor was slick, squishy, and populated by all the beasts and beetles that scrounge and scavenge in this rich banquet in the twilight world of the cave. Usually I got used to the ammonia smell, but at Bracken this was so strong that it just about shut down my breathing apparatus. We took our pictures and retired topside.

The action at Bracken started a couple of hours later, around five-thirty, with a gentle rumbling coming from the cave's mouth. As we watched from the rim, we could see a great tornado of bats, flying counterclockwise but still far back in the dark throat of the cave. Little by little, the mass of flying bats came closer to the mouth, sounding and looking like a West Texas whirlwind. Then it would withdraw back into the cave's darkness, as if fearful of the light. After numerous advances and retreats, the cylinder cautiously moved out of the mouth and into the breakdown pit and entrance to the cave. I believe the bats would have hung there, outside the cave but below ground level, circling forever, timidly and nervously, had they not been pushed from the inner cave by more bats working themselves into the bottom of the rotating circle. Slowly they rose as high as the ground, then higher, then up finally into the evening sky, where they peeled off and fanned out into smoky flights in all directions to harass the insect population of central Texas.

We watched them for an hour or more, calibrating the slowness of their ascent by the occasional albino bat that flew in their midst. We were joined by a bull snake poking along the ledges, looking for those bats which had not made it to the top of the flight. A skunk showed up, and later some 'coons. A hoot owl observed the ritual from a snag on a nearby live oak. This was definitely suppertime. Should I live long and late into life, this magnificent whirlwind of bats flying out of the ground, over the mesquite, and off into the Texas night always will remain spectacular in my memory.

The wild caves can be dangerous and are not for the inexperienced. Their exploration requires special skills and equipment. Cavers of the Golden Age soon realized, too, that the flood of explorers entering the delicately balanced underworld soon would destroy the fragile place that they most treasured. Every touch and every breath in the subterranean alters a cave's life and can lead to the demise of stalactite or isopod. Enough visitors, even though they take nothing but pictures and leave nothing but footprints, eventually can make a fatal difference in the life of a cave. Going caving nowadays is not so casual or careless as it was a generation ago.

However, the urge to see the world under the world endures, and the Texas Parks and Wildlife Department and commercial cave developers have provided the public with a way to visit the caves of Texas without further damaging the cave systems or putting lives at hazard. Then there are claustrophobic individuals who want the opportunity to see and admire the geological beauties of the cave world without the psychological trauma of being completely enclosed in a vast, dark hole in the ground. *Texas Caves* covers half a century and more of the people and places which opened the cave world to the general public. So if you can't go caving yourself, you can read about that world and look at the pictures.

*Francis Edward Abernethy*

# Preface

From prehistoric times to the present, caves have represented a mysterious world—a world of the unknown, a world of darkness—that often was believed to be the haunt of the supernatural. The entrances to caves offered early humans, like wild animals before them, shelter and protection; and cultures evolved around the openings. The mystery of the blackness beyond the entrances always attracted curiosity, however. Some of these cultures placed the afterlife in the dark of the cave. Caves were a mystery, and their darkness raised questions about life and death.

Long after people's first use of caves as shelter, humans still were searching for answers. In the Dark Ages, caves were considered the realm of dragons and the homes of mythical beasts. It is fairly easy to understand why humans assigned so much importance to the mysterious dark places.

It was not until the nineteenth century that this curiosity about caves took on a more serious, investigative approach. Hand-made torches were replaced by dependable sources of light; kerosene lamps and eventually carbide lights made deeper and longer trips into the unknown possible. By the twentieth century, caves finally were being understood as parts of the natural world. The study of caves grew into a science known as speleology. Those who took part in this activity were known as speleologists, spelunkers, or cavers. The ignorance and superstition about caves that had come down through the ages were replaced by a new knowledge, a new awareness that offered natural explanations of this special, isolated world of darkness.

In 1941, the National Speleological Society (NSS) was founded. This organization formed a clearinghouse for cave information. Members' reports were published in its periodical, the *NSS News*. In these initial stages, exploration and adventure underground were considered to be of primary importance. As speleologists published more scientific studies and reports, however, values shifted. Scientific study revealed that this underground world was fragile. The formations were the results of thousands of years of growth. By the 1950s and 1960s, adventure had been replaced by a new and growing desire to understand this unique realm. Today, a major goal of the NSS is to protect and conserve caves.

In the 1950s and 1960s, cavers in Texas were making some important cave discoveries. In those decades, the Caverns of Sonora, Natural Bridge Caverns, and Inner Space Cavern were discovered and developed, and our list of known caves in Texas grew. Texas caves became regarded as some of the most beautiful in the world. The geology of caves became a special field of study. Many sciences contributed to a greater understanding of the miracles of the cave. Hydrology, paleontology, archaeology, and biology added to a growing awareness that the delicate cave environment was being destroyed by unqualified "explorers" and even by increasing numbers of experienced cavers visiting wild, noncommercial caves. Protection became more important than exploration.

Growing awareness of the fragility of the underground environment has led to the pro-

1. (left) Paleoanthropologist Ernest Lundelius at an excavation in Inner Space Cave.

2. (right) A human molar found in the excavation in Inner Space Cave.

3. (below) In addition to the tooth, the excavation also uncovered evidence of larger animals in Inner Space Cave. Here, paleoanthropologist Ernest Lundelius brushes dirt away from a fossilized mammoth tusk.

tection of endangered cave life forms that, over hundreds of thousands of years, have become adapted to life in a world with little or no light. Today many cavers are almost secretive about their caves and activities. They are not adventure seekers, but rather seekers after knowledge. They have learned not to talk very much about their caving activities, so caving has become a very low-key, exclusive means of studying a fascinating dark world.

I was one of the workers who helped develop the Caverns of Sonora in the early 1960s. We built the trails using jackhammers and dynamite when needed, then buried the wiring and placed the lights. In defense of turning a wild cave into a show cave, I must point out that, once the trail is complete, the cave is protected, and then the public can enjoy its beauty.

My intention here is to offer a basic understanding of caves and cave formations, much as I used to do as a guide in the Caverns of Sonora. This book has two purposes. The first is to reveal the glories of our Texas caves to people who may never see some of the unique "wild" caves and their formations in our state because of their fragility. The second aim is to describe the show caves that have been opened and developed for public touring.

In this book I wanted to show the many different types of cave formations. Some photographs were made in show caves and others in wild caves. It would have been impossible for any one photographer to visit this many caves, so other cave photographers kindly provided their favorite photographs.

Cave photography is a very special art that requires a great deal of care. A careless photographer can destroy fragile formations. One picture is not worth a broken formation. That is another reason I chose not to return to some of the delicate rooms in a number of caves but instead used photographs that were taken when the rooms were first explored. I want to show the beauty of Texas caves but do not want to contribute to their destruction in the process.

Not enough people understand caves. This book is designed to offer the public some insight into the miracles to be found in, and under, our nation's most unusual state. We need public awareness of this beauty, because in future years we may have to protect our caves more vigorously than ever before. We may need legislation; we will need the cooperation of landowners, the general public, and the caving community. I think it may require a unified front to accomplish this goal. We need to let everyone learn why this unique underground world is so very special.

Fortunately, I had forgotten how difficult caving and cave photography can be. It had been a number of years since I had worked seriously on the subject, so when Texas A&M University Press asked me about working on this book, I remembered only the good experiences— mostly the feeling of satisfaction I got from seeing underground wonders in the photographs. The memories of muddy crawlways, heavy cases of gear, sweat, exhaustion, and difficulties had been clouded by the many intervening years. It didn't take me long, however, to remember what a team effort successful cave photography is.

I reentered the caving world after thirty-five years of going caving only occasionally. For the last five years, my life has been back-to-back trips, covering some fifty thousand miles. I also renewed old friendships. They reminded me how special cavers and the caving community are. I became aware of how much I had missed them during my newspaper and magazine years. There is a level of comfort with these friends that I have found nowhere else.

4. In this example of the Pecos River style of pictographs, it is believed that the White Shaman, a mystical man of wisdom for these early Texans, is rising from his body. Even five thousand years ago, people wondered what happened after death. One interpretation of this painting is that the spirit must pass the monster above to gain everlasting life, symbolically representing everything the people were afraid of. Such archaeology should be protected by cavers.

I owe debts of gratitude to many who believed in this book. My thanks go to the show cave owners and managers, many of them my long-time friends. My thanks also go to Jack Burch, Orion Knox, and James Brummett; to Robert Burnett, Dave Stuart, and the Texas Parks and Wildlife Department for their help with the state-owned caves; to the landowners of the wild caves I photographed; to Bill Mixon, who read the draft manuscript and provided the list of suggested readings; to Dwight Deal and James Reddell, who checked facts; to Pete Lindsley, Carl Kunath, and Bob Parvin, other longtime friends who provided photographs and useful advice; to Louise Shelby, who helped with the glossary; and to Gill Ediger, chair of the Texas Speleo-logical Association, whose support made this a better book.

For me, this book has been a journey through the past, present, and future of caving and cave photography. A circle is complete.

# Part I

## THE MARRIAGE OF ROCK AND WATER

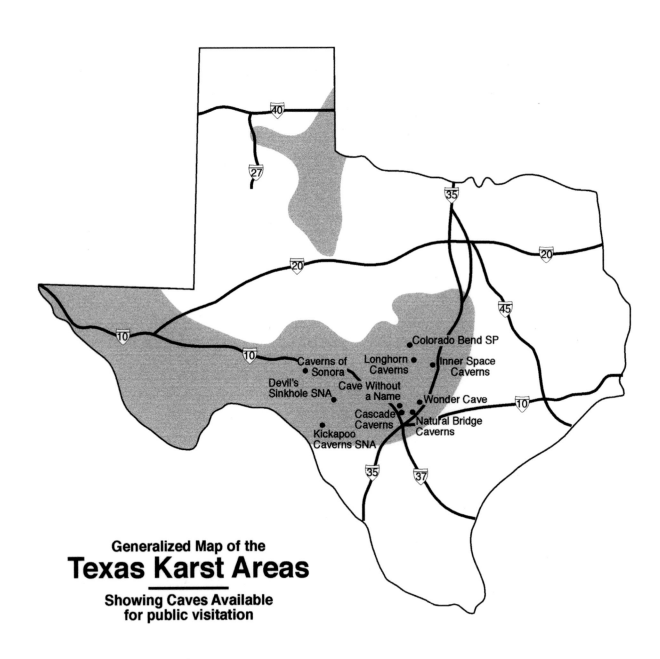

**Generalized Map of the**

# Texas Karst Areas

**Showing Caves Available
for public visitation**

# The Geologic Origins of Texas Caves

Even a modest cave is awe-inspiring to someone who has never been inside the earth before. The magnificence of a cave full of dramatic formations is even greater when you know how much time and geologic coincidence went into its creation. To help readers appreciate the invaluable beauty and fragility of Texas' wonderful caves, I asked my friend S. Christopher Caran to prepare the overview of Texas cave geology that follows.

## Geology of Texas:
### Establishing a Firm Foundation

In a very real sense, Texas was made for caves. About three thousand large and small subterranean openings have been explored and mapped at least partially, but it is likely that many more are as yet undiscovered, and some may remain unknown forever. The reason for this abundance is the combination of a suitable rock type and underground water. The rock in which caves are most common is limestone, which is found at or near the surface in at least one-third of Texas. A few other kinds of rock—most notably gypsum in West Texas—contain caves as well, but they are comparatively rare in the state.

In general, rocks may be classified as igneous, metamorphic, or sedimentary, depending on their mineral and chemical composition, internal structure, and other characteristics that reflect their origin. Sedimentary rocks are the kind most common in Texas, and the kind of which most Texas caves are formed. Sedimentary rocks form on land or under water (or, in other climatic regions, under glacial ice). There are three general categories of sedimentary rocks: (1) those composed primarily of fragments of other rocks or minerals, whether igneous, metamorphic, or sedimentary; (2) those produced from the hard parts of dead organisms; and (3) those that solidify (precipitate) directly from water. The ages of sedimentary rocks range from at least six hundred million years to the present—for, indeed, these rocks actively are forming in many areas today.

Limestone, sandstone, and conglomerate are the most familiar types of sedimentary rock. Conglomerate and sandstone are made up of rock and mineral fragments that adhere because of one or more natural cements. The cements crystallize from waters rich in dissolved minerals and fill the spaces between the sand grains and pebbles. The most common naturally occurring cement is the mineral calcite. Calcite is also the principal mineral in limestone.

Over the six hundred million years or so of sedimentation, the region that now includes Texas has been covered time and again by shallow seas. The hard, calcite-rich skeletons and shells of dead marine organisms combined with calcite precipitates from the water and the fine sand of earlier rivers and seas, settling in layer upon layer on the bottom. As those layers of sediment built up, their weight pressed down on the layers below, and with the cementing action of the calcite, they formed hard limestone, sandstone, and other sedimentary rocks.

The remains of the organisms often are preserved as fossils—mineralized bones, wood, mollusk shells, coral, and the like—in Texas limestone. Some limestone also may include fragments of older rocks, bound together with lesser amounts of mineral precipitates, whereas other limestone may be more "pure," with few rock fragments present. Such limestone is made up almost entirely of precipitates and the hard shells of microscopic life forms.

## Cave Formation

As those layers of limestone were building, the floor of the shallow seas rose and fell with the long, slow movement of the earth's crust underneath. Eventually, about a hundred million years ago, the sea floor emerged and became land and was exposed to the temperatures of the surface and the effects of wind and rain. That limestone now is on or near the surface across much of central, north central, western, and northwestern Texas, and caves are encountered most frequently in these regions. All the major caves in Texas are in limestone, although other kinds of rock also are found at a few of these cave sites. Under the right conditions—mild acidity and moderate temperatures—calcite slowly dissolves in water. For this reason, true caves, formed primarily by this progressive process of dissolution, are more common in limestone than in any other rock.

The most important factor in cave formation is the solution of carbon dioxide in water to form carbonated water, or weak carbonic acid. Carbon dioxide gas, a component of the atmosphere, is exhaled by air-breathing animals and is used by photosynthetic plants to create sugars and starches. As rain falls, it dissolves a minute amount of carbon dioxide from the atmosphere and carries it to the ground. Long ago, investigators concluded that the mild acid formed in this way can dissolve limestone and create caves.

A far more important source of acid, however, is found in the soil. As organic matter decomposes in porous, well-aerated soils, it produces humus acids and carbon dioxide that dissolves in moisture trapped in the spaces between soil particles. There, the concentration of carbonic acid may be ten to a thousand times that in rain. As heavy rains saturate the soil, they force the trapped acidic moisture downward. If limestone underlies the soil, it is dissolved by these acidic waters.

More important, fractures in the limestone allow the water to penetrate deeply and carry with it some of the organic matter, which continues to produce acid within the fractured rock. The acidic water dissolves the walls of the frac-

5. Aragonite crystals and other calcite formations grow above and below water in Natural Bridge Caverns, South Cave.

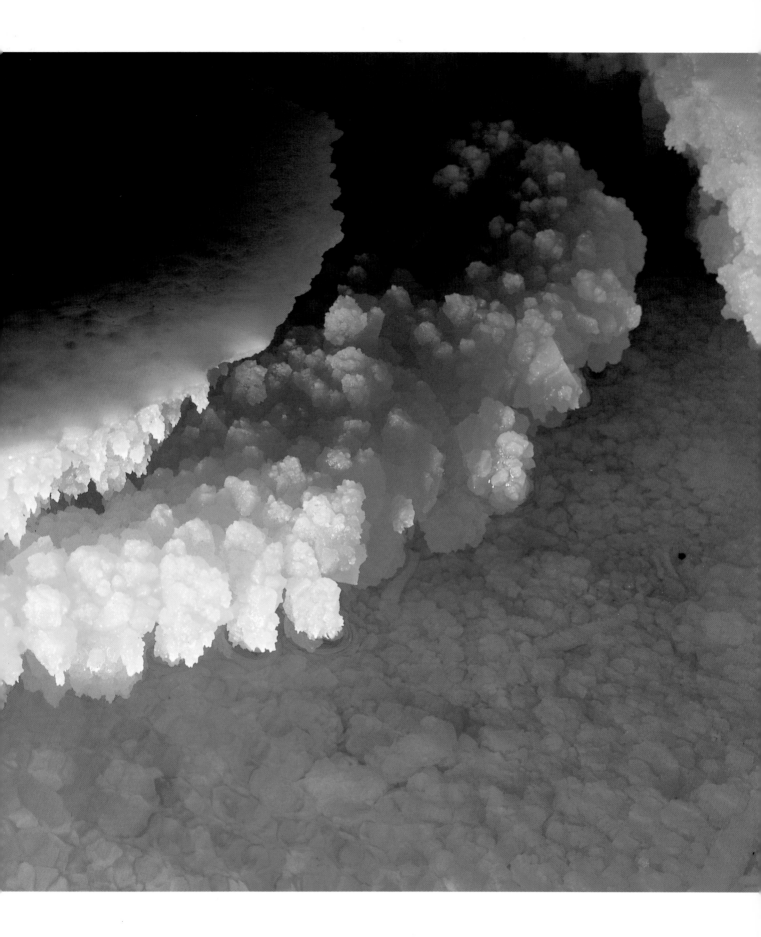

ter and water-borne sediment after heavy rains. As the amount of water and its rate of flow increase, the limestone may become a significant aquifer (water-filled rock layer) containing large cave systems. If the water table recedes over a period of time, the cave will be left dry or partly dry. Once an air space is established, the next phase of cave development begins.

What the waters take away, they also may give back by degrees. As water seeps into air-filled caves, some of the carbon dioxide that was dissolved in the soil to form carbonic acid is lost into the cave atmosphere. As a result, the water becomes less acid, and eventually the calcium carbonate that was dissolved in it begins to form tiny crystals (precipitate). Gradually, the individual crystals form a layer, then layer upon layer, building stalactites, stalagmites, and myriad other speleothems.

A steady drip through the cave ceiling cre-

6. One-of-a-kind formation, Big Mutha Cave. Photograph by Carl Kunath.

7. In these drops of water, one can see the tiny crystals that form the helictites. A hair-thin helictite defies gravity. Caverns of Sonora.

tures, further widening the openings and thereby allowing more water to collect and more quickly infiltrate the rock. This process extends ever deeper through time, causing the cavities to enlarge. Intersecting fractures become passageways through which water can flow rapidly, allowing the walls, floors, and even the ceilings of these passages to be eroded by turbulent wa-

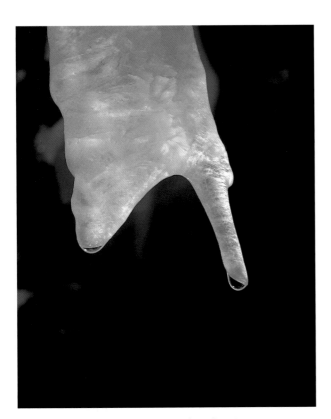

8. Double stalactite in Natural Bridge Caverns, South Cave.

## Age of Caves and Cave Deposits

A popular conception is that tens or even hundreds of millions of years are needed to create a cave and its speleothems. While this may be true in some places, the available evidence indicates that most caves in Texas are much younger, perhaps only a few million years old or less. The first clue to the age of a cave is the age of the rock strata in which it formed. Even if cavern development began during or immediately after the rocks were deposited, their age defines

9. Carrot stalactites in Natural Bridge Caverns, South Cave.

ates a downward-building *stalactite,* and if the drops fall to the floor below, they form a matching, upward-growing *stalagmite.* Should these formations bridge the gap, they will form a *column.* Drops of water trickling down an inclined wall deposit a ribbon of stone that may grow into a sheetlike formation known as a *drapery.*

If the groundwater level then rises, flooding the passage, other types of speleothems may grow outward into the surrounding water rather than vertically. In this way, older cave formations may become coated with deposits such as *cave popcorn, cave grapes, cave shelves,* and other forms. Or perhaps the water level may fall, causing loose sediment on the cave floor to dry and slough off. This may reduce support for massive but delicately balanced columns, leading to their destruction. Cycles of decimation and renewal may follow one another for millennia.

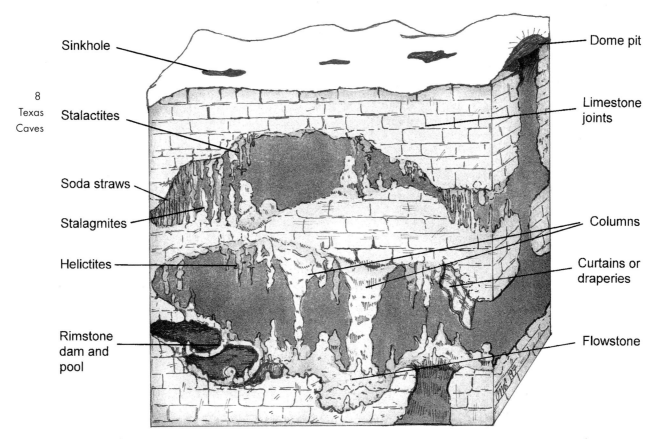

Sinkhole

Stalactites

Soda straws

Stalagmites

Helictites

Rimstone
dam and
pool

Dome pit

Limestone
joints

Columns

Curtains or
draperies

Flowstone

10. As carbonic acid water moves downward through cracks and fissures in the limestone, it dissolves calcium carbonate and other minor minerals, carrying them toward the air-filled cave passage. If the water has all of the minerals that it can hold, it is called "saturated." As the water comes into contact with the air, some of the carbon dioxide, which forms the carbonic acid, is absorbed into the air, leaving more mineral in the water than it can hold—a condition called "super saturated." The dissolved minerals are forced to recrystalize. Conditions within the cave such as humidity, temperature, wind, water velocity, volume and surface angle, and others will determine the types of speleothems that will be formed. Courtesy Christa McLeland

the maximum time available for cave formation.

Limestone deposits throughout the state span every geological age from the Cambrian period, almost six hundred million years ago, to the present. Indeed, caves were forming early in this interval, during the Ordovician period, half a billion years in the past. We know this because we find deposits very near this old in depressions formed when caves' roofs collapsed or the caves opened to the surface. The irregular surface and filled depressions later were buried beneath additional layers of sedimentary rock. In some areas, ancient eroded landscape has been reexposed by recent erosion, but the caves

found in it actually are *paleokarst*, meaning that they are the remains of a cave system that became inactive long ago. No caves that continue to form today are known to be anywhere near this old.

Local conditions produced varying degrees of cave development over the next 250 million years. In the Panhandle and parts of West Texas, beds of Permian salt and gypsum were undergoing relatively minor cave-forming processes while they were still accumulating some 250

11. (right) Punkin Cave. Photograph by Carl Kunath.

12. Westcave Preserve, near Austin, is an example of a cave that has collapsed. Its formations are eroded almost to disappearance.

Another major episode of cave development began in the early Cretaceous period, about 135 million years ago. Some of these rocks were relatively porous, allowing water to filter through them to produce caves and establish aquifers that are important sources of groundwater today. This phase of cave development may have ended relatively soon after it began, although a few investigators believe that some cave organisms found today have survived and evolved in those caves since the Cretaceous.

One of the most important periods of cave formation in central and southwestern Texas probably began in the late Miocene epoch, ten million years ago. An arc of faulting bisects the state from near the present Red River, northeast of Dallas, southward through the Austin–San Antonio area, and westward to Del Rio. The main line of faults is called the Balcones Fault System, but there were other faults as well. Limestones of early Cretaceous age were heavily fractured, and on the southern and eastern sides of these faults they dropped more than a thousand feet. That change caused coastward-draining streams to carve deep valleys, which further modified the aquifers in those layers.

Although the Balcones faults would become important later, it is not clear whether caves underwent a major period of development at or soon after the faulting. Certainly no caves of that age are known to have opened to the surface, because the oldest known well-dated fossils and deposits in caves of this region are much younger—about one million years old, dating from early in the Pleistocene epoch. Other evidence, related to the disruption of aquifers when surface streams cut down into them, suggests that none of the caves with existing outlets are much older than one to three million years.

Although it is reasonable to assume, then, that these caves may have had a somewhat

million years ago. In fact, these easily soluble deposits have continued to dissolve ever since, at least in some areas, producing underground cavities that cause the ground above to collapse but that do not open to the surface.

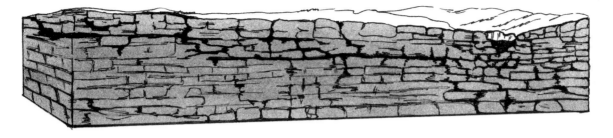

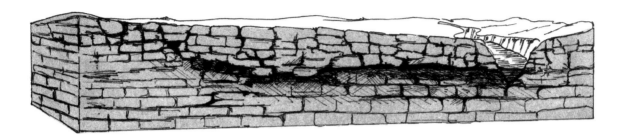

**13. The Making of a Cave—Chemistry and Time**
Note: This is by no means the only way caves can be formed, but it is the most common. Some caves are formed in a similar manner by acidic water which enters the natural cracks in the limestone from below, rather than above. Cave scientists are actively studying the many aspects of cave development and we should expect many variations on the theory shown here. All drawings courtesy Christa McLeland

longer history of development, they do not appear to have opened to the surface until relatively recently in geological time. Throughout the late Pleistocene and Holocene epochs (up to a million years ago or so), the caves of the state have had a rich evolutionary history. Evidence of this history is revealed by fossils found in caves, by the variety of creatures that live in them now, by cave sediments that can be dated, and by the signs of vigorous use of caves by humans over the past twelve thousand years. The truly remarkable story of Texas caves has, perhaps, reached a new beginning, with many more chapters yet to be written.

# Cave Biology

Before members of the *Homo sapiens* species venture into a cave, they have to gather a lot of equipment. Cavers have all sorts of special lights, ropes, and tools to help them navigate cave environments safely. The species that naturally occur in caves have a lot of special equipment, too. Whereas we cavers buy and borrow our equipment, the cave species, like the caves themselves, evolved over a long period.

To describe some of these incredibly special Texas cave dwellers, I invited Robert Mitchell, a biologist and expert on cave insects, to present this overview of cave biology.

Caves are unusual environments. There is constant darkness, temperature, and relative humidity, at least in the caves' remote regions. There are extremely few primary food makers in caves—that is, there are no green plants to provide the basis for a food web. So energy must be imported from outside the cave. Most caves, then, are food poor. Interestingly enough, similar conditions are found in the ocean depths. In that darkness, sea creatures tend to be without pigment and eyes, much like cave-adapted

forms. So the adaptations seen in cave animals are related in some way to these features of their environment.

How did cave animals arrive in their unusual habitat? Based on the distribution of related surface animals, scientists believe that many cave animals are "relict" species—that is, they evolved from remnant populations that at some time in the past were cut off from others of their kind. They might be Pleistocene relicts or perhaps marine relicts—they might have been left behind in caves as the Pleistocene ice sheets receded or when ocean waters receded from rising land masses. Then, isolated from any surface relatives with which they might interbreed, they were left to follow their own evolutionary course, isolated within the confines of their distinct environment.

In many instances, cave populations of the same widespread colonizer later were further isolated from each other as streams cut through the cave-bearing limestone strata, eliminating any subterranean routes of communication between the caves. Individual populations were positioned to follow their separate evolutionary routes of adaptation. This is a major reason why there are so many cave animal species in the limestone caves of central Texas. No doubt other cave animals were isolated and evolved in ways that as yet are little understood.

Many people know cave animals as "blind and white." These are, in fact, two common adaptations. Those species truly adapted to caves usually have no pigment in their skin, or little pigment; some have so little pigment that they are transparent. They also show eye reduction; their eyes may be gone entirely or may be present only as vestiges, pinpoints of remaining eye tissue.

There are other characteristics of cave-adapted species as well. In those species with legs, the legs generally are much longer and more delicate than they are in related surface creatures. This probably is an adaptation that allows the animal to spread itself over more surface area in the search for food in a food-poor environment. The cave animal's body also may be much more slender than that of its surface relatives. Such delicacy probably can be tolerated in the calm of the cave environment and in the general absence of predators, when otherwise it would make such a delicate animal easy prey.

It long had been assumed that cave animals were general feeders, not specialists—that is, that they ate nothing in particular but everything in general. That would make sense, as there isn't very much food to be had in most caves. But, surprisingly, it turned out that, for example, Texas cave beetles, *Rhadine subterranea,* were food specialists; they fed mostly on cave cricket eggs. Female cave crickets would inject their eggs in the silt of the cave floor with a long ovipositor, and the cricket would then cover the hole by dragging silt over it with the tip of the ovipositor. The cave beetles proved to be very adept at finding these buried eggs, evidently by detecting marks in the silt made by the cricket's ovipositor. Cave communities probably are a bit more complicated than we once thought.

Cave-adapted animals also are presumed to have very low basal metabolic rates. The value of this adaptation is obvious, given the nutritional poverty of the cave environment. Like so many assumptions, this one is not well supported by research. However, one researcher, Suzanne Wiley, has provided some good support for this idea. In a study of a series of Texas cave beetles, she found that the more cave-adapted the beetle is (based on eye and pigment reduction and leg and body slenderness), the lower is its metabolic rate.

Of course, not all cave-inhabiting animals show the extreme adaptations mentioned above. There are degrees of adaptation—and restriction—to the cave environment. Biospeleologists tend to recognize several categories of cave animals, as follows:

*Cavernicoles* are cave-dwelling animals in general. James Reddell reports that about twelve hundred species have been recorded from Texas caves. Among them are some specific types: trogloxenes, troglophiles, troglobites, and guanophiles.

*Trogloxenes* show the least adaptation and restriction to caves. These animals live in caves a large part of the time but occasionally, or routinely, leave through the cave entrance to feed outside. Best known to all are the cave bats, which typically depart the cave each evening to feed.

Several species of bats inhabit Texas caves. The most widespread and commonly seen is the Mexican brown bat, *Myotis velifer.* But the most abundant, by far, is the Mexican freetail bat, *Tadarida brasiliensis.* The number of these bats in several Texas caves is staggering—almost one hundred million in about a dozen caves. Bracken Cave is estimated to house more than twenty

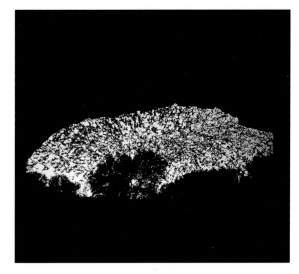

14. Thousands of Mexican freetail bats exit Bracken Cave at dusk. Photograph by Robert Mitchell.

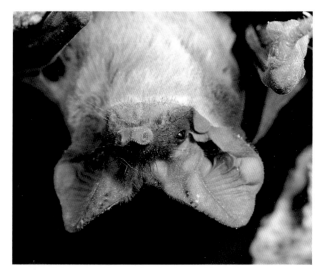

16. The Mexican freetail bat, *Tadarida brasiliensis.* Photograph by Robert Mitchell.

million bats, the largest number in any cave in Texas or the world.

These freetail bat colonies are "maternal," consisting primarily of females that come to Texas caves in about April from Mexico and beyond to give birth. They and their young head south in October. There is possibly no greater concentration of mammalian life on earth than the bats roosting in Bracken Cave, where each summer night they consume about two hundred tons of insects.

Another important example of a trogloxene in Texas caves (and in caves elsewhere) is the "cave cricket," which is not a cricket at all but a little hump-backed grasshopper relative otherwise known as the "camel cricket." These cave crickets are very important transporters of energy into cave ecosystems, and in many Texas caves they may be the chief source of energy upon which the food web in the cave is built.

15. This photograph of a small group of Mexican freetail bats shows how they hang by their hind limbs from the ceilings of caves. Photograph by Robert Mitchell.

Some of the cave harvestmen, or "daddy-long-legs," also fit here.

*Troglophiles* show some of the adaptations mentioned above—reduced eyes, reduced pigment, and long legs—but not in the extreme. While these animals may complete their entire life cycle within the cave, they may be capable of doing so, too, in appropriate above-ground environments—in leaf litter, under rocks, and in similar dark places. Many species of cave animals, such as varieties of beetles and spiders, are in this group. There also is a widespread troglophile scorpion and some troglophile crayfishes.

*Troglobites* show the extreme adaptations—lack of pigmentation and vision—discussed above. They are "obligate" cave dwellers, incapable of living outside the cave. It is this group of Texas cave fauna that is truly distinctive and justifiably famous. The first example of this type was discovered at the turn of the century, when the Texas blind cave salamander, *Typhlomolge rathbuni,* was described. This is a remarkable cave animal, embodying all the classic cave adaptations. Famous the world over in biological and caving circles, it is exactly what a cave animal should be. Attesting to its rarity, it was in the first group of animals, and was the first cave species, formally to be declared endangered.

But many more troglobite species live in Texas caves, enough to make the Edwards Plateau the most important center of cave-adapted animals on earth. About 250 species of troglobites from Texas caves now are known, including species of blind cave catfish, salamanders, beetles, spiders, millipedes, silverfish, shrimp, isopods, amphipods, pseudoscorpions, planarians, harvestmen (also known as daddy-long-legs), and others. About one-fourth of these troglobites are spiders; one of them, at less than a millimeter in length, is the world's smallest spider. Six spe-

17. Cave crickets are extremely common in caves and sometimes can be found in moist, shaded places above ground. Photograph by Robert Mitchell.

18. Another relative of spiders is this cave scorpion, *Vejovis reddelli,* which has caught a cave cricket. Photograph by Robert Mitchell.

cies of these invertebrates currently are on the endangered-species list.

*Guanophiles* constitute a distinctive group of cavernicoles. These are small animals that live, often in unbelievable numbers, upon the guano deposited beneath bat colonies and the bodies of dead bats that fall to the cave floor. They show

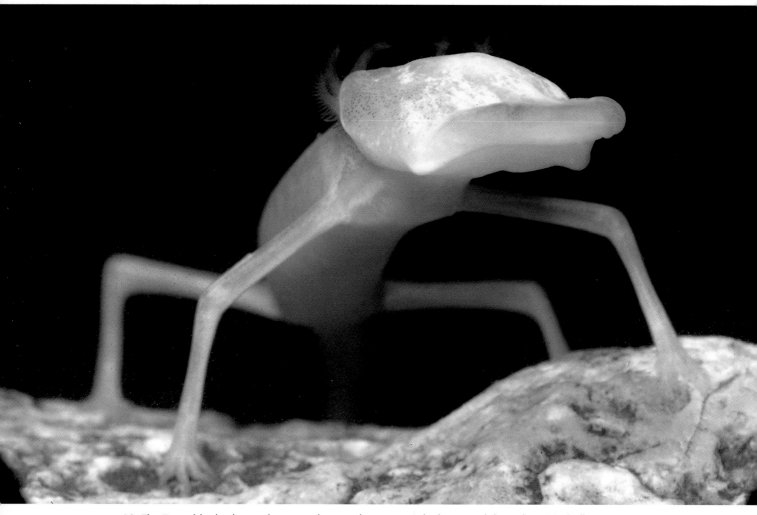

19. The Texas blind salamander, an endangered cave animal. Photograph by Robert Mitchell.

20. The Purgatory Creek cave shrimp is an eyeless, dark-adapted troglobite. Photograph by Robert Mitchell.

21. Another crustacean troglobite is the Texas cave isopod. These were photographed in Ezell's Cave by Robert Mitchell.

22. This small troglobitic flatworm is Zesch's cave planarian. Because of its lack of pigment it is almost transparent, and in this example the animal's gut is outlined by the food contained therein. Photograph by Robert Mitchell.

23. The Bee Creek Cave harvestman, *Texella reddelli,* is typical of troglobitic "daddy-long-legs." Blind and completely cave-adapted, this relative of the spiders is an endangered species. Photograph by Robert Mitchell.

24. Relics of bat guano mining still lie on the floor of Frio Bat Cave, where daylight filters in from the entrance. Mining of the rich guano deposits has been carried on here since the Civil War. Photograph by Orion Knox.

no cave adaptations, living as they do in an area of high energy content. They are there not so much because of the cave as because of the bats.

In one study, my students and I looked at guanophile numbers on the guano mound beneath the bat colony in Fern Cave. Random samples of guano measuring 10 x 10 x 2 centimeters (about 4 x 4 x 4¾ inches) showed an average of 268 animals in this small volume, including bedbugs, spider beetles, skin beetle adults and larvae, fleas, and pseudoscorpions. One sample had 426 fleas, and another had 335 pseudoscorpions.

Mind you, skin beetles don't distinguish well between bats fallen to the floor and biologists attempting to count them. Scientists who do field work, whether in caves, rainforests, or deserts, are accustomed to the creature discomforts of their research. Fortunately, the general public can learn a great deal about caves vicariously, with various levels of creature comfort, from armchair reading to taking a guided tour. The following pages describe Texas' wonderful show caves, where you can stroll through millions of years of natural wonders without getting too personal with skin beetles.

# The Seven Show Caves

When I first meet someone, it does not take long for them to learn that I am a cave fanatic with many caves in my past and, I hope, many new ones in my future. The most common question they ask is "What's your favorite cave?" My stock answer is "The one I am going into next."

Most people are surprised to learn that Texas has over three thousand known caves, seven of which are commercial, or "show," caves. Each of the show caves is different, but each has its own individual appeal. Some have wetter, more active formations. Some have few formations but large rooms. Some are tunnels eroded into the limestone by swift-flowing underground streams, while others are examples of the effects of long, slow action by tiny drops of water. Together they offer insights into the variety and beauty of Texas' caves.

All show caves once were "wild" caves, and before they were transformed into commercial caves the developers had to take several things into consideration. What unique qualities set this cave apart from all others? Why would the public be interested in touring the cave? Is the cave near highways or major population areas? If not, is the road to the cave well maintained?

As in any successfully operated business, cave owners and managers find it necessary to promote and market their product. One cave is promoted as the largest in the state, another as the most beautiful. Yet another cave touts accessibility and actually is located underneath an interstate highway. The owner of each of these caves attempts to publicize the cave's natural features and make it better known to the public.

To transform a wild cave into a show cave is a very expensive and labor-intensive process. Trails are designed carefully both to provide for visitors' comfort and to minimize the impact on the cave. Electrical wiring is buried out of sight, and smaller wires lead to each series of light bulbs. Lights are arranged to highlight unusual features of the cave, as well as to illuminate the path.

25. Bob Crisman looks over a group of delicate formations, including long, fragile soda straws, in the Helictite Room, Caverns of Sonora. Photograph by Bart Crisman.

26. Hair-thin helictites with water drops, Caverns of Sonora. Photograph by Carl Kunath.

27. Tilted stalagmites as a result of breakage of the base, The Cave Without a Name.

28. The Grapes, in The Cave Without a Name.

29. A double stalactite, Caverns of Sonora. Unfortunately, this formation has been broken since this photograph was made.

of no one who ever has seen a dangerous rock fall in any of Texas' show caves. Millions of visitors have gone safely through Texas' seven commercial caves.

Hollywood movies and bad gothic novels notwithstanding, bats are not dangerous; besides, they are not common in all caves. Bats require specialized conditions to flourish, and some caves simply do not always offer the right environment. Although some Texas caves harbor millions of bats during part of the year, the flying mammals are not found in most caves, and they never bother the public in Texas' show caves.

Nor is the air in caves "dead," or gas-filled. In fact, people who suffer from allergies find it easier to breathe the air in caves. Pollen and dust settle, and the air deep inside a cave is clean. For those affected by these problems, a cave would be a healthy place to live.

As with any trip, when planning a cave tour it is a good idea to call your destination before leaving home. Guidebooks and brochures contain tour times and information on facilities, but that information may have changed since the book or pamphlet was prepared. Along with general considerations such as accommodations, directions, and hours, some questions are specific to cave tours. How long is the trail, and how long does the tour take? If the tour is

In most of the show caves, a manager or head guide is responsible for training the tour guides. The manager places special emphasis on understanding the geology responsible for the existence of the cave and the conditions that cause the formations to grow as they do. A knowledgeable guide will help the visitor understand the "whys" and "hows" of caves.

In show caves, visitor safety is the first priority. Any loose rocks have been either carefully cemented in place or simply removed from the cave. After nearly fifty years of caving, I know

30. Cave pearls. Natural Bridge Caverns.

strenuous, or if stamina or mobility may be a problem, are the elevation changes or stairs manageable? If necessary, are trails wheelchair accessible? Are there convenient places to stop and rest while in the cave? Is time for rest stops built into the tour? How large is the average tour group? Do tours operate on a fixed time schedule? If not, what is the usual wait for a tour to leave? Advance planning will make the trip much more enjoyable.

For photographers, there are still more questions. Does the cave operator offer special trips for photography? Does the cave allow the use of tripods or remote flash units? I have learned some of the pitfalls of cave photography the hard way—by experience. The challenge is to not make the same mistake twice, which I have managed to do a few times. In the chapter on cave photography, I share a few of the more important lessons I've learned over the years.

A cave tour is designed to be a pleasant learning experience. A visitor who understands caves will enjoy them more, will appreciate them, and may even come to agree with me that the *next* cave is always the best.

## Cascade Caverns

Cascade Caverns were first opened to the public in 1932. The cave was closed during World War II but reopened after the war's end; it has been in continual operation since.

The original entrance is a limestone pit sixty feet deep, named Peep in the Deep. In it developers were able to build a series of switchbacks with steps for public access. After the entrance, the trail is level walking.

The cave opens into a series of three large rooms, in which many of the formations are wet and active. The water collects in crystal-clear pools on the cave floor. A highlight of the tour is the Diamond Ceiling, covered with hundreds

31. Caver among a group of long soda straws, Caverns of Sonora. Photograph by Carl Kunath.

33. Tink Brummett under the Diamond Ceiling, Cascade Caverns.

of small, rounded stalactites with a water drop at the tip of each. Cave drapery is still forming in the cave as well.

The tour ends in the largest room in the cave, the Cathedral Room. The main feature there is a waterfall cascading down a wall, filling the room with sound.

Cascade Caverns is home to a species of colorless, blind salamander; for the protection of the salamanders, the lighting in parts of the cave is more subdued than in most caves.

32. Cascade Cavern. Visitors view the lake and waterfall in the Cathedral Room. Solution domes pocket the ceiling.

| Location: | Three miles east of Boerne. Exit Cascade Caverns Road, exit 543 on I-10 west of San Antonio. |
|---|---|
| Tour length: | One-quarter mile, round trip; about forty minutes. |
| Facilities: | Gift shop, snack bar, restrooms, meeting rooms. |
| Camping: | On cave property. |
| Motels: | Boerne. |

## The Cave Without a Name

The Cave Without a Name was commercialized in 1939. The entrance stairs spiral down ninety feet to the main level of the cave. The highly

34. Eugene Ebell with several exceptional examples of cave bacon, in The Cave Without a Name. Note the translucency of the formation.

35. Frozen Waterfall, a flowstone formation, overhangs the river in The Cave Without a Name.

36. Cave Without a Name. Visitors with guide Eugene Ebell at the Queen's Throne.

decorated quarter-mile of cave certainly is worth the climb back out the same way.

A contest to name the cave was held before it was opened to the public. The winner was a local grade-school student whose entry claimed, "The cave is too pretty to have a name." For a few years in the 1970s the cave was given the name Century Caverns, but the owners later reverted to its original name.

The graveled trail is level, winding through a large cavern filled with formations. Clusters of large stalactites and stalagmites divide the large chamber into smaller rooms. Layers upon layers of flowstone attest to the age of the cave.

37. Modern sculpture, with Mary, Joseph, and Baby Jesus to the right, in The Cave Without a Name.

The cave is still dripping water, so many of the formations are colorful and wet. The best cave bacon, a type of limestone drapery alternating bands of red-brown and white, known in the state is found here. One strip of cave bacon is twenty-two feet long.

Other formations remind the visitor of a nativity scene, a modern-art mushroom, an ice cream cone with multiple dips, and clusters of grapes. Organ pipes, a queen's throne, and thousands of soda straws and odd little helictites are other colorful features of this cave.

The tour ends at the edge of an underground river and returns along the single trail.

The road to Cave Without a Name is narrow and winding, but it is well worth the drive through the Texas Hill Country to find the cave. The more you know about caves, the more you will enjoy this out-of-the-way one.

| | |
|---|---|
| Location: | From Boerne, follow FM 474 north for six miles. Turn right at the cave sign and follow Kreutzberg Road five miles. Another cave sign marks the right turn onto a gravel road. The drive itself is scenic and well worth the trip. |
| Tour Length: | One-quarter mile; about one hour and fifteen minutes. |
| Facilities: | Soft drink machine, restrooms. |
| Camping: | Guadalupe River State Park, twenty miles away. |
| Motels: | Boerne. |

## Caverns of Sonora

Since the early 1900s, local ranch hands would enter the small, drop-in cave entrance and explore the quarter-mile of passages that ended in a large room. The cave was known as Mayfield Cave, after the landowner, Stanley Mayfield, and exploring it was cowboy entertainment on a day off. In that part of the cave there was very little cave formation, only some popcorn and a hint of cave coral.

In 1955, four Dallas cavers received permission from the landowner to explore the cave. They entered what is now called the Pit Room by an upper-level passage and, after careful exploration, discovered the most beautiful part. This was the first room leading to seven and one-half miles of what has been called one of the most spectacular caves in the world.

According to Bill Stephenson, founder of the National Speleological Society, "The beauty of the Caverns of Sonora cannot be exaggerated, not even by a Texan." Almost every square inch of the walls, floor, and ceiling is covered with a staggering variety of formations. Cave coral trees, as fragile as china and as much as three feet tall, grow from the floor. Helictites grow at gravity-defying angles from the walls and even on stalactites. Crystals of yellow dog-tooth spar grow in pools of water. Draperies cling to the walls along with fragile soda straws up to six feet long. Colorful and dripping water, the formations resemble their names: Butterscotch Falls, Ice Cream Sundae, Valley of Ice, Palace of the Angels, Crystal Palace, Moon Milk Falls.

The commercial trail winds amid this profusion of formations. At the beginning of the Diamond Room Passage is the famed Butterfly, seven and a half inches from wingtip to wingtip;

38. Caverns of Sonora. Translucent stalagmites in the Valley of Ice.

39. A Fishtail helictite, Caverns of Sonora.

actually it is two fishtail helictites that just happened to grow side by side.

The natural humidity of the cave is protected by doors, so 95 percent of the cave contains formations that are still growing. The temperature in the cave remains constant at 70 degrees Fahrenheit.

Stairs were unavoidable because of the topography of the cave. Ending the extended tour is the climb to a man-made exit tunnel. Rest stops are available.

40. Helictites, Caverns of Sonora.

41. Moon milk pool, Caverns of Sonora.

42. The Butterfly, Caverns of Sonora, about 1966. Note the droplet of water in the center of the formation. Photograph by Carl Kunath

43. The Butterfly, Caverns of Sonora, 1996. Note that the droplet in the center has crystallized.

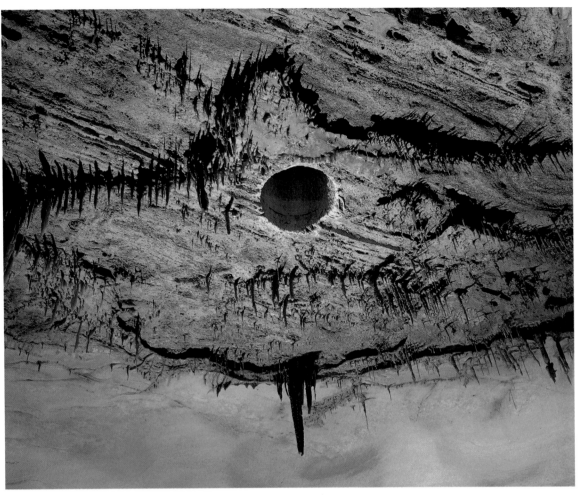

44. The discovery drill hole where it enters Inner Space Cavern. Note the thirty-five years' growth of formation around the edge of the hole.

Caverns of Sonora have been designated a National Natural Landmark.

| | |
|---|---|
| Location: | 8 miles west of Sonora on I-10, exit 392 at the cave sign, south 7 miles on FM 1989. |
| Tour Length: | 1.5 miles, two hours. |
| Facilities: | Gift shop, snack bar, picnic grounds; Covered Wagon Dinner Theater in summer. |
| Camping: | RV sites, showers, tent camping. |
| Motels: | Sonora and Ozona. |

## Inner Space Cavern

Inner Space Cavern was discovered in 1963, during construction of Interstate Highway 35. While drilling for core samples to determine if the footing was strong enough for a highway overpass, the crew watched as the drill bit dropped twenty-six feet. The supervisor, concerned with making sure that the footing was solid for the overpass, decided to enlarge the hole and lower workmen in for an inspection. Members of the Texas Speleological Association were contacted, and cavers made several trips into the drill-hole,

mapping more than seven thousand feet of cave.

In 1964, developers began constructing a tunnel to open the cave to the public. Workers building the trail discovered several collapsed entrances which were found to contain the remains of mammoths, sabertooth cats, and many other Pleistocene animals. The cave itself is thought to be sixty million to one hundred million years old.

Tours began in the summer of 1965. A cable car, called the Scenic Subway, delivers visitors from the main building down into the cave. From there the trail is flat and wide throughout the cave, with a few ups and downs along the way, but no stairs. This is the only show cave in Texas that is fully wheelchair accessible.

This 95-percent active limestone cave has several large rooms decorated with various types of formations, including cave drapery, flowstone, stalactites, and stalagmites. Visitors also will see some delicate formations such as soda straws, rim pools, and helictites.

Two light-and-sound shows in a unique underground theater stimulate visitors' imaginations. This is the only cave in Texas to use this technique.

Location:      Beneath I-35 in Georgetown, exit 259.
Tour length:   1 mile, round trip; about one hour and fifteen minutes.
Facilities:    Gift shop, snack bar, restrooms, picnic grounds.
Camping:       Nearby state parks.
Motels:        Georgetown, Round Rock, Austin.

45. Inner Space Cavern. Lake of the Moon reflects guide Dan Brown.

## Longhorn Cavern

Longhorn Cavern was developed in the 1930s by the U.S. Civilian Conservation Corps (CCC), a federal New Deal program. The original visitors' center, built by the CCC, now houses a museum dedicated to the era of the Great Depression.

Millions of years ago, an underground river sculpted the limestone into the distinctive fluted shapes for which this cave is noted. Caves formed in this manner are not common and typically do not develop the extensive assortment of formations usually associated with show caves, although there are some flowstone and dripstone formations in Longhorn Cavern.

The trail enters the cave through the largest of three natural entrances. A short flight of stairs leads down to the main cave floor. This is a pleasant, cool place to meet the guide. The cave tour follows the meanders of the ancient stream bed through several large rooms, while the guide describes the geological processes by which the cave was formed. Large calcite crystals cover the walls in parts of the tour.

Interspersed with the geology lesson come tales of the more recent history of the cave: Fossils and bones found by the developers in the entrances show that wild animals used the cave as a shelter. Comanche Indians, it is known, used one chamber of the cave as a council site and made weapons of the flint found there. During the Civil War, the Confederate Army manufactured gunpowder there. Sam Bass, the outlaw of the late 1800s, it is claimed, used the cave as a hideout, and hundreds of Prohibition-era revelers, it is recorded, used a room of the cave as a speakeasy and dance hall.

Longhorn Cavern is a registered U.S. Natural Landmark. It is operated for the State of Texas by a private corporation.

46. Longhorn Cavern. Karren Flowers looks up at the Eagle's Wing and Viking's Prow.

| | |
|---|---|
| Location: | From Burnet, south on U.S. Highway 281 six miles to Park Road 4 and then west five miles on the park road. |
| Tour length: | 1-¼ miles, round trip; about one hour and twenty-five minutes. |
| Facilities: | Gift shop, snack bar, CCC Museum, picnic area, hiking trails. No pets are allowed. |
| Camping: | Inks Lake State Park, five miles west on Park Road 4. |
| Motels: | Several a short drive away in Marble Falls or Burnet. |

47. Detail of rimstone dams at Castle of the White Giants, Natural Bridge Caverns.

## Natural Bridge Caverns

Natural Bridge Caverns, discovered in 1960, were developed soon after. At the entrance the excavators found evidence of human occupation from about 5,000 B.C. and bones of a kind of bear that became extinct more than eight thousand years ago. The cave is named for the sixty-foot-long natural bridge of limestone that stretches across the cave entrance.

Not only is this the largest commercial cave in Texas, but it is also one of the most spectacular. It is still almost completely an active cave, and its temperature remains at a constant 70 degrees. The rooms offer panoramic views and vistas. Stretching more than a mile down to Purgatory Creek, an underground stream, they contain rows of wet, colorful stalactites, stalagmites, columns, travertine dams, and draperies. Massive formations fifty feet high and delicate soda straws an eighth-inch in diameter grow side by side. Numerous lakes and pools of crystal-clear water reflect the cave formations.

The room known as Sherwood Forest has some unusual formations, including tall, slim stalagmites reminiscent of totem poles. In the Hall of the Mountain Kings, which is longer than a football field and one hundred feet wide, the totem poles are eccentric and seem to twist toward the ceiling, a hundred feet above. Some of the cave's rare "fried eggs," which look just like their namesakes, are found in this room as well. From the Hall of the Mountain Kings an artificial tunnel leads back to the surface.

Natural Bridge Caverns has been a U.S. Natural Landmark since 1971.

49. (above) A drop of water hits cave pearls in Natural Bridge Caverns. Cave pearls are formed by concentric layers of mineral that form around a central particle. The impact of the water drops keeps the pearls from adhering to the surrounding walls of the pocket or to each other.

50. (right) This "fried egg" is one of many in Natural Bridge Caverns.

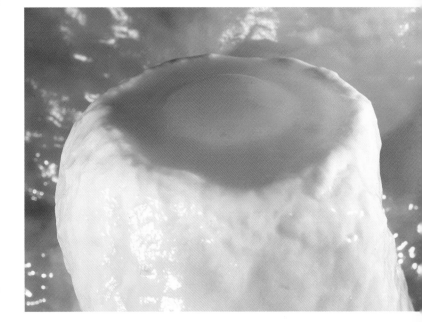

48. (left) Natural Bridge Caverns. Castle of the White Giants.

51. Wonder Cave. A visitor views the Main Hall.

| | | | |
|---|---|---|---|
| Location: | I-35 between New Braunfels and San Antonio; exit at Natural Bridge Caverns Road and follow the signs. | Camping: | State parks and private campgrounds nearby. |
| | | Motels: | Numerous on I-35 in New Braunfels or San Antonio. |
| Tour Length: | ¾ mile; one hour and fifteen minutes. | | |
| Facilities: | Gift shop, snack bar, displays in visitor center, restrooms. | | |

## Wonder Cave

Wonder Cave is the oldest commercially operated cave in Texas, first opened to the public in 1903. The cave is operated as one of several attractions at Wonder World, an amusement park located in San Marcos.

The cave was discovered by a farmer, Mark Beavers, when his drill bit fell into a void while he was drilling for water. He opened an entrance to what he called Beavers Cave and began offering tours, and it is said that he hid an illegal whiskey-making and gambling operation there as well.

Wonder Cave is a dry cave, the result of an earthquake. It lies within the three-hundred-mile-long Balcones Fault Zone that was created when the earth shifted during the uplifting of the Edwards Plateau some thirty-five million years ago. The fault line is visible in the ceiling of the cave.

Although Wonder Cave is not noted for typical cave formations, it is interesting as an example of the shifting and faulting of the earth's crust during a major earthquake.

The deepest point in the cave is the Wishing Well, 160 feet below the surface, where visitors can view the waters of the Edwards Aquifer. Steps allow guests to negotiate the ups and downs of the cave floor. The guides offer a good introduction to geology.

The forty-five-minute lecture-tour concludes in the Fossil Room, where guests can see some excellent examples of marine fossils while waiting for the elevator ride to the surface or to a higher observation tower overlooking a segment of the Balcones Escarpment.

| | |
|---|---|
| Location: | San Marcos. Take the Wonder World Drive exit (exit 202) from I-35. It is a short drive to the park. |
| Tour length: | 400 feet; about forty-five minutes. |
| Facilities: | Gift shop, snack bar, restrooms, amusement park, wildlife park and train ride, observation tower. |
| Camping: | San Marcos. |
| Motels: | San Marcos. |

# State Speleological Parks

Show caves offer a first-class excursion into the subterranean splendors of Texas, but they are just one option available for cave visitors. The Texas Parks and Wildlife Department (TPWD) offers alternatives: professionally guided tours to caves that are otherwise closed. For anyone who wants a very down-to-earth cave experience, crawling through a wild cave in one of TPWD's speleological parks may be just the thing.

G. Elaine Acker, an award-winning outdoor writer, tells us more about these cave parks.

Many of Texas' caves are found in state parks and wildlife management areas, and the Texas Parks and Wildlife Department now is making the speleological experience available to the public. Tours, led by experienced guides or professional speleologists, take you through a subterranean scrapbook of history, geology, and archeology.

Caver Bob Burnett was a resource specialist with TPWD. "Our largest water reserve is ground water, and caves are like storm sewers into our aquifer," said Burnett. "That's why they are so incredibly critical. For years, landowners filled in caves and sinkholes with garbage: household trash, appliances. Sheep and goats or other livestock would fall into the holes, and it seemed to make sense to fill them in. But water picks up any pollutants in the trash and flows on into the underground water supply. Trash accumulation in caves really is a problem."

Extensive cleaning and a thorough cave inventory are the first steps in management. Next, the TPWD maps the caves and conducts biological observations and collections. Many cave species are considered endangered, and all collection procedures require special permits. Based on the information, the department develops management plans, carefully considering public safety as well as the cave's need for protection.

"I am torn about cave visitation and rarely encourage people to go caving just for adventure and exploration," Burnett says. "I know we can't all be scientists, but the impact is so great. A little thoughtless behavior can alter or damage something that has been there for eons." Burnett does wish for others the peaceful sense of wonder that he associates with caves. "I feel a

52. Texas Park Ranger Dave Stuart climbs out of the entrance to Kickapoo Cave, part of the Texas Speleological Park System. The cave is protected by a locked iron gate to prevent unauthorized entry and possible damage.

spiritual connection with caves," he said. "Caves give you a place to contemplate things and place yourself in the overall timeline. These caves have been here and have taken thousands, if not hundreds of thousands, of years to build and form. It gives you a better perspective."

If you are interested in exploring the TPWD caves, you might begin with Longhorn Cavern State Park, near Burnet. It is the most highly developed of the state-owned caves, being operated by a private concessionaire, and is one of Texas' most popular show caves. The tour is not physically challenging and is accessible to the average visitor.

An elaborate lighting system, installed by the Civilian Conservation Corps during the 1930s, illuminates the cavern walls and ceiling, and a smooth pathway curves along the one-and-one-quarter-mile tour route. The route inside the cave is wheelchair accessible, although it is necessary first to negotiate steep steps leading to the cave entrance.

The cavern features some formations and tunnels that have been used for thousands of years, first by animals that preyed on prehistoric camels, elephants, and bison, and later by man. Archeologists working in the cavern have discovered animal bones, arrowheads, bullet molds, guns, a bayonet, and human skeletons. The limestone walls also have sequestered Texas outlaws, inspiring tales of lost maps and buried treasure.

Near Bend, west of Lampasas, Colorado Bend State Park offers "wild" cave tours. "A 'wild' cave means that you visit the cave in its natural state, with no trails or electrical lighting," says Park

53. Entrance to Longhorn Caverns.

Ranger Ed Young. You may participate in either a walking cave tour or a crawling cave tour, or both. Colorado Bend is a 5,300-acre park, and there are more than 150 caves on the property. All the caves are strictly closed, except for guided tours.

An eight-hundred-foot section of Gorman Cave is explored on the walking cave tour. Inside the cave, rimstone dams crisscross the floor, trapping water in shallow pools. Crystalline stalagmites stretch upward toward the ceiling, while clusters of stalactites point rigidly toward the floor. The hike to Gorman Cave is a rugged mile, and sturdy footwear is recommended.

If you would like to get an introduction to caving, the crawling cave tour may be more appealing. You'll visit two or three caves, climb through layers of daddy-long-legs (harvestmen), crawl past six-inch centipedes, and satisfy your quest for adventure. "We'll see some caves with very pretty formations, and some with almost no formations," said Young. "Sometimes you're standing in a fifty-foot room, and sometimes you're on the ground, crawling through spaces no more than a foot high. This is not just a simple tour of the caves. It is the equivalent of a course in basic caving. I like for people to leave with information on how to be safe in caves, and how to take care of the cave."

Kickapoo Cavern State Natural Area is a 6,368-acre site, just north of Brackettville, that offers a natural cave experience. Kickapoo Cavern is about fourteen hundred feet long. It is a massive cave with large rooms, and it has a wide representation of different types of cave formations: stalactites, stalagmites, and huge columns that are the largest in the state. About one percent of the cave is still active.

The cave has been the site of much human activity, including occupation by prehistoric populations who first used the cave for shelter. Indian middens can be found outside the mouth of the cave and historical graffiti, dating back to the 1880s, is present. Although the cave was damaged by early visitors, who broke formations and scrawled on the walls, the undeveloped cave now is protected and open for guided tours.

Tours of Kickapoo Cavern often are followed by observing the evening bat flight at nearby Green Cave. There are no bats in Kickapoo Cavern, but Green Cave is 1,068 feet long and supports a significant population of Mexican freetail bats.

North of Kickapoo Cavern is the vertical cavern called the Devil's Sinkhole. Dave Stuart describes the formation of the sinkhole: "An orb-shaped hole formed below the ground, measuring about 300 feet by 200 feet. Once the water receded, it no longer supported the rock strata above the cavern, and the rock started caving in." Eventually an oval 40 by 60 feet

eroded through several layers of rock. "If you walked up to the edge and stepped in, you'd fall about 150 feet," Stuart continues. "We don't take any tours into the hole. We're concerned about safety, and we're concerned about the bat population."

During the late spring and early fall, bat flights at the Devil's Sinkhole are popular. "The bats put on a good show," says Stuart. "When they fly from the sinkhole, they spiral in a counterclockwise vortex, forming a column as they rise out of the earth. One night there were so many, it looked as though you could cross the cavern by walking across the bats."

Exploring any cave can be dangerous to the untrained, but by offering guided tours and instructions, the TPWD makes it possible for anyone to walk from the warm sunlight into the cool darkness and safely experience the unknown—the mystery of the caves.

54. State Park Ranger Jon Byrd explores a tight crawlway in Dynamite Cave.

# Part 2

## THE CAVE EXPERIENCE

# Reverend Cunningham in the Great Kickapoo Cave

Imagine what it was like to discover the Grand Canyon, to first set human eyes on Niagara Falls, to put the first footprint on the moon. That sense of awe and discovery has also sent folks underground to explore caves. The first-person caving travelogues in this section are a fascinating sample of exploratory zeal at a time when modern Texans were just becoming aware the ancient underground wonders. S. Christopher Caran shares the following account, the earliest known written record of a cave exploration in Texas.

The earliest known written account by a visitor to a Texas cave dates from 1889. Hal T. Cunningham, then a twenty-four-year-old Methodist minister, recorded a description of his trip into "the Great Kickapoo Cave" in what is now Kickapoo Cavern State Natural Area in Kinney and Edwards counties, one hundred miles west of San Antonio:

I am writing this on the morning of the 23rd [of April, 1889]. [We] reached our destination last evening at about six o'clock; had supper and made preparations at once to explore the great cavern. We were well provided with torches and lanterns, and with our blankets and quilts, and lights in hand, we began the ascent of the hill in the side of which is the entrance to the cave.

There is an opening in the rock, 12 feet square, more or less, overgrown with shrubbery and grass. By bending our bodies almost double, the ingress was easily made. [After] an abrupt descent of a few feet . . . we were on our feet, and with raised torches, peered into the Egyptian darkness of the subterranean wonder.

Massive rocks and huge boulders lay before us and around us on all sides. Over [these] we stumblingly passed into the silent and awful depths of the cave, now constantly increasing in dimensions, to a distance of about 100 yards. A massive pillar, extending from the floor to the gracefully arched top, and about 30 feet in diameter, stood before us while immense perpendicular gorges lay on either

55. Kickapoo Cavern. The eighty-foot-tall twin columns are the largest known formation in Texas.

56. A pool in Haby Cave. Photograph by Orion Knox.

side. . . . Entering another passageway by a defile in the rock, . . . [we] stood in another apartment, known as the "Crystal Palace," [and] were overwhelmed with wonder and admiration. The scene here beggars description. The most beautiful stalactites, [descending] from above in every conceivable way, and blending into each other in the most fantastical manner, are opposed by formations below, both made by percolations through the rock. Frequently, the stalactite and stalagmite formations meet, and the result is a solid column from the vaulted roof to the rock strewn floor. These columns, or pillars, are numerous throughout the cavern[,] varying from a few inches to many feet in diameter. We did not explore the cave thoroughly by any means [yet] it took over four hours to make this subterranean tour. I shall never regret having made this visit.

Despite its early date, Reverend Cunningham's description of a Texas cave is remarkably detailed and essentially accurate. His comments regarding the development of stalactites, stalagmites, and columns are consistent with present knowledge. His fascination with the cave environment and his sense of the adventure of cave

exploration mirror the sentiments of modern cavers.

It is possible to compare Reverend Cunningham's important historical record with observations of Kickapoo Cavern today. It has, in fact, changed very little in the more than one hundred years since his visit. The "massive pillar" he observed is the largest known cave formation in Texas and one of the largest in the world; it is shown on the cover of this book. The "beautiful stalactites, [descending] from above in every conceivable way" are helictites, which grow irregularly instead of straight downward.

Kickapoo Cavern contains many outstanding helictites and other formations, which collectively are referred to as *speleothems*. Caves and the speleothems in them have their origins in the constant interplay of rock and groundwater.

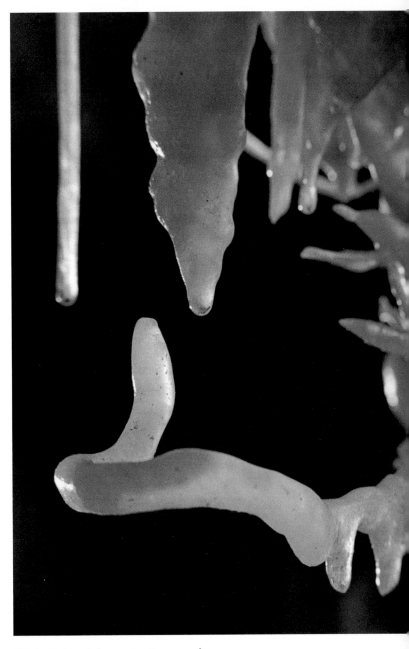

58. Helictites defy gravity, Caverns of Sonora.

57. Helictites grow in all directions on this stalagmite in Natural Bridge Caverns, South Cave. Note the small spider in the lower right.

# Blair Pittman, Preteen Caver

The Devil's Sinkhole is an awesome place. My first trip there was on a cool autumn day in 1949, when I was eleven years old. Now, nearly half a century later, I was lying on the same edge, peering down the same 150 feet at the top of the same underground mountain, formed when the roof of a giant cave collapsed thousands or maybe even hundreds of thousands of years ago. My stomach still wasn't quite sure about making the descent, even after years of visiting the sinkhole. Every time, before rappelling in, it was this way. Some things don't change, and I couldn't help remembering the early years.

My Fort Worth school library had a copy of the 1948 National Speleological Society's Bulletin 10, which featured a trip into the Devil's Sinkhole. The cave was right here in Texas, near Rocksprings, and I wanted to see it, so I found an adult, Mason Lisk, who had done some caving and who had two important assets: he wanted to make the trip, and he had a car.

On that first trip, we didn't have rope. Heavygauge sheep-wire fencing was tied to a metal stake outside the entrance and extended all the way to the top of the mountain. The ranch owner assured us that others had climbed in and out on the fencing material. As I peered down into the hole, it sure looked like a long way to climb. That distance was then, and still is, the equivalent of a fifteen-story office building.

No, this is not recommended procedure, but it turned out to be sturdy wire. I wrapped my arms around it as I climbed down. The view from the inside looking up at the entrance was even more spectacular than looking in. The daylight and the outside world seemed far away.

After the descent, we found our way down the mountain to the lake rooms—actually the water table, 385 feet below the surface. Now we were in total darkness, with carbide lanterns to light the way. The water was crystal clear, so clear it was hard to see where the edge really was, and 68° cool. I was intrigued by the other side of the body of water, where there seemed to be a passage continuing underwater. There had to be more cave than the part we had found, but I was helpless to explore any further with no underwater gear.

While climbing the sheep fence back to daylight, I knew I would come back and explore that passage, but there was a lot that I needed to learn. Where could I learn vertical rope work? Where could I get underwater breathing gear? This was 1950, and scuba diving wasn't very common then.

A friend of mine was technically inclined and intrigued by the challenge, so we set to work. We scrounged a used air tank from a local welding supply distributor, who also filled the tank with compressed, filtered air.

Our first attempt wasn't very sophisticated. We rigged a hose from the air tank to a surplus diver's mask and thought we had the problem licked, so we went swimming. The first try at breathing underwater was interesting. I cranked the air valve open, and twelve hundred pounds of air pressure blew the mask off my face, breaking the rubber strap. We went back to the drawing board.

*Popular Mechanics* magazine came to the rescue with an article and instructions for building underwater breathing equipment. Now we prowled army surplus stores, looking for an "AN-6004-1 diluter demand control valve," as specified in the magazine. In a dusty back corner of an old store, we finally found one. Following the instructions, we got the regulator converted for underwater use, then hooked it to the air tank. It was time for another test.

The rig didn't have a mouthpiece, and the air hose fed directly into the surplus face mask. The instructions said that after you took a breath and held it, the air would stop flowing until you wanted another breath. This time I barely cracked the air valve. Nothing happened, but at least I still had my mask on. I cautiously slipped my head underwater and took a breath. Air came flowing in until I stopped breathing. I went deeper and tried again. A breath of fresh air flowed into the mask. I sat on the bottom at ten feet breathing for fifteen minutes. It worked.

Now I needed to learn about ropes—rap-pelling and ascending with prusik knots. My army mountaineering manual taught only a body rappel, which was intended for combat conditions. In a body rappel, the rope goes under one leg, then across the chest, and over the shoulder. After I got some minor rope burns, my mother sewed leather patches on those points of jeans and shoulder where the rope produced the most friction.

I quickly learned that it is easier to rappel down a rope than to climb up one, but after experimenting with small loops of rope tied onto a larger, longer rope with a climber's knot, called a prusik, I got the trick of it. I learned to lift one foot, slide its loop up the main rope, then repeat on the other side, not unlike a toy monkey climbing a string. After some searching, I found a two-hundred-foot length of half-inch sisal rope, and for the next year I stayed busy on weekends, either practicing with the home-made scuba or on trips, not only to caves but also to cliff locations in Texas and Oklahoma.

A year after that first trip into the Devil's Sinkhole, I felt ready to explore the rest of the Lake Room. My father was more than curious about what I was doing, so he offered to take me and a couple of caver friends in the family car.

Again, as I gaped over the edge, my stomach wondered why I insisted on doing this. But in a body rappel I backed over the ledge, then hung in midair, suspended above the bottom. Very slowly I let the rope slide across my body. I had learned that too much speed and friction can create enough heat to be uncomfortable. Finally, I touched down on the bottom and climbed out of the rope. My friends pulled the rope up, tied the underwater gear securely, and lowered it to me. Then each of them rappelled in. We carried the gear down the mountain to the largest lake room.

Oh, that water was cold. For warmth I wore a long-sleeved shirt and blue jeans. My underwater light was a flashlight in a fruit jar with a

59. Devil's Sinkhole. A caver ascends the 150-foot cave entrance.

60. Rappelling into Devil's Sinkhole.

strap taped to it. I eased underwater, breathing as I went. My friends fed out parachute cord as I moved to the possible passage. For a year I had dreamed of swimming through this passage and coming out of the water on the other side into a big room full of cave formations. Excited and a little nervous, I swam around the corner . . . and found a dead end.

A few things do change, and now, in 1996, on a cool October day, I was preparing for yet another trip into the Devil's Sinkhole. For one thing, since 1985, the cave has been part of the Texas State Parks System, and access to it is tightly controlled. Although anyone can make arrangements to see the bat flight, entry into the cave itself is restricted to scientists and researchers. I received permission to enter this time only, to make photographs for this book.

Too, this time I was working with the assistance of members of the San Angelo Fire Department, who brought the latest in climbing gear. This was a far cry from climbing in and out of the sinkhole using sheep fence. Still, even with the comfort of high-tech climbing gear and experienced people, when I hooked onto the rope, backed up to the edge, and looked down, my stomach registered the same old objection. A moment later, though, I was over the ledge and hanging on the rope, poised for a free rappel. My stomach relaxed as I let the rope slide slowly over my familiar brake bars.

The walls of the sinkhole belled out farther and farther away from the rope as I slid slowly downward. I had the sensation of floating in midair and didn't want it to end. It gave me an opportunity to look around, up at the entrance growing smaller and down at the mountaintop looking bigger. The slow descent left me time to admire the foliage growing stubbornly in the cracks of the layered limestone. I turned slowly, revolving on the rope, trying to look every direction at once, soaking it all in. The memories of my previous trips here stayed with me all the way down.

Too soon I touched down on top of the mountain. The entrance was far above me, and the world beyond seemed much smaller now. As I unhooked myself from the rope and looked down the steep mountainside into the darkness that eventually became total blackness, I heard bats clicking and calling.

This cave world of mammoth proportions offers a special environment. It is a world of darkness, deep below the surface of West Texas. At the bottom of the mountain, crystal-clear lakes sit at the water table. More than twelve million bats make themselves at home in here.

With camera case and tripod, I found my way down the mountain to the spot where I wanted to spend the day watching the light play on the limestone walls, waiting for the magic light I needed. As the afternoon drifted on, the walls soaring up to the surface became coated with a buttery light, soft and warm.

It was 4:30 in the afternoon when I shot my last pictures, packed up the camera gear, and headed up the mountain to the waiting rope and the ascent back to the sunlight and that other world 150 feet above. I hooked my climbing rig to the rope and started upward, one foot after the other, each step taking me closer to the surface. Again I took my time, soaking in the vistas surrounding me. It was only fifteen minutes before friendly hands pulled me over the edge and out into the sunlight of a warm autumn day in West Texas.

I'll be back.

# Orion Knox's Discovery

Natural Bridge Cave's striking entrance had long attracted visitors by the time Orion Knox and his friends went exploring there in 1960. They went farther into the cave than any previous visitor and found rooms whose formations rivaled the gargantuan splendors of Carlsbad Caverns. In an interview, Orion described to me how he and his friends named room after room in the extended caverns of Natural Bridge Cave, near New Braunfels.

College students haven't changed much over the years. In San Antonio in 1960, when the weekend arrived after a tough week of studies at Saint Mary's University, it was time for some relaxation. To me that meant caving. Several friends and I were members of the Saint Mary's University Speleological Society.

There were numerous wild caves near San Antonio that we could have picked to visit, but one that had captured our attention that weekend in January 1960 was a place called Natural Bridge Cave, named for the sixty-five-foot natural span of limestone that stretched over its entrance. It was a pretty place, covered with foliage and trees. It was a well-known natural feature often visited since before the turn of the century. Even before that, it had been a popular camping area for prehistoric Native Americans.

On our first trip, we visited the areas near the entrance that had been seen by many curious picnickers with idle time. There were a few formations there, but nothing unusual or outstanding. We kept checking leads, crawling through small passages and descending pits until we were more than a hundred feet below the entrance. At that level we noticed a possible passage nearly plugged with mud and rocks. I thought I felt a breeze, but we had better leads to follow. We explored a passage we named the South Fault, without reaching its end. It was a good weekend of fun, and we left with more cave to explore in the future.

With high hopes, we set out on our second trip the following weekend. Our hopes were rewarded with the discovery of the 'Coon Rooms, a nicely decorated passage near the entrance. We also explored Saint Mary's Hall, a well-decorated passage that had been visited previously by the University of Texas Speleological Society in the

late 1950s. By now we were getting excited about the cave, because of both its extent and its beauty. On the third trip, we photographed and surveyed our previous finds and explored a portion of a small, very muddy passage. Leaving the cave, we agreed that much more exploring remained to be done. Many leads were left unchecked.

On the fourth trip, we had enough people to split up. One group was pushing the South Fault, while Preston Knodell, Al Brandt, Joe Cantú, and I were going to try the nearly plugged crawlway we had noticed on our first trip. Being the smallest, I usually was "urged" to go first into crawlways. Shoving debris to the sides, I dug enough mud and rock to wriggle in and crawled about twenty feet to a small room. I had been in a solution passage, but now I was in a cavity formed by breakdown wedged against a steeply sloping bedrock wall. I asked Preston to follow me through the space left between the boulders. They had fallen thousands of years ago, so we hoped they wouldn't shift now. I had a climber's piton hammer with me and had to break off some pieces of rock to continue through the breakdown crawl.

Preston followed me part of the way, and after I had covered about sixty feet, I could see only blackness at the end of the crawl, indicating that it opened up. This was getting more interesting. At least it was better than more crawlway. I yelled back to the others, "Hey, we've got some cave up here."

I went on into the room while they were crawling to me. It was a muddy slope. I was trying to see the formations and turned my carbide lantern up high, trying to see through the black. I took a step, slipped, and fell down the muddy incline. My lantern spewed, water bubbled, and the flame went out. Just about the time the others got there, I was getting myself back together and my lantern going again.

This was a spectacular room compared with what we had seen. The right wall was covered with very nice formations. There were no footprints ahead of us; the only ones were ours, left behind.

Leading to our left, we could see what now is called Chapel Hall. Preston and I headed into it. It was a walking passage, and we thought it was the main cave. Al headed down the mud slope. In a few moments he yelled up to us, "Hey, here is where the main cave goes." Feeling like fools, we named our passage Fools Hall.

We made our way to where Al was. It was a

61. (left) Brian Vauter at Castle of the White Giants, Natural Bridge Caverns. Rimstone dams in the lower portion of this scene hold pools of water.

62. James Redell, after a day of caving. Natural Bridge Caverns. Photograph by Orion Knox.

very steep slope. We weren't sure we could get back out if we went down it. We debated a little, then I thought I saw a way. We didn't have any rope with us, as we had no idea we would be getting into anything like this, and the floor was steep and slick with mud. We climbed with care; we didn't want any accidents. We made our way down the slope and could see the beginning of Sherwood Forest, full of stalagmites like totem poles and walls of flowstone.

Moving on into the cave, we got to the point where the sloping ceiling flattened out. All we could see was black. Carbide lamps are good for putting light right in front of you, but now we were in a big, big cave. The lamps wouldn't show us what was in the distance.

We were slapping each other on the back in sheer excitement. We took a break and just stood there, not believing what we were seeing. It was fantastic; we were getting into a really major cave. I had never seen anything like this. We knew we were deeper than any cave we knew of in the Bexar County area.

We moved over to the edge of another steep drop and looked down into Purgatory Creek. Ahead of us was blackness. We estimated that the ceiling was a hundred feet high. When we surveyed later, it was eighty feet. We overestimated most of our distances because of the dim carbide lights.

We barely could make out the bottom below us but could see far enough ahead to know that the cave continued. I went to the left side of the passage, where some formations formed a kind of stair. I climbed down those. I'm still excited about it, just remembering. In my wildest dreams, I never thought of finding anything like that—it was a caver's dream come true.

The mud at the bottom was knee deep, making for slow going. Then we started up the other side. The slope was at about forty degrees; it was a bit like climbing a steep snowbank. I kicked

my boots into the mud, making steps for the others to follow. As we got near the top of the mud slope, the ceiling seemed to lower to only fifteen feet high, as if the passage was ending. Then we got a glimpse of the Castle of the White Giants room, with its huge formations. We had seen some nice formations, but nothing like this—mammoth formations, dripping with water; white columns, stalactites, stalagmites; a series of rimstone dams on the cave floor.

Of our group of four, only Joe Cantú had seen anything comparable: Carlsbad Caverns. This was Joe's first wild cave, and he had tried it just to find out if he liked caving. What luck! We kept asking him, "How does this compare to Carlsbad?" He assured us that these formations were as big as those in Carlsbad. We thought we had found the next wonder of the world. It took us a while to get to the other end of the room; we kept stopping to look. It was one wonder after another.

Once again it began to look as if the cave might be ending. From a distance, the ceiling seemed to come down to the floor. But when we reached the end of the room, we saw a five-foot-high duck-under leading to another passage, which dropped into another canyon we named Grendel's Canyon. There another mud slope awaited us. This area has some of the best echoes in the cave, so we did some caver hollering: clapping hands, whistling, timing the echoes. Reaching the steepest part of the canyon, we weren't at all sure that we could get back up. So, rather than all of us taking a chance, I went down first, kicking steps down and then back up the other side. I retraced my steps to make

63. The bridge over Purgatory Creek, Natural Bridge Caverns. The high water level seen here resulted from unusually heavy rains on the surface. Photograph by Orion Knox.

sure we could get back. When I found I could, the others came on and joined me.

We climbed to about the same level as the Castle of the White Giants and entered the largest room I had ever seen, which we called the Hall of the Mountain Kings. We couldn't see the ceiling or the other end of the room. Formations everywhere were different from the White Giants. Stalagmites made turns, kind of squiggly shapes. There were so many formations at one point that they created a visual barrier, obscuring the big room beyond. We climbed up and up through the formations. Strangely enough, the route we traveled then is about the same as the one the commercial trail now follows. We took the easiest route that would disturb the fewest formations.

We couldn't see the ceiling until we were almost to the top; it was so high we thought we ought to be nearing the surface. The room was so large that we couldn't tell exactly where we were going. We stopped at the top and took a break. We sat on the old, soft guano, looking back at what we had just climbed through. It was a vast chamber, but the other side where we were going was even larger. The sheer size of the room and the formations were mind-boggling. We drank some water, ate a snack, and tried to take it all in. Our adrenaline was pumping like crazy.

The only thing I can compare this experience to is reaching the summit of a great mountain. I had the same deep sense of internal reward. At the same time, I felt very humbled by the majesty of what I was seeing. I sat there at the top of the Hall of the Mountain Kings, feeling sheer wonder at the beauty of nature. In this instance at Natural Bridge Caverns, all these elements were combined. I really can't think of words fully to describe my feelings.

We worked our way farther into the cave. Down the other side of the Hall of the Mountain Kings was the place we later named the Valley of the Fallen Lords, as there were huge rocks that had fallen from the ceiling. Preston was taking an English literature course at the time, so many of our names came from well-known English classics.

Beyond the bottom of the Valley of the Fallen Lords, we again had to climb a long, muddy slope to a solution passage, small in comparison with what we had come through. Because of the deep layer of guano and mud we had to walk through, we named it the Moors.

We passed several smaller side passages, proceeding straight ahead on the obvious largest route. We finally got to a point where it narrowed to a stoop-over walkway and then grew smaller, becoming a crawlway. I thought, "Well, we've finally done it. We've reached the end." All of us were pretty tired at this point, but I didn't want to quit. I wanted to know what was up ahead. The rest took a break while I crawled seventy-five feet or more. The passage opened up again, about eight feet high and six to eight feet wide. It was a nice walking passage with a mud floor.

After walking about three hundred feet, I saw a hole in the floor and walked over to its edge. Standing in ankle-deep mud, I looked down into a pit which opened up just beyond my feet. I couldn't see the bottom or the far side. All alone, my first reaction was panic. I quickly backed away as if the pit had been a rattlesnake. Turning up my carbide lantern and looking again, I could barely see a wall on the other side. Wow! The cave didn't end after all. The others joined me, and we sat there overwhelmed that the cave continued, with no end in sight. Later we named this the Inferno Room. The edge of the pit, where we sat, became Belayman's Bluff. As we had no ropes or cable ladders for the descent, we turned back toward the entrance. We were tired but elated, planning our next trip, as we passed back through all the wonderful cave we had discovered.

Little did I realize how this day would affect the rest of my life. I dropped out of school for two years to help Jack Burch and the owners commercialize Natural Bridge. I wanted the world to see this cave, but my viewpoint was a selfish one. I wanted this cavern protected, and at the same time I wanted to share it with the world. I agree with Jack Burch's philosophy that the best way to protect a world-class cave is to commercialize it, then make sure it is operated right and protected for future generations.

I think people can appreciate the cave more by understanding how it was discovered. There is an element of risk and endurance involved in caving, creating a deep bond among cavers. We trust each other with our lives. In caving I have received satisfaction and exhilaration paralleled, in my experience, only through trekking in the Himalayan mountains. But caving is more affordable and more available than Mount Everest. Caving is the only activity in which the average person can hope to go places and see things no one ever has seen before.

# Jack Burch Develops a Show Cave

Jack Burch's caving hobby became a mission of helping the public see the wonders, without endangering themselves or the cave. In our interview he told me that he feels he has fulfilled his mission by helping to develop two show caves in Texas, but is thinking about new, futuristic ways for people to visit these ancient wonders.

I have helped commercialize two Texas caves, Caverns of Sonora and Natural Bridge Caverns, so that people can see how beautiful underground places can be. Caves are some of nature's most fantastic work, but they are hidden from view. They aren't like the Grand Canyon or Yosemite. The public can't go see a cave until trails are built and lights installed. I guess I found that it was up to me to make it possible for people to see the beauty I enjoyed underground.

The 1950s and 1960s have been called the Golden Age of Texas cave exploration. Many of Texas' finest caves were discovered in that period—for example, Caverns of Sonora (1955), Natural Bridge Caverns (1963), and Inner Space Caverns (1965). The number of known caves in

Texas grew quickly. Stories about new caves were published. Cavers were interviewed for feature stories in many major newspapers. Locations were given, so more and more people found out about the caves and wanted to go see them for themselves. It wasn't unusual for cave formations to be broken for souvenirs. People just didn't know any better.

## Caverns of Sonora

After Caverns of Sonora was discovered, Bob and Bart Crisman, brothers and respected cavers, published an article about it. Their photographs showed formations that I had never seen before. I had to see that cave. The article didn't reveal the cave's location, so I went to Bart's home in Abilene to talk to him. It took some talking, but Bart finally was satisfied that I could be trusted and would take care of the cave. He gave me the location and the ranch owner's name. The cave was known as Mayfield Cave, or Secret Cave, at that time.

Every square inch of the pretty part of Cav-

64. Soda Straw Room, Caverns of Sonora. Photograph by Carl Kunath

65. Jewel Jennings near stalactites covered with cave coral, lower level, Caverns of Sonora.

erns of Sonora was covered with cave formations: popcorn, cave coral, helictites. There was no mud or bats; "pristine" describes it pretty well. Sonora was like crawling inside a beautiful geode. I had never seen anything to compare with it, but from 1956 to 1959, destruction had spread everywhere. It began to look as if a football game had been played in the cave.

Photographers were the worst. They wanted people in the picture, so that meant someone had to climb on a fragile formation to pose. Cavers were not following in the footsteps left by others. Everyone wanted to start their own new trail. I believed that the only way to save

Sonora was to commercialize it. Then it could be protected.

In 1960, my caving partner, Jim Papadakis, worked out a lease agreement with the ranch owner, Stanley Mayfield. We moved to Sonora and went to work. First we accurately surveyed the cave, so we could plan the trail. Then the work really began. It took us only four months of hard, fast work to complete the first half-mile. We opened for tours that same year.

Our main consideration in building the trail was to keep the formations safe. We wanted to keep the trail away from walls of fragile helictites and at the same time lose as little of the forma-

66. A maze of helictites, Caverns of Sonora.

67. A fishtail, Caverns of Sonora, caver Jack White. Photograph by Carl Kunath

When we first opened to the public with a half-mile of trail, the end of the tour was a turn-around, and the trail backtracked to the entrance. I knew we would extend the trail later, so I built an elevated trail to double back. It was more like a bridge sitting on two-by-fours, doing as little damage as possible. After it was carefully removed, you couldn't tell a trail had ever been there.

The next year I extended the trail into the Diamond Room passage which included the Butterfly. That is when Blair Pittman came to work with me. We built wooden bridges with rock walls and footing for them. Then there was

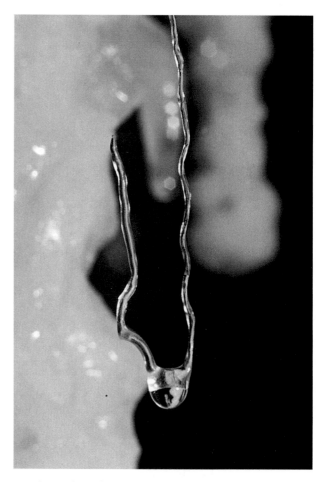

68. Thin outline of crystal around a drop of water forms two helictites, Caverns of Sonora. Photograph by Carl Kunath

tions on the floor as possible. We did a lot of thinking before making decisions. My basic approach, though, was to build the trail just as our Texas Highway Department builds a road. If you dig here, you have to fill there. So before I started digging out a high place, I had to find a low place to fill with the rubble. This was also the path of least resistance. We worked by hand with a wheelbarrow. We never did use machinery in the cave.

69. Stanley Mayfield and cave coral, Diamond Room Passage.

the electrical work, burying wires under the trail and figuring where to place the light bulbs and how many were needed. The Diamond Room passage was opened to the public in 1962.

Most of the trail and lighting was built by cavers. They respect the formations. Mills Tandy, a caver from Ozona, helped me in the first part of the cave. My friend Calvin Perryman helped, for free, with the transit survey. Then Blair helped with the Diamond Room passage, and Richard Doak, a caver from Tennessee, helped

build the north loop. Cavers are also dedicated. They will work harder than any other human being you could hire. At one point I hired a couple of high-school football players who wanted to get in shape, but it was more work than they expected. They quit after one day.

It wasn't until 1978 that I extended the trail again, this time into the north part of the cave, to the Hall of the White Giants. That part took us almost a year to finish. It was all fragile formations around us. One of the toughest parts

70. Glenda Kunath at the Diamond Horseshoe, Caverns of Sonora. Note the size of the crystals in the formation.

was a seventy-one-foot-long tunnel we had to dig through solid limestone by hand. We finished the extended loop, which comes back into the Diamond Room trail below the Red-Topped Stalagmite. In 1979 we opened up another beautiful part of Sonora, but that's it. I don't think any more of the cave will ever be opened. Off the trail is now closed to cavers or anyone else.

I had no idea that crystals could form as they did in Caverns of Sonora. Conditions had to be perfect. After seeing it for thirty-seven years now, I still find it hard to believe. The more you try to understand what happened, the more you realize that a miracle happened.

You can't measure the growth of a crystal in a lifetime. I have been watching for thirty-seven years now, and I haven't noticed one crystal grow. I found a stalactite that was only one three-thousandth of an inch from the stalagmite below it. I carefully measured the gap. Ten years later I measured it again; no change. Twenty years later, I checked again; it was the same. Now, thirty-seven years later, it still hasn't grown.

## Natural Bridge Caverns

Back in 1962, Orion Knox showed up at Sonora, excited, telling me about a big cave he had discovered near San Antonio. He went on and on about how beautiful it was. Passages went in six different directions, and he hadn't found the end of any of them. He wanted me to come look at it. That sounded like a good thing to do, so we headed for San Antonio.

Orion was right. It was a large, impressive cave, with lots of huge cave formations. It was far different from the Caverns of Sonora, but it was unique in its own way. The location was excellent, near New Braunfels, between San Antonio and Austin. We talked about turning it into a show cave and met with the landowner, Clara Heideman. We worked out a verbal contract, and I finished up at Sonora in a couple of weeks and moved to New Braunfels. Orion took some time off from college. As the discoverer, Orion had a sincere desire to be part of the development. He and I, with Reggie Wuest and Harry Heideman, started work on opening Natural Bridge Caverns in 1963.

Our philosophy was to avoid the use of stairs. If we followed the discovery route, opening up the crawlway to walking passage, we would have had at least one hundred steps just to get to Pluto's Anteroom. There had to be another way. I quizzed Orion, who knew so much more about the cave than I did. He agreed that the best way would be to tunnel around, but we needed to know at what grade to slope the tunnel. That's where James Reddell, caver and cave surveyor, got involved. He just happened to be there, visiting and caving. We put him to work. He surveyed through Bear Pit drop and came up with an angle for us. We saw what we had to do. The tunnel would have to be at least one hundred feet long.

With the cave survey in hand, we figured where to start digging outside the cave. We had to move a lot of rubble and gravel, and needed to dig at least twenty feet down to start tunneling. It took a couple of weeks, but we finally came into Saint Mary's Hall, right where we had hoped. We jack-hammered the floor, continuing the survey angle, then were stopped by forty feet of solid rock. We had to go through it. Day

71. Pete Lindsley, cave surveying with Brunton Compass, 1965.

after day we drilled and dynamited, being careful not to break any cave formations with our blasting. Again, we came out right on the nose. Finally we were in the main cave, and we hadn't had to use stairs so far. The real challenge was the topography, as it was up and down forty or fifty feet the entire length of the cave.

Next we had to build a trail on a 38-degree slope of rubble down to Sherwood Forest. We zigzagged the trail back and forth with switchbacks. We were torturing the fool out of

72. Jack Burch building the tunnel in Natural Bridge Caverns. Photograph by Orion Knox

that slope, digging as much as five feet deep. It was either that or put in stairs.

Then there we were, at Purgatory Creek, with knee-deep mud and another steep slope to the bottom of the creek, then back up the other side. Orion asked me about sinking concrete blocks in the mud for a trail base. I didn't like that idea at all. I looked at the cliff wall; it was vertical and 150 feet to the other side, 50 feet above the bottom. I turned to Orion, "Let's build a bridge, anchor it to the cliff, all the way across. That way we can keep the trail level."

"How are we going to do that?" was Orion's response.

I didn't know, but I sat down and started thinking. A plan began to form. It wasn't complete yet, but it was the beginning of an idea.

I sent out for some oilfield cable, enough to stretch across the cliff. We wrestled one end of the cable through the mud to the other side, secured both ends with eyebolts cemented in place, and started taking out the slack with borrowed fence stretchers. To get it good and tight, we used a twenty-inch oilfield turnbuckle. We tightened and tightened until I thought it wouldn't sag with weight on it.

Then we made a little seat that would hook onto the cable, and on that we could slide, pulling ourselves across the cliff. Orion, skinny and unafraid as he was, slid along drilling holes.

Then he cemented 1-1/4-inch rebar into the holes, all the way to the other side. We used a cutting torch to heat the rebar, bending it till it was level. All we had to do then was wire boards to the rebar, and we could walk over Purgatory Creek.

On the north side of the cave, past the Castle of the White Giants, we drilled a hole from the surface. We could shovel gravel and sand down the hole into the cave, then wheelbarrow it to the White Giants room and dump it in. It was another long haul to get everything to the bridge. We even brought in a concrete mixer one part at a time—the barrel, running gear, and the electric motor. We put it all back together down there in the cave and mixed our concrete. We toted in the sacks of cement, ninety-four pounds each, and used water from nearby pools.

In a cave, as you have a constant temperature, there is no expansion or contraction. The concrete we poured one day, we could safely walk on the next, so we could pour again. That's how we finished, from the north side, building the bridge toward the entrance. Every eight feet, we built a concrete buttress for support. It seemed plenty stout to me, but Clara Heideman wanted to know for sure that it was safe for twenty people. I could understand her viewpoint. She was the one to be held responsible if the bridge wasn't strong enough.

I got all the information together—the formula I used of cement and sand, how much rebar, the supports for the bridge—and mailed it to an engineer friend. It didn't take him long to write back to us. He claimed it was over-engineered—that you could stack lead bricks across the bridge, all the way up to the ceiling, and it wouldn't hurt anything. He said the eight-foot spans between supports would hold fifty thousand pounds per running foot. Clara was satisfied. Twenty or thirty people on that bridge would be as safe as they could be. We finished

73. Orion Knox building the bridge in Natural Bridge Caverns. Photograph by Jack Burch

the trail and the electrical lighting, opening the cave in 1964. It was an immediate success.

## South Cave

For several years, all of us involved with Natural Bridge Caverns had speculated about the possibility of more cave to the south of the entrance. The geology looked good, but we

75. Several kinds of formations clustered in Natural Bridge Caverns, South Cave.

74. Jan Knox descending through the bore hole into
Natural Bridge Caverns, South Cave. Photograph by
Orion Knox

76. Brian Vauter at a new discovery, the Broom Closet, a group of slender columns and stalagmites in Natural Bridge Caverns, South Cave.

*77.* Brian Vauter in front of flowstone that forms an "organ-pipe" formation in Natural Bridge Caverns, South Cave.

couldn't find any passages going in that direction. If there was more cave, it had been sealed up for many thousands of years. The only way really to find out was to drill from the surface and see what we would find.

On December 6, 1966, we hired a drilling rig to give it a try. At about forty feet the drill bit entered a large cavity. There was more cave. How big was it? What formations?

That night we tied a camera to a line and lowered it into the well hole. It was rigged with the shutter open and a flash attachment. We had the flash wired so we could shoot it remotely. We lowered the camera down the six-inch hole, about fifty feet, and set off the flash. We turned the film in and waited for the results. We didn't have two-hour photo labs back then. We had to wait two days, even with a rush request.

Finally, there it was, a big room. The flashbulb we used didn't have enough power, but you could barely see formations in the distance. We had a new cave. The next step was to drill the six-inch hole out to twenty inches so we could go in and see what was down below.

On January 8, 1967, three of us—me, Reggie Wuest, and Myles Kuykendall—were lowered in.

78. Stalactite, drapery, and soda straws in Natural Bridge Caverns, South Cave.

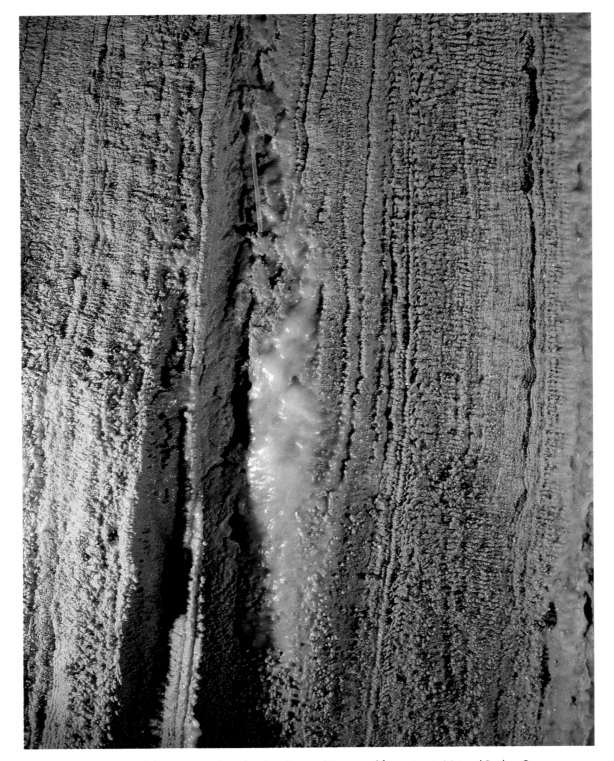

79. Over ages, layers of clay were replaced with calcite in this unusual formation in Natural Bridge Caverns, South Cave. A soda straw grows in the upper part of the picture.

We named that discovery the Jaremy Room, from the first letters of our names. What we found was far different from the commercial north cave. Not only was it a big room with stalactites, stalagmites, columns, and lots of flowstone, but also, surprisingly, it had soda straws, up to sixteen feet long, and helictites. Nothing like this was in the known part of Natural Bridge Caverns.

More and more people are interested in nature, and a cave is certainly one of nature's most beautiful works of art, but cave development in the future may be in for some drastic changes. One idea is to let people tour a cave from inside a transparent tube. That way not even breathing would affect the cave, and there would be no lint from clothes to stick on formations.

Or someday we may see a representation of the cave, a copy, rather than the real thing. We might be able to show some fragile areas with the use of holograms, in three dimensions, or with closed-circuit cameras. It might not be like seeing the real cave, but it would beat not seeing these fragile areas at all. Who knows—we might be able to see them better, and the cave would be protected. Let's see what happens.

# Jim Brummett
# Runs the Show

Anyone who plans to visit a show cave should pay attention to Jim Brummett's interview with me about managing such a site. To cavers and the cave manager, these sites are sacred. Those visitors who worship with respect will be rewarded; deface the site, and be prepared to face the consequences.

Any commercial cave manager is responsible to the owners, but as a caver myself, I feel a personal responsibility to take care of the cave and protect it. A major part of the job is trail and cave maintenance. I also train the guides, keep the tours on time, and do everything possible to help visitors enjoy their trip as comfortably as possible. Then there is always the book work—accounting and souvenir sales. Sometimes marketing, promotion, and advertising are part of the job. But the bottom line is—caves have always been special to me.

By the time I was fifteen years old, I had been in every cave I could find near Menard, where I grew up. I went to every commercial cave I could find. In 1963 I started working at Caverns of Sonora. Blair Pittman had quit working at the cave when he married my daughter, and I took his job. Blair wanted to turn his cave photography into a newspaper job, and he did.

The first thing they started me doing at the Caverns of Sonora was replacing the wooden stairs and bridges with concrete. That was hard work, and I was mostly by myself. I had to carry in the lumber, cement, and water and set the forms. At the same time, tours had to be able to get through where I was working. I also was a guide when the cave got busy and when I had time.

After a few years at Sonora, I got a job offer to be the manager of Cascade Caverns. So with my wife, Ann, I moved to Boerne. The cave needed the electrical wiring updated, and the trail needed lots of work. When there was a big rain, water flowed through the entrance into the cave. That kept the trail in need of frequent repair. I figured out a system of concrete dams that carried the water away from the entrance, and I made a lot of other outside improvements. The owner wanted me to build a gravity house—

you know, a house of optical illusions, where the floor, walls, and ceiling go off at angles. Very carefully I measured everything to build a house that wasn't straight. That was harder than building a regular house. The public really enjoyed it, though.

For extra business, the owner wanted to cater private and company parties and get-togethers, so, in addition to running the cave, I built a barbecue pit.

In 1975, a manager was needed for Inner Space Caverns. It has miles of passages not on the commercial trail. With some well-known and trusted cavers, I was able to start caving again.

Most of the passages are pretty small, but they usually open up into some nice rooms with beautiful formations. One of these formations is named the Dragon's Mouth. The cavers wanted to go caving more than I had time to do, so I let them go without me. They were most cooperative, reporting to me where they had been and what they had found. Our cave map was growing. That's when we bumped into a problem. It came to my attention that the Dragon's Mouth had been defaced with muddy footprints and initials carved into the formation. Photographs were sent to me showing the damage. I don't think the trusted cavers were responsible. They probably had brought someone new with them who just didn't understand proper caving manners. When the owners found out, all of that group of cavers was prohibited from going off-trail again at Inner Space.

We also had a few break-ins and cases of vandalism at the cave. One time someone stole a mastodon tusk and a sabertooth-tiger tooth. The tusk and tooth were pretty crumbly, so the thieves didn't get away with much.

For safety, we installed telephones for the guides in the cave. In case they needed help, they could call us on the surface at the visitor center. One of those busy holidays, the cave phone rang. One of the guides reported that someone on her tour had scratched initials on a painted diorama of mastodons. She had asked the people on the tour who did it, but no one seemed to know. I told her to keep them right there, I was on my way.

The first thing I saw were the initials scratched, two feet high, on the painting. I asked each one on the tour to show me a driver's license. Everyone did except one man—the same one who had been giving the guide a rough time. I explained to him that he could show his driver's license to me, or he could show it to the sheriff. He pulled out his license. Sure enough, his initials were the same as those on the painting. I apologized to the rest of the tour for the inconvenience and told the man to come with me, his tour was over. That's when he took a swing at me. I ducked, then my paratrooper training took over. I grabbed his arm, turned my back into him, and threw him over my shoulder.

A few years earlier, at Sonora, some formations were broken on a tour, but legally there wasn't anything we could do about it then. The same thing happened at Cave Without a Name, where the cave manager couldn't prosecute. Now we have laws to protect the caves of Texas, and the sheriff arrested the man who defaced our mural and took him to court. The judge found him guilty and ordered him to pay a five-hundred-dollar fine or serve out jail time. He paid his fine.

Most of the time, if you have a good staff, everything goes pretty smoothly. As in any business, if you get it set up right, it will almost run itself. In Georgetown, we chose as guides college students who had good personalities and genuinely liked people and the cave. One young man, a high school student, applied for a job as a guide. He had never had a job before and was a little young to be a guide, but he told me he had been through the cave and wanted nothing

80. Scene along the trail, Inner Space Cavern.

81. Jim Brummett looks at a flowstone formation, Cascade Caverns.

more than to work there. I decided to give him a chance with a part-time job mowing the grass and picking up the parking lot and picnic area. That was fine with him, but he asked if he could be an assistant guide. I told him we would see.

That young man was just crazy about the cave, so I started taking him with me to change light bulbs. Sometimes we had to replace a switch. He was happy just being in the cave. When we got busy, I would ask him to be a rear guide. That way he could listen to the various guides give their tour. He asked me questions. He wanted to know everything about a cave. He just couldn't learn enough, fast enough.

One of the big holiday weekends, all the guides were in the cave. We don't like to get too many people on one tour, because then many of them can't hear the guide. The young man was mowing grass, so I went out to him and asked him if he thought he was ready to be a guide. He said he was ready, all right; so I told him to change clothes. He had fifteen minutes. There were about twenty-five people lined up and waiting when he was ready. I introduced him to the people, explaining that this was his first tour and asking them for a report on how well he did. Off they went. One hour and forty-five minutes later, he brought them out. Every person on the tour came over to me with a big smile. All of them agreed that this was the best cave tour they had ever taken. They liked how he explained everything so they could understand it. I had a new guide. He stayed with me until he graduated from college.

Sometimes it is rewarding to be a cave manager. Those are the times I like to remember.

# Gill Ediger's Guide to Caving Etiquette

A leader in the state's caving organizations, Gill Ediger has some advice for anyone who may be coming down with the caving bug. Among his words of wisdom is one that bears repeating: never go caving without other folks who've been bitten by the same bug. Read on.

The mysterious underworld of caves is both frightening and fascinating. Caves often are thought of as dark, dirty, uninviting holes in the ground, posing unknown dangers, the risk of getting lost, and a good chance of injury or death for those who explore them. Yet that unknown also exerts a strong pull on human curiosity—the quality that moves people to explore the mysteries of the world about them.

The caves that lie beneath Texas are complicated systems. Each cave is a unique world where living organisms interact with air and water and the chemicals of the earth, where hard limestone slowly is dissolved and redeposited somewhere else, where the forces of nature are playing as important a role as they are playing on the surface. And caves are places where the presence of man can have a serious impact. As a cave explorer—a caver—for more than thirty years, I view caves and cavers as being in a reciprocal relationship. Caves are not much good to us as human beings if we can't enjoy them, and we as human beings are not much good to caves if we don't protect them. We cavers by default take on the stewardship of caves, even those we don't explore. If you like the pictures in this book, if you have even a passing interest in caves, if you harbor a latent curiosity concerning what is down there, then you probably hold in your soul the stuff of which cavers are made.

Cavers are a strange branch of the diverse tree of humanity. Like most interest groups, they want to be recognized, because of what they do, as something special in society. The reasons cavers go caving differ with each caver: blatant curiosity, a sense of adventure, scientific study, an adrenaline rush. Although each caver may have her or his own driving forces, all share a bond that is closer to that of family than of fellowship. And that bond, of course, is based upon an above-average interest in, and awareness of, caves.

83. Bob Crisman examines the Snake Dancers closely. Helictite Room, Caverns of Sonora. Photograph by Bart Crisman.

If you want to become a caver—if you want to become a good caver—the very best way to do so is to take up with someone who already is an experienced caver or to join one of the caving clubs active in the larger cities and at some universities in Texas and elsewhere. You can learn a lot from books, but there is no substitute for learning directly from highly experienced cavers. They have the interest and awareness, and they want you to be the very best caver you can be—it's in your best interest and it's in their best interest. If you want to go caving, it is best to contact cavers in your area and start attend-

82. Bob Crisman inspects the Snake Dancers on the floor of the Helictite Room, Caverns of Sonora. Photograph by Bart Crisman.

ing some of their cave exploration projects. These are the perfect training ground for new cavers. Not only do you get to learn about caving in a cave, but you also get to go caving with some of the best and most experienced cavers in the world.

Caving is a group sport, and cavers are encouraged to join and participate in the various caving organizations. The statewide caving organization is the Texas Speleological Association (TSA). It is a regional group of the National Speleological Society (NSS). Addresses for these organizations are provided below. If you are interested in Texas caves, you can contact the TSA for the caving club or project nearest you. If you are from another state, contact the NSS for similar information.

No discussion of caves and cavers would be

84. "Let nothing you dismay." Photograph by Carl Kunath.

complete without mentioning the real stewards of the caves—cave owners. To cavers, the cave owner is a special person, the one who holds the key to caving happiness. It is overwhelmingly important that cavers treat the cave owner with utmost respect. Without the good graces and generosity of cave owners, we would have no caves to explore. If you are a caver, or if you want to be a caver, remember that you are required to ask the cave's owner for permission to visit the cave. Find out what the rules are while on her or his property, and then respect those rules.

If you are lucky enough to own a cave, then you are a member of a fairly small group. While there are a few cave owners who view their caves as liabilities, most are curious about "what's down there." Most cave owners are well educated, cosmopolitan, environmentally aware,

and scientifically curious people who feel a stewardship for their land and its related features. Many also are adventurous and like travel and outdoor activities. We find that most really want to know "what's down there" but realize that they do not have the training or equipment to check it out for themselves. If you fit into that category, we would like you to contact cavers of the TSA. We can get you in and get you out safely. But whether or not you want to see what's down there for yourself, we can explore your cave and provide you with a map, photographs, and any other details you might need, such as the location of water into which you can drill a well. Contact the TSA if you want assistance in studying or managing your cave resource.

As a cave owner, you have certain rights that you should expect cavers to respect. First, you can specify who goes into your cave, when they go, and what they do there. You have the right to require that cavers sign and provide you with a release and waiver absolving you of any liability and agreeing to any restrictions you wish to impose. While cavers have very strict rules against ever holding any landowner liable for negative consequences of a visit, the release and waiver serves as a contract between the caver and the cave owner, outlining the caver's responsibility. We want cavers to be aware of those responsibilities every time they go caving. We pro-

vide established cavers with these standard forms. You should request the completed forms and refuse access to any cavers who can't produce them. In Texas, the so-called Texas Sportsman's Law further absolves the landowner of virtually all liability for harm to visitors, so long as no fee was charged.

As cavers, we try to instill a sense of stewardship of caves, not only in cavers but also in cave owners and the general public. Locating caves, studying them, and then managing them are necessary parts of that stewardship. They require

85. Robin Havens and Mae Zhon in Honey Creek Cave. Photograph by Andy G. Grubbs.

that everybody work together. We older cavers teach younger cavers how to cave and how to take care of the caves they explore. We provide cave owners with the information to understand and manage their caves and the related resources.

## Caver Courtesy

These common-sense rules for behavior while on someone else's property will help make you welcome again.

- Leave gates as you find them—open or closed.
- Drive slowly, and don't disturb livestock—they have the right-of-way.
- Don't build fires without permission—grass and brush fires destroy property.
- Don't shoot guns or fireworks without permission.
- Don't swim in stock tanks without permission.
- Just go caving—leave everything else alone.
- Call, leave a note, or personally say good-bye and thank the owner when you are out of the cave.

86. Caving can involve the whole family.

87. Cavers follow a wet passage.

## How to Cave Safely

Cave exploring can be dangerous if you're not properly trained or equipped. Here's how to reduce the risk.

- Join an experienced group for proper training in safe caving. Never go caving alone—three or four cavers is a safe minimum.
- Each caver should carry three dependable sources of light and extra batteries and bulbs.
- Use the proper gear, including a good hardhat and suitable boots and clothing.
- Don't attempt to explore caves or perform caving maneuvers that are beyond your training or ability.
- Get proper training before entering pits that require ropes or ladders.
- Leave word with family or friends about the cave locationand the time you expect to return. Try to be on time.
- Always choose the safer option when you have alternatives.
- Use good judgment. Most accidents are the result of stupid mistakes.

## Who to Contact

Texas Speleological Association
P.O. Box 8026
Austin, TX 78713

National Speleological Society
2813 Cave Avenue
Huntsville, AL 35810

# Pittman's and Kunath's Guide to Cave Photography

Leaving the sunlit world behind to capture the beauty of a cave on film poses some unique challenges. Fortunately, technology, experience, and a bit of common sense give the well-equipped photographer the ability to meet them.

For years, dedicated cavers have practiced, and enforced, a simple ethic: "Take nothing but pictures; leave nothing but footprints." Caves are delicate environments and demand a special approach and special precautions. Respect for the cave, for the creatures that live in the cave, and for other visitors who will see the cave is the single most important imperative in cave photography. Damage done by a thoughtless photographer never can be undone, and no photograph ever will begin to repay that loss. Caves grow on a geological time scale, not a human one. The print of a muddy boot will deface a pristine formation for millennia to come; the mark of a tripod is permanent.

Respect for a cave means remaining on the trail and not risking a broken formation by trying to get just a little closer. Formations can be unbelievably fragile; the same delicacy that makes them wonderful picture subjects also makes them easy to break. Long soda straws, for example, can be broken by the breeze stirred by a visitor's passing. Experienced cave photographers, like experienced cavers, don't work alone; there is always another person present to watch the photographer and warn of the presence of nearby formations that might be damaged.

The greatest challenge in cave photography, of course, is lighting. Cave photography is totally dependent upon artificial light, whether from the photographer's flash units or the bulbs installed by the cave's developers. The quality of the lighting available varies tremendously, and even the best-lit commercial cave is woefully dark by a photographer's usual standards. Tour lights are installed for viewing the cave, not for photography; because the human eye is more sensitive than most cameras, tour lights are not always useful for photography. Although many good pictures can be made with the installed tour lighting, a solid tripod, and a long exposure, most photographs require the pho-

88. Translucent stalactites grow from soda straw bases in Caverns of Sonora.

tographer to provide suitable lighting. Many serious photographers prefer to provide their own lighting in any case.

Many cave photographs, especially in larger rooms, are made using a technique referred to as light painting. Essentially, this means that the camera is mounted on a tripod and the shutter is locked open while multiple flashes are fired into specific areas of the cave to highlight desired features, creating a sense of depth. This technique requires several people to work together if it is to be done successfully. After the camera is set and the photographer has decided what the composition will be, the lighting is planned and the assistants are placed and pointed. Then the shutter is opened, the assistants fire their flashes in the appropriate directions, and the shutter is closed. For extremely large rooms or very small crews, it sometimes is necessary to repeat this entire procedure several times on the same exposure. This is not something that can be done successfully on a standard visitors' tour.

This is not to say that the casual cave visitor is condemned to boring photographs. Although it is quite simple to attach a flash to a camera and fire the shutter, and even easier to use a camera with a flash built in, the resulting picture almost never is the best that can be had. On-

89. Barriers Passage. Photograph by Carl Kunath.

camera flash is simple, fast, and convenient, but those are its only advantages. The limitation of the technique is that the flash comes from the direction of the camera, resulting in extremely "flat" lighting, which does not lend itself to interesting pictures. Lighting from the back or side of the subject, in addition to, or instead of, lighting from the direction of the camera, gives the subject a realistic depth by creating shadows and highlights, revealing the texture and unique translucence of the formations.

The easiest way to add back or side light to a photograph is by using additional flashes and a special adapter that makes them fire when the camera flash fires. These are called "slave lights," or simply "slaves"; because the light from the primary flash triggers them, they don't need to be connected to the camera at all. Slave adapters, available at most large camera stores and many small ones, are not particularly expensive. A battery-powered flash equipped with a slave unit can be hand-held or attached to a pole or monopod. A ball-and-socket joint between the pole and the flash will allow the photographer or an assistant to place the flash exactly where it is needed and aim it in the right direction without leaving the trail.

Almost all flash units available today have some way that the photographer can adjust the amount of light they put out. By varying the output of the flash units, the photographer can adjust the lighting to produce the desired effect. A problem arises with slave units when the camera itself does not allow the photographer to control the intensity of the flash built into the camera. This is a problem with many small "point-and-shoot" cameras, which are not designed for sophisticated lighting effects. There usually are ways to work around the problem, however, and a simple camera in expert hands is capable of some very high-quality work. In general, however, a photographer looking for better

90. Pit entrance room in Midnight Cave. Photograph by Orion Knox.

91. The Canopy, Midnight Cave. Photograph by Orion Knox.

92. An example of dry or dormant formations, Fawcett's Cave. Photograph by Carl Kunath.

93. A large room of dry formations, Big Mutha Cave. Photograph by Carl Kunath.

than snapshot-quality photographs will find a more advanced camera far easier to use in a cave.

For most amateur cave photography, a 35-millimeter single-lens reflex (SLR) camera will serve quite well. It need not be an expensive model; in fact, given that it will probably receive more than a little abuse in the course of getting the photographs, a less expensive camera is probably preferable. The fully automatic elec-tronic marvels currently being sold are nice, and they can, under some circumstances, make photography easier. However, almost all of the photography in this book was done using older, manual, mechanical cameras. In part this is because many of the photographs were taken some years back, but there are other advantages to mechanical cameras. They don't require batteries, which always seem to go dead at the wrong moment and which can be quite expensive. In

94. First Lake Room, Haby Cave. Photograph by Carl Kunath.

many cases, cave photographs will require long shutter times (sometimes several minutes), and these drain batteries. It would not be unusual on a single trip to use four or five batteries, at up to fifteen dollars each.

The most important features in a camera to be used for cave photography are interchangeable lenses and the ability to operate the camera in a manual exposure mode. If the camera has a flash synchronization socket, or PC terminal, which is used to fire the flash off-camera, so much the better. PC connections once were standard on all SLRs, but recently they seem to have become less common. Zoom lenses, which change focal length, are a valuable addition to any cave photographer's arsenal. They are lighter, easier to handle, and faster to use than the bagful of single-length lenses photographers carried for many years. A zoom lens on the order of 35–135 millimeter, or possibly 28–105 millimeter, is most useful. Of course, the wider the range of focal lengths available,

95. Tink Brummett shows a backlit drapery in the upper level of Caverns of Sonora.

the wider the photographer's range of options becomes, but the heavier and more unwieldy the photographer's kit becomes, too.

Close-focusing lenses, sometimes referred to in advertisements as "macro" lenses, add the ability to photograph small formations or detail areas of larger ones. Close-up filters also are available from a number of suppliers, and, although the quality of the filters varies, often these work well enough. As with many things, price is a fairly reliable guide to quality.

A stout tripod is essential in cave photography. The purpose of a tripod is simply to hold the camera steady while the film is being exposed. There are many variations of tripods in style, appearance, and so on, but these are simply questions of taste; there are no right or wrong types. A good tripod should be stable; unfortunately, usually this means that it will be somewhat heavy. Lightweight tripods, under about six pounds, tend to vibrate and flex, resulting in pictures that are not sharp. Ideally, a tripod will have independently adjustable legs which open to different angles, to enable the camera to be placed almost anywhere. Independent leg angles allow the camera to be stable on uneven or sloped trails. The tripod also should allow the camera to be placed at, or close to, ground level to allow a different perspective. Some sort of quick-release fastener that enables the camera to be put on and taken off the tripod easily makes using the tripod much more convenient.

Film manufacturers provide a bewildering array of choices—color or black and white, slides or prints, high speed or fine grain. Each cave, each photographer, each shot will be different, and again there are no right or wrong selections.

96. Lighted columns, Jack Burch, Caverns of Sonora.

The first decision probably should be whether the picture will be shot in color or in black and white. This is determined primarily by personal preference and the intended use of the photographs, although economics can play a role as well. Done well, black-and-white photographs can be spectacular, but they can lack subtle shadings and nuances of color which can make a photograph more interesting. In general, black-and-white photography requires a different approach from color photography, and in a cave the differences become pronounced. The lighting must be carefully planned and placed, and composition becomes more critical. Most serious black-and-white cave photography is done by avid photographers who have access to darkroom facilities. Commercial black-and-white

97. Unusual wavy helictite, Caverns of Sonora.

labs can do an adequate job but rarely are willing or able to offer the type of individualized service required for truly memorable results, and the cost of custom processing and printing generally is prohibitive.

Color film generally is simpler and easier for the amateur to work with, since there are fewer technical variables involved in the film processing. The primary decision is whether to opt for the working convenience of a high-speed film or the finer grain and brighter color of a slower film. The other major decision for color photography is whether to use slide film or negative (print) film.

The choice of fine-grain versus high-speed film probably makes the greatest difference in the appearance of the color photograph. Fine-grain films produce sharper, crisper prints, but at the cost of requiring more light. This translates into more power from the flash units, a longer exposure if available light is being used, or a wider lens aperture, which reduces the depth of field—the portion of the photograph that will be acceptably sharp. Low-light films, commonly referred to as "fast" films, require less light and therefore are more convenient to use in a cave. However, prints from them will be grainy and will appear to be less sharp.

A film's relative sensitivity to light is indicated by the film speed, sometimes referred to as the DIN or ASA rating. Commercially available films range in speed from 25 to 3200. The lower the number, the finer the grain of the film and the more light it requires. Photographers generally refer to films with ratings in the 25 to 100 range as slow films. Films with ratings of 400 or more are fast films that require less light but produce grainier images and do not enlarge as well as slower varieties.

The intended use of the photographs will make the slide-versus-negative decision simpler. Although slides generally offer brighter, more saturated colors and are preferred by magazines and publishers, slide film has a much narrower range of acceptable exposure and must be "balanced" to the kind of lighting in use.

Most cave lighting uses tungsten or tungsten-halogen bulbs similar to normal household lighting. These bulbs produce a light that is considerably more yellow-orange in color than normal daylight. Since photographic film cannot adjust for this color automatically, the way the brain does, the correction must be made in the photographic process. Specialized types of slide film are made to counteract the yellow-orange of tungsten lighting. These films usually are marketed as "tungsten-balanced" films, and they generally are well suited for use with commercial tour lighting in caves.

Electronic flash units, unlike tour lighting, do not have the yellow-orange cast of tungsten bulbs. Electronic flash produces a light which reproduces the color balance of normal midday sunlight and therefore calls for "daylight-balanced" films. Cross-balancing, using daylight film with tungsten lighting or tungsten slide film with flash, results in false colors that sometimes are interesting but more often are merely very strange and not particularly appealing. It is possible to add filters to the camera lens to correct for cross-balancing or to adjust the light to the exact balance the photographer desires. It is far easier, however, to start with the appropriate film.

Negative film has some distinct advantages for the amateur in terms of color balance. The printing allows for a great deal of control over the final color of the print, so it is possible to correct the effect of off-color lighting almost completely. The effect of tungsten lighting on the negative is both obvious and unmistakable, and a good lab should make this correction automatically.

The humidity in some caves can approach 100 percent. Condensation on lenses, cameras, flash units, and photographer's glasses is common, and frustrating, when the equipment is cooler than the ambient temperature in the cave. In addition, in that kind of wetness, electronic devices become unreliable. Flash units may not fire or may fire repeatedly without prompting from the photographer. Cameras may suffer a variety of electronic ills. Although the effects of humidity are to some extent unavoidable, many of them can be minimized by the simple expedient of warming the equipment before entering the cave or by placing the equipment in the cave ahead of time and allowing it to adjust to the cave temperature. Otherwise, a clean, lint-free cloth and a can of compressed air can help—somewhat.

Cave photography is both a demanding and an intensely rewarding art form. Its techniques take time and effort to master, and its logistical problems can be fierce, but the rewards can be spectacular. In many cases, a well-executed photograph will reveal details and shapes that were not apparent in the cave. Most important, cave photographs allow the photographer to share with others the wonders of the subterranean world.

I always considered cave photography a great challenge. I was fascinated by the natural beauty that nature provides and especially with the smaller details that often escape our attention. I discovered a beautiful, often perplexing world that was commonly no larger than a postage stamp. To capture those images in a "photographically hostile" environment and with a minimum of equipment presented a challenge that I never really mastered.

The few images that I treasure from those efforts represent but a small portion of the film I exposed. To capture the beauty of a flower in the garden on a sunny day was one thing, but to get the image of a water drop where my physical position, difficult to begin with, was made almost impossible by the close proximity of other fragile beauties and without sufficient light to properly compose and focus the image was quite another thing. Then, to make an educated guess as to the best angle for the light source and, almost as an afterthought, to carefully work through the exposure problems of close-up photography—the circumstances argue poorly for a successful photograph.

I also made photographs of rooms large enough for football stadiums and used flash bulbs as big as normal 60-watt household bulbs, but the close-ups were my first love.

Cave photography is a tricky thing. Just as sports, portraiture and landscape photography have their

98. A drop of water hangs by a thin crystal thread.

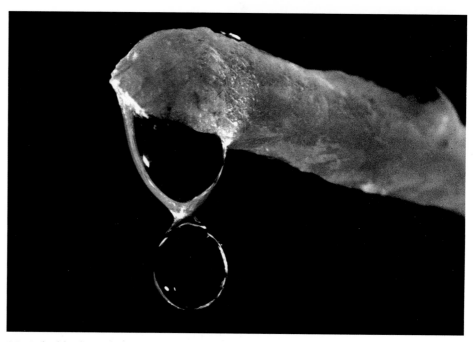

99. A double drop of water held together by a shell of crystal.

"secrets," so it is with cave photography. I'd guess it took me two years and a thousand pictures before I was confident that my technique would produce an image that was at least acceptable if not a world class image.

My interest in cave photography led me into a life-long affair with cameras, but it was the cave photography that came first—then the rest of photography followed.

100. Photographing a small crystaline formation. The photographer uses the light on his helmet lantern to focus the lense.

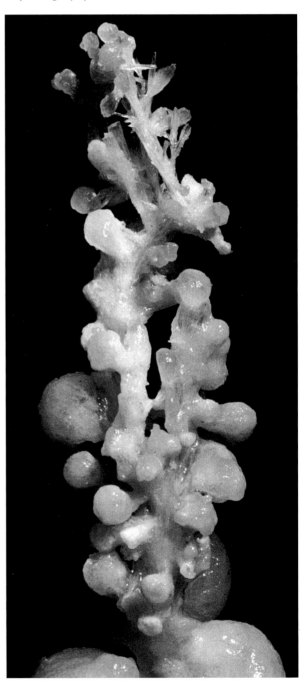

101. Results of the photographic effort made in figure 100.

# Contributors

BLAIR PITTMAN (National Speleological Society no. 4594) learned photographic technique as a caver in the 1950s and while helping to develop Caverns of Sonora in the early 1960s. Since then he has gone on to a career as a photojournalist and fine art photographer. He is author and photographer of *The Natural World of the Big Thicket* (Texas A&M University Press) and *The Stories of I. C. Eason, King of the Dog People* (University of North Texas Press).

FRANCIS EDWARD "AB" ABERNETHY is a retired Regents Professor of English at Stephen F. Austin State University, Nacogdoches, Texas. A caver since the 1960s, he has also served as executive director and editor of the Texas Folklore Society since the early 1970s and is a member of the Texas Institute of Letters. He has edited many of the publications of the Texas Folklore Society, and in addition to his educational and editorial pursuits, he plays and sings Texas folk music.

G. ELAINE ACKER, who lives in Austin, received her master's degree in English from the University of St. Thomas in 1994. She is author of the book *Life in a Rock Shelter* (1996) and more than 150 articles in such periodicals as *Texas Parks and Wildlife* magazine, *Backpacker Magazine,* and the *Houston Chronicle.* She has received writing awards from the Texas Outdoor Writers Association and the Regional Publishers Association.

JIM BRUMMETT, who grew up near Menard, Texas, developed an obsession for caving in his teen years. After service as a paratrooper in World War II, he returned to his home state and worked as a mechanic until 1963, when he began working at Caverns of Sonora. He and his wife, Ann, became a cave management team and in addition to Caverns of Sonora have managed Cascade Caverns and Inner Space Caverns. Jim is now retired. Ann died in 1995.

JACK BURCH grew up in Oklahoma near the Arbuckle Mountains, where he learned cave exploration. After service as a B-17 gunner in the Army Air Corps in World War II, he returned and resumed caving, joining the National Speleological Society in 1952 (member number 2175). He has commercialized three caves: Caverns of Sonora and Natural Bridge Caverns in Texas and Río Camuy in Puerto Rico.

S. CHRISTOPHER CARAN, a research and consulting geologist formerly with the U.S. Geological Survey and the Bureau of Economic Geology at the University of Texas at Austin, now is president of a geological and environmental consulting firm in Austin, Texas. He has written for both technical journals and popular magazines and is author of six books.

GILL EDIGER (National Speleological Society no. 10010), Austin builder and designer, grew up in Sinton, in South Texas. He received a bachelor's degree in geography from Texas A&I University, Kingsville, and began caving in 1967. He has served as Texas Speleological Association chair in 1970, 1997, and 1998, and he is editor of the *Texas Caver.* He served on the board of the National Speleological Society from 1973 to 1976.

ORION KNOX was a college student at St. Mary's University in San Antonio in 1960 when he and other members of the university's speleological society explored Natural Bridge Caverns. He later finished college with a degree in architecture and made a career with the Texas Parks and Wildlife Department, from which he is retired. His lifelong interest in caving continues, and he is now a consultant on cave conservation and commercial development, working from his home in Austin.

CARL E. KUNATH (National Speleological Society no. 6230) began caving in 1961. He received a bachelor of science in mathematics from Sul Ross University in 1964. Editor and co-editor of several books on caves, he served as Texas Speleological Association vice-chair and chair in 1965 and 1966, respectively. He currently owns a sporting goods store in San Angelo, Texas.

ROBERT MITCHELL is a retired biologist and caver who lives in Bandera, Texas. He received his bachelor's and master's degrees from Texas Tech University and his doctorate in biology from the University of Texas at Austin. He is author of several books and many scholarly articles on cave biology, and is one of the leading authorities on cave insects.

# Glossary

ACTIVE CAVE. Cave containing a running stream or in which speleothems are growing.

AQUIFER. A ground-water reservoir. Pervious rock that is completely saturated and will yield water to a well or spring.

BACON. Thin, elongated, translucent flowstone having parallel colored bands on or projecting from roofs and walls of some caves.

BED. A layer in sedimentary rocks; a stratum.

BIOSPELEOLOGY. The study of subterranean living organisms, particularly in caves in limestone regions.

BRAKE BARS. A metal bar that is part of a device creating friction for a controlling the speed of the decent on the rope.

BRIDGE. In a cave, a residual rock span across a passage.

CALCITE. A mineral composed of calcium carbonate, like aragonite but differing in crystal form; the principal constituent of limestone.

CARBIDE LIGHT. A lantern operated by controlled drip of water on calcium carbide, acetylene, to provide flammable gas.

CARBONATE. A salt or ester of carbonic acid. A rock consisting mainly of carbonate minerals, such as limestone or dolomite.

CAVE. A natural underground room or series of rooms and passages large enough to be entered by man; generally formed by solution of limestone.

CAVE BREAKDOWN. Enlargement of parts of a cave system by fall of rock masses from walls and ceiling.

CAVE CORAL. A rough, knobby growth of calcite resembling coral in shape, generally small; found on floor, walls, or ceiling of a cave.

CAVE FORMATION. Secondary mineral deposit formed by the accumulation, dripping, or flowing of water in a cave.

CAVE GUANO. Accumulations of dung in caves, generally from bats; in some places partially mineralized.

CAVE ICE. Ice formed in a cave by natural freezing of water.

CAVE PEARL. Small concretion of calcite or aragonite formed by concentric precipitation around a nucleus.

CAVER. One who explores caves as a sport.

CAVERN. A cave, often used poetically or to connote larger-than-average size.

CAVERNOUS. Containing numerous cavities or caverns.

CAVE SYSTEM. An underground network of passages, chambers, or other cavities.

CAVING. The sport of exploring caves.

CEILING BLOCK. Roughly cubical joint-bounded large block, which has fallen from the ceiling of a cave.

CEILING CAVITY. Solutional concavity in the ceiling of a cave. The orientation is determined by joints or a bedding plane.

CHAMBER. The largest order of cavity in a cave or cave system; it has considerable length and breadth but not necessarily great height.

CHIMNEY. A narrow vertical shaft in the roof of a cave; a dome pit.

CHOKE. Rock debris or cave fill completely blocking a passage.

CHUTE. An inclined channel or trough in a cave.

CLAY FILL. Dry or wet clay that fills a cave passage.

COLLAPSE SINK. A closed depression formed by the collapse of the roof of a cave.

COLUMN. A flowstone formation, generally cylindrical, formed by the union of a stalactite and stalagmite.

CORRIDOR Relatively narrow passageway permitting travel between two larger areas.

CRAWL, CRAWLWAY. A cave passage that must be negotiated on hands and knees.

CURTAIN. A wavy or folded sheet of flowstone hanging from the roof or projecting from the wall of a cave; often translucent and resonant.

DEAD CAVE. A dry cave in which all solution and precipitation has ceased.

DECALCIFICATION. Removal of calcium carbonate from a rock, leaving a residuum of noncalcareous material.

DOG-TOOTH CRYSTAL, DOG-TOOTH SPAR. A variety of calcite in the form of sharp-pointed crystals.

DRAPERY. A thin sheet of dripstone, equivalent to curtain.

DRIPSTONE. Calcium carbonate deposited from water dripping from the ceiling or wall of a cave or from the overhanging edge of a rock shelter; commonly refers to the rock in stalactites, stalagmites, and other similar speleothems; in some places composed of aragonite or gypsum.

DRY CAVE. A cave without a running stream.

FAULT CAVE. A cave developed along a fault or fault zone.

FISSURE CAVE. A narrow vertical cave or cave passage along a fissure.

FLOWSTONE. Deposits of calcium carbonate, gypsum, and other mineral matter which have accumulated on the walls or floors of caves at places where water trickles or flows over the rock.

FORMATION. The fundamental unit in rock-stratigraphic classification, consisting of a distinctive mappable body of rock.

GALLERY. A rather large, nearly horizontal passage in a cave.

GEODE. Hollow globular bodies varying in size from a few centimeters to several decimeters, coated on the interior with crystals.

GROTTO. A small cave, natural or artificial.

GYPSUM. A mineral composed of hydrous calcium sulfate.

HALL. In a cave, a lofty chamber which is much longer than it is wide.

HELICTITE. A curved or angular twiglike lateral projection of calcium carbonate having a tiny central canal, found in caves.

JUMAR ASCENDER. (brand name) One of several devices that will ascend a rope using a camming device.

KARST. A terrain, generally underlain by limestone, in which the topography is chiefly formed by the dissolving of rock, and which is commonly characterized by channels or crevices, closed depressions, subterranean drainage, and caves.

KARSTIFICATION. Action by water, mainly chemical but also mechanical, that produces features of a karst topography, including such subsurface features as caves and shafts.

LAKE. As used in speleology, a body of standing water too deep to walk across.

LIMESTONE. A sedimentary rock consisting chiefly of calcium carbonate.

LIVE CAVE. Cave in which there is river action or active deposition of speleothems.

MAZE CAVE. A complex pattern of repeatedly connected passages in a cave system.

MOONMILK. A white plastic calcareous cave deposit composed of calcite, huntite, or magnesite.

NATURAL BRIDGE. A rock bridge spanning a ravine and not yet eroded away.

OUTFLOW CAVE. Cave from which stream flows out or formerly did so.

PALEOKARST. A karstified rock or area that has been buried by later sediments.

PASSAGE. In a cave, the opening between rooms or chambers.

PERMEABILITY. The ability of a rock or soil to permit water or other fluids to pass through it.

PILLAR. A column of rock remaining after solution of the surrounding rock.

PIT. A deep hole, generally circular in outline, having vertical or nearly vertical walls.

POCKET. Solution cavity in ceiling, floor, or walls of a cave, shaped like the interior of a round-bottomed kettle; unrelated to joints or bedding.

POTHOLE. A small rounded hole worn into rock in a streambed, at a waterfall, or near sea level by sand, gravel, and stones being spun around by force of the currents; a natural mill.

Prusik loop. A special sliding knot used to ascend a rope.

Pseudokarst. Karstlike terrain produced by a process other than the dissolving of rock, such as the rough surface above a lava Weld, where the ceilings of lava tubes have collapsed.

Rappel. The descent of a rope using friction to control speed and safety.

Rimstone. Calcareous deposits formed around the rims of overflowing basins, especially in caves.

Rimstone dam. A wall-shaped deposit that impounds pools of water in caves, around springs, and in cascades of streams saturated with calcium bicarbonate.

Rimstone pool. Pool kept in place by a rimstone dam.

Rock shelter. Shallow cave under an overhanging rock ledge.

Room. A part of a cave system that is wider than a passage.

Sheet. A thin coating of calcium carbonate formed on walls, shelves, benches, and terraces by trickling water.

Shield. A disk-shaped speleothem standing edgewise at a high angle.

Sink, sinkhole. General terms for closed depressions. They may be basin, funnel, or cylindrical shaped.

Siphon. In speleology, a cave passage in which the ceiling dips below a water surface.

Soda straw. Thin tubular stalactite, generally less than a centimeter in diameter and of very great length.

Solution. The change of matter from a solid or gaseous state to a liquid state by combination with a liquid.

Speleologist. A scientist engaged in the study and exploration of caves, their environment, and their biota.

Speleology. The scientific study, exploration, and description of caves and related features.

Speleothem. A secondary mineral deposit formed in caves, such as stalactite or stalagmite.

Spring. Any natural discharge of water from rock or soil onto the surface of the land or into a body of surface water.

Squeeze. A narrow passage or opening just passable with effort.

Stalactite. A cylindrical or conical deposit of minerals, generally calcite, formed by dripping water, hanging from the roof of a cave, generally having a hollow tube at its center.

Stalagmite. A deposit of calcium carbonate rising from the floor of a limestone cave, formed by precipitation from a bicarbonate solution through loss of $CO_2$.

Sump. A water trap.

Terra rossa. Reddish-brown soil mantling limestone bedrock; may be residual in some places.

Travertine. Calcium carbonate, light in color and generally concretionary and compact, deposited from solution in ground and surface waters.

TROGLOBITE. An animal living permanently underground in the dark zone of caves and only accidentally leaving it.

TROGLOPHILE. An animal habitually entering the dark zone of a cave but necessarily spending part of its existence outside such as some species of bats.

TROGLOXENE. An animal entering a cave for various reasons but not living there permanently.

TUBE. A smooth surfaced cave passage of elliptical or nearly circular cross section.

WATER TABLE. The upper boundary of an unconfined zone of saturation, along which the hydrostatic pressure is equal to the atmospheric pressure.

WATER TRAP. A place where the roof of a chamber or passage of a cave dips under water but lifts again farther on.

WILD CAVE. A cave in its natural state with no man-made improvements.

# Index